INTRODUCTION TO
The Philosophy of Being

IMPRIMI POTEST:

John J. Foley, S.J.
Provincial, Wisconsin Province,
September 18, 1962

IMPRIMATUR:

✠ Joseph Cardinal Ritter
Archbishop of St. Louis
January 10, 1963

GEORGE P. KLUBERTANZ, S. J.
Saint Louis University

INTRODUCTION TO
The Philosophy of Being

SECOND EDITION

Wipf & Stock
PUBLISHERS
Eugene, Oregon

Wipf and Stock Publishers
199 W 8th Ave, Suite 3
Eugene, OR 97401

Introduction to the Philosophy of Being, Second Edition
By Klubertanz, George P.
ISBN: 1-59752-263-5
Publication date 7/1/2005
Previously published by Appleton-Century-Crofts, 1963

Preface

This is an introductory textbook of metaphysics, whose aim is to help a beginning student; it is not a profound study directed to the scholar. The reason for writing this textbook, Thomistic in inspiration, was twofold; there was question both of manner of presentation and of doctrine.

With many others I believe that metaphysics is *not* an analysis of concepts. As an example of a purely conceptual analysis, I would like to point out the procedure of those who take a concept of being, compare it with a concept of nonbeing, and derive the principle of contradiction. From this they deduce the principle of sufficient reason. Then, by applying the principle of sufficient reason to change, they deduce the principle of causality. In this procedure, before we have ever experienced a cause, we know that a cause is necessary for change. This entire procedure of analysis and deduction seeems to me to be hypothetico-deductive (a priori), and far from St. Thomas's method. "Aristotle," says St. Thomas,* "proceeded along another way. For first he showed in many ways that there is something stable in sensible things."

According to St. Thomas, the human intellect must begin with sensible things, and hence all principles must somehow be found in sense experience. The discovery of principles is an induction, as I hope to prove in this text. But there is no danger of empiricism or sensism, if we remember that point on which Aristotle and St. Thomas were ready to stake their whole philosophy, namely, that sensible things are potentially *intelligible*. If this

* *On Spiritual Creatures,* art. 10, ad 8, trans. Mary C. Fitzpatrick and John J. Wellmuth (Milwaukee, Marquette University Press, 1949), p. 122.

means anything, it means that sensible things can be understood as being. How we can build a metaphysics upon our experience of sensible things may be difficult to explain, but according to St. Thomas we must find in the being of our direct experience all the intrinsic principles of being. Being is simply the first principle; there are other principles which we find in concrete being through the intelligible light of being. These principles are connected with being, but they cannot be deduced from it by any purely conceptual process.

The decision to base metaphysics on sensible being as it is presented to us in immediate experience entailed other departures from systematized Thomism. Act and potency could no longer be presented according to their "concepts," but had to grow out of the consideration of substance and accident, matter and form, essence and the act of existence. Similarly, analogy turned out not to be a simple scheme of predication but a complex group of relations. Naturally, in an introductory textbook, the historical and textual evidence that confirms the experiential evidence cannot be presented; the reader—student or teacher—is referred to the last chapter and to the studies there cited.

With regard to the manner of presentation, this book is not "St. Thomas made simple." St. Thomas's thought is not simple, and attempted simplifications usually end by simplifying the positions and letting the reasoning go. The method of this book attempts to provide for the necessary introductory character of the course by selecting only a few of the problems of metaphysics for study and by giving as concrete a presentation of the evidence as possible.

As far as course work is concerned, these suggestions can be made. In the preliminary presentation, the first three chapters should be covered rapidly and then taken thoroughly at the end of the course by way of review. The course could also be begun with Chapter IV, without any serious difficulties. It would even be possible to begin with Chapter IX, but this procedure would entail quite a few difficulties in teaching. It is also suggested that Chapters XI to XIII inclusive be studied very briefly, and that, if the time is short, preference be given to a review of the first ten chapters. Chapter XIV is not intended to be taken as such in a regular class; pertinent parts can be taken up in connection with earlier parts as indicated by the cross references to the last chapter, and better students can be directed to study parts of it privately. The footnotes are in general of two types: cross references and clarifications. The cross references will help the student to become aware of the connections between the various topics. The explanatory footnotes will sometimes be helpful for classwork, but in the main they are not intended to be given full attention by all the students the first time through the book. Better students can find in them suggestions for further study and comparison with what they have learned. In review classes, the footnote material will often be useful, but the individual teacher will be able to judge the capabilities and interests of particular classes.

Some passages from St. Thomas are included in the text. It is presumed that the student will have ready access to the English translations of St. Thomas and that readings be assigned from the passages indicated in the readings at the end of the chapters. Perhaps the review sessions are also the best time to study the passages from St. Thomas more thoroughly.

A word to the student may be in order here. Philosophy is a distinct kind of knowledge, different from history, science, languages, mathematics, and so on. Hence, it must be studied in a special way. Particularly in the philosophy of being, the great need is for understanding. There are few new facts to be learned, but explanations must be grasped. Definitions and proofs need to be memorized; at best they are but tools. Knowing the answer the teacher wants is by no means the same as knowing philosophy. Real knowledge of philosophy is an intellectual understanding, an insight. It is something like a contemplation, a long, hard look at reality and its intelligible manifestations. There are no mechanical rules or formulas that can substitute for understanding. Time, thinking, reading, discussion—these will generate the habit of metaphysics. To many students, philosophy will seem at first a strange pursuit. But if it is faithfully worked at, it can be one of the truly rewarding experiences of education.

If the author were to mention by name all who have helped him in the learning of metaphysics or the writing of this book, he would have to mention some who would not agree with the final form this book has taken. Prominent among those who have given suggestions and constructive criticism have been the teachers in the fourteen schools where the preliminary edition was used.

My gratitude is also due to those teachers who, on the one hand, welcomed the experiential basis on which this textbook tried to place a Thomistic metaphysics and, on the other, indicated places where they found difficulties and gaps in the exposition. These I have tried to take into account in the second edition. In addition, my own further studies in St. Thomas's doctrine of analogy showed me that I had dealt with this topic in a rigid and overrefined way and that simplification was both possible and desirable. Finally, more emphasis could be placed on the subjective side of metaphysics and on the naturally known differences between persons and things. I have taken the occasion to add some references where particularly helpful books and articles have appeared in English.

In particular, I should like to recall with special gratitude the many helpful suggestions of the Reverend Lothar Nurnberger, S.J., of Loyola University in Chicago.

The mature reflections of one's teachers, one's colleagues, and even one's students influence the writing of any philosophical work. Yet in spite of this social or group aspect which philosophy has in common with the sciences, there is a highly personal character to all philosophical thinking, so that in the last analysis no one except the author of a philosophical work is responsible for its inadequacies.

G.P.K.

Contents

III. THE ANALOGY OF BEING: FIRST APPROACH

IV. BECOMING—CHANGE—MOTION

V. THE INTRINSIC PRINCIPLES OF CHANGE AND BEING: I. IN PARTICULAR

VI. THE INTRINSIC PRINCIPLES OF BEING: II. AS ANALOGOUSLY ONE

VII. THE EXTRINSIC PRINCIPLES OF BEING: I. THE AGENT

VIII. THE EXTRINSIC PRINCIPLES OF BEING: II. THE GOAL OF ACTION

IX. GOD, THE CAUSE OF LIMITED BEING

X. THE TRANSCENDENTALS

XI. THE PREDICAMENTS: SUBSTANCE AND SUPPOSIT

XII. ACCIDENTS IN GENERAL: QUANTITY AND QUALITY

XIII. THE FORMALIZED ACCIDENTS

XIV. CORRELATIONS

If we wish to distinguish more accurately the various demonstrative knowledges, we must examine (*a*) precisely what they intend to investigate and (*b*) how this is to be done. These two questions will accurately determine the specific, or proper, matter of a demonstrative knowledge. The concrete subject matter designates the "things" a knowledge is about indeterminately and in their entirety. What we precisely consider about these "things" is the *abstract* subject matter: number (not, the numbers), life (not, living things). For example, we might say that the abstract matter of the natural sciences is "what can be known about the things around us which come into being by natural processes," and that of the social sciences is "what can be known about men in their relationships to each other, especially as they are formed into groups."

But such a limitation does not yet distinguish demonstrative knowledges. For we find that there are distinct knowledges about the same matter; for example, biology, psychology, and the philosophy of human nature have, at least in part, the same matter, man. And they all intend to find out what can be known about man. What then is the difference between them? Their ways of knowing and the kind of knowledge they obtain are different; this sort of difference is the abstract matter considered explicitly according to the way or ways it is known in the particular knowledges. That is why the manner of our knowledge, the principles we use, the kind of argumentation we employ, are included in the adequate notion of a particular demonstrative knowledge. The abstract matter explicitly designated as it is knowable will be called the "proper subject matter" (or, "proper matter") of a knowledge, and the "particular way in which an abstract matter is knowable" will be called its "formal intelligibility." Thus, to give a complete and accurate description of a demonstrative knowledge, we designate its proper matter, that is, we name its abstract matter together with the formal intelligibility under which it is considered.

3. Characteristics of scientific knowledge

Not only is a scientific knowledge unified and organized by having a complete set of similar data, by having a self-coherent

or internally consistent set of propositions in which these data
are expressed, and especially by having a single set of principles
(in some knowledges this is merely an ideal not yet realized)
by means of which everything in that field of knowledge is
related, but there must be an explicit *showing* of these relationships. A man who has a scientific knowledge not only knows
something, but he knows that he knows. In other words, an
organized knowledge is in some sense a *certain* knowledge. From
this point of view, an organized knowledge contains not only
data or facts but also conclusions, which are arrived at by some
form of reasoning or demonstration; hence, organized knowledge
is properly a *demonstrative* knowledge (*scientia*).

A second characteristic of organized or demonstrative knowledge is that (with the exception of history) no demonstrative
knowledge deals with a singular thing as singular. Physics, for
example, is not interested in the individual peculiarities of this
falling body (for example, that it is a dark-green object falling at
11:03 A.M. in a second-story classroom in Idaho); similar examples can easily be found in the case of biology, chemistry, or
mathematics. (An exception might seem to be "individual psychology," but the individual is included in this science not as *this*
individual—for example, John Smith—but in terms of the common characteristic of being *an* individual with an individualized
set of values or common variable traits.) In other words, organized, demonstrative knowledge is not of the individual and consequently is not expressed through the use of proper names. Put
positively, demonstrative knowledge uses general or common
terms. Sometimes, also, an equivalently universal proposition is
expressed in the form of an indefinite particular (for example,
"A man is a rational animal"). We should not be misled by the
grammatical form of propositions into thinking that some sciences do not use universal or at least common terms. In the
fifth chapter we will examine the implications of universal knowledge more fully.[5]

But first it will be necessary to consider other demonstrative
knowledge with which we are more familiar in order to see
similarities and differences. Knowledge, of course, is not a thing

[5] See below, sec. 42.

in itself. As an act, it is the act of a man who knows by his senses or his intellect or both; as a habit, it is a quality of a man. (Here we simply accept the fact that sense and intellect are different; in the philosophy of human nature these powers are considered in detail, and the kind of difference between them is proved.)⁶ The knowing subject is a man, not an intellect or a sense. It is by a figure of speech that we say, "The senses know this," and "The intellect knows that." It is, however, a convenient, shorthand way of speaking, and we shall often use it.

We have already seen that no demonstrative (scientific) knowledge concerns the singular as singular, in other words, that demonstrative knowledge is common or general in character. We should be careful not to assume from the start that all scientific knowledge is general in exactly the same way.⁷ Most demonstrative knowledges are universal, in the sense that they employ univocal concepts and terms.⁸ Univocal concepts deal with one characteristic of things that is common to many and leave differences out of consideration. Univocal concepts are derived, either immediately or mediately, by abstraction from material things.⁹ When, in the understanding of a material thing, we consider one characteristic, trait, or aspect of it and omit others, we are said to "abstract" from the latter. The two simplest kinds of abstraction are called "total" and "formal."

The very name, "total abstraction," is a kind of misnomer, but it is traditional and has a certain value. Suppose we consider the existing individual or being as fully determinate (for example,

---

⁶ By spontaneous knowledge we know that intellect and sense are different. For a philosophical examination of the nature of the difference and a proof that intellect and sense are essentially different, see G. P. Klubertanz, S.J., *Philosophy of Human Nature* (New York, Appleton-Century-Crofts, Inc., 1953), pp. 158–164.

⁷ The kind of generality which metaphysical knowledge has will be examined in Chap. III.

⁸ A univocal term, as we know from logic, is one that is applied in exactly the same sense to many individual things, for example, "gold," "frog," "chair."

⁹ There are various ways in which univocal concepts arise. Those derived immediately from sensible things are gained by simple abstraction. Other univocal concepts are made by combinations of the first kind, by second-level abstraction (see n. 11), and by mental construction (see secs. 115 and 123). For the relation of such concepts to real things, see below, sec. 88.

Peter) and then drop out of consideration the individual determinations and limitations; the result is an abstract consideration
of the whole being indeterminately. When I look at a particular
pencil, a particular piece of paper, a particular human being and
know them as pencil, paper, and man, I have performed an act of
total abstraction ("total," because each of these nouns designates
a whole and entire thing [not merely a part]; "abstraction," because the definite individual characteristics are omitted from
consideration). Total abstraction can be carried further than this;
that is, the being can be known more indeterminately, according
to a more and more ultimate genus. For example, Peter can be
known not only as man but as animal or living thing. The limit
of this kind of abstraction is "material substance";[10] this is the
matter with which some physical sciences deal. Total abstraction
is sometimes called the "first degree of abstraction."

".Formal abstraction" is almost a reverse type of abstraction. In
this second type, a formal determinant is considered apart from,
and independently of, others. A very clear example is found in
the knowledge of number, figure, and surface, which can be considered by the intellect apart from the sensible qualities with
which they are associated in the real order. This kind of abstraction consists in considering an accidental form (or a perfection
considered after the manner of an accidental form—see Chapters
XII and XIII) apart from the other perfections of a being, provided that this accidental form does not depend upon these
other perfections for its intelligibility. "Formal abstraction" is
often called the "second degree of abstraction"; it is connected
with such operations as counting and measuring.

In general, abstraction[11] in its proper sense is an act of sim-

[10] If we attempt to carry total abstraction further, we no longer have
knowledge of a real thing; perhaps we come to a being of reason, "no-thing
conceived of as the indeterminate possibility of being" (cf. sec. 88, on beings
of reason). It is true that we can understand "substance" without understanding it as material, but this is done, not by way of abstraction but by
way of separation; see below, sec. 17.
[11] In addition to these two basic types of abstraction, there are other,
more complicated types of abstraction, that for convenience' sake we will
call "second-level" abstraction. Whereas both total and formal abstractions
have their point of departure in the real thing, a second-level abstraction
has its point of departure in a previous knowledge; for example, "humanity,"

ple and absolute consideration, which consists in apprehending one characteristic or intelligibility (*ratio*) without another with which it is associated in the real order. Now, we learn in logic that an act of absolute consideration belongs to the first act of the mind, the simple apprehension. We also know from logic that the object of simple apprehension is an essence or quiddity.

In summary, a consideration of most scientific knowledge yields these general conclusions. Most scientific knowledges deal with strictly universal and univocal concepts. Such concepts are the result of at least total abstraction; formal abstraction may also be involved, as well as other types of abstraction. In any abstraction something is always omitted from the object, and an abstraction, in the strict sense, is an act of simple apprehension directed to an absolute consideration of an essence.

We can now, using the definitions of other sciences as models, give a preliminary and descriptive definition of the philosophy of being. Its subject matter, in general, is reality, or real things; its abstract subject matter is reality as we find it in experience; its formal intelligibility is what is real inasmuch as it is real. Its proper matter can therefore be stated briefly: what is real as real. We can see at once that most other knowledges deal with, or are concerned with, some particular aspect or part of reality (for example, physics, biology, sociology). Thus at first sight the philosophy of being seems to differ from all other organized knowledges even by its general subject matter, for it deals with all of reality, and the others with aspects or parts of reality.

But we may wonder whether there is anything more to the philosophy of being than the sum total of all other knowledges. Is there any room for, and any point to, an alleged organized knowledge about the real as such? Some people (positivists, empiricists) say that there is no such thing at all as the philosophy of being. "It is usually supposed that if you publicly

which is the intelligible form (intelligibility) of man, arises by second-level abstraction from "man," which is itself a product of total abstraction. Second-level abstractions are more properly called constructions than abstractions, but there is some similarity, in that the products of second-level abstraction also contain less than the initial stage from which they are derived.

dismiss ontology, it will go away quietly. . . ."[12] Others hold that there is a kind of collected and digested summary of all the various kinds of particular knowledges and that this digest could be called a philosophy of being. Perhaps the best preliminary way to see that there is a place for a distinct and special kind of knowledge called "the philosophy of being" is to look at the type of question that is asked in it. For example. What is it to be real? Why do we call a thing a being? Is there more than one kind of reality? What is change? Is every being changeable, or is there unchanging permanent reality? Is being simple or complex? Is being limited or unlimited? Is a limited being caused? How many kinds of causes are there? What are truth and goodness? What is an individual? A person? Is there a cause of the various beings which we experience? Is this cause God? What kind of being is God, and what is His relationship to us? Even if we do not understand these questions now, it is easy to see that no other organized knowledge asks or answers them and that no collection or summary of other knowledges touches on them.

4. Why should I study philosophy?

For these reasons, there are persons who admit that there is a kind of knowledge called philosophy of being, but think it is an unnecessary luxury, like the pastoral poetry of the eighteenth century or elaborate lacework. We may put this position in the form of a concrete question: What does the philosophy of being mean to me? What difference does it make to me whether I bother answering these questions at all or answer them wrongly? Here a distinction must be made. Some kind of knowledge of the real, at the lowest level of our everyday knowledge and as the implicit background of all our other knowledge, is the absolutely indispensable condition of all other knowledge in any mode—this we hope to see more clearly at the end of the course than we do now. But even now we can see that in a sense every man is implicitly a philosopher. For everyone distinguishes between fact and fiction, between dream and reality; everyone deals with reality, takes it quietly or rebels against it.

[12] James K. Feibleman, *Ontology* (Baltimore, The Johns Hopkins Press, 1951), p. 100.

These distinctions and modes of action include and involve phil-osophical knowledge in the everyday mode. For example, the distinction between fact and fiction is actually made even by uneducated persons, though not very clearly and accurately; and these same persons implicitly accept the principle of contradic-tion in all their thinking and doing. Furthermore, we see that many persons know, with everyday or even refined knowledge, that there is a God, but they are unable to prove it in any organ-ized way. Is it not enough to know that there is a God without being able to prove it? Can we not rest satisfied with our every-day and our refined knowledge of the real (supported and enlarged by faith) and let it go at that? It is true that not every-body needs to have philosophical knowledge in an organized way, just as not everybody needs to know higher mathematics. But suppose no one explicitly knew the philosophy of being. The probable result would be the acceptance of a large amount of error and superstition by many people. For everyday and refined knowledges contain a greater or smaller percentage of error, and they are incomplete. They contain no safeguards against error; they do not enable a person to meet difficulties and objections. Thus, the common good requires that some of those who can learn philosophy do so. Hence, a person who is trying to become an educated man or woman and who con-sequently will meet with erroneous philosophical positions both in his reading and in his contacts with other people needs for his own sake as well as that of society to know at least the essentials of philosophy. Intellectual ability is a responsibility as well as a gift.

There is a personal advantage in the study of philosophy. A person cannot be mature and confident without an organized and unified outlook on life. A person who is highly educated only in certain specialized areas finds that the world for him is broken up piecemeal. How is he to organize and master this multiplicity? If he attempts an organization by means of limited principles— limited principles are all that can be found from a specialized (that is, partial) point of view—something will have to be left out. He can organize and order all his knowledge and all the aspects and parts of the world that confront him only from the point of view of, and by means of the principles discovered in, his study of philosophy.

But why must *I* in particular organize my outlook on life? Why must *I* engage in these very subtle investigations about things apparently so remote from everyday life? Because, ultimately, I am a man and I want to be fully a man. A man is an animal, and so he does have needs and interests directed to the sustenance and enhancement of his bodily life. This is his biological sphere of activities, and it is to some extent the basic condition of all other activities. Man is also a gregarious animal, and enjoys his activities with others—the social sphere. But he is a special kind of animal, and not merely because of the moral and religious dimension of his activities. (This dimension not only extends beyond all the others but also permeates them all, and so is more than a part of his activities alongside other parts.) Man is also an intellectual animal. Almost as soon as he can talk, he is asking "What?" and "Why?" All his life, he wants to know what is going on and why. True enough, most people let the preoccupations of biological life limit their questions to what is immediately practical, in the narrow sense of "useful." But man remains a questioning animal; and in itself this tendency to question is not limited to a particular set of questions, to a particular class of things. It is open to literally everything and in its deepest reality. It has been well said that "man is a being who questions being"—and primarily perhaps even his own being.

Our contemporary culture both reinforces this tendency and turns aside from it. On the one hand, we are constantly questioning ourselves and our world. Our art and our literature are the most introspective; even common conversation turns on the hidden feelings and motives of ourselves and others; world problems make us question our common values and our ways of attempting to realize them. On the other hand, this very questioning is sophisticated and fearful—it questions with more than half a mind that our analysis is not a revelation of the truth and with somewhat of a fear of the answers we might find if we push the question far enough. At the same time, we are surrounded with more opportunities for distraction than any other civilization has offered, and so it requires a great effort to continue serious questioning in an organized way.

necessary, even from the viewpoint of revealed religion, that some believers become skilled in philosophical thinking. So philosophy indirectly helps faith. Secondly, a believer, because he has an intellect with an innate drive toward understanding, wants to understand the content of his faith as much as possible. The organized effort to understand faith is called theology, and a large part of scientific theology consists in the use of philosophical principles and methods to help in the understanding of faith.

On the other hand, historically speaking, faith has helped philosophy. For example, a man who believes what the Christian revelation has to tell him about the nature of God cannot make the philosophical error of thinking that God is an impersonal force. Theology thus is a "negative norm" for philosophy, inasmuch as a man's faith may warn him of errors he is making in philosophy. It must be noted, however, that faith can tell a man *that* he is making an error; it does not tell him *why* the error was made or *how* to correct it—this is a properly philosophical task. Secondly, there is a positive influence of faith on philosophy. Faith suggests new problems to philosophical reflection (for example, Christian thinkers go as deeply as they do into the nature of personality because of the problems raised by the Incarnation and the Trinity); and faith often presents truths that serve as hints for the properly *philosophical* solutions of problems (for example, St. Thomas's statement, "*Deus est ipsum esse*," owes much to the revelation of God's name, "I am who am," in Exod. 3:13).

Akin to this is the advantage that a Christian student has in the very learning of philosophy.[16] Through his faith and the Christian traditions, a Christian has accepted as certain and has become familiar with truths like the dependence of the sensible universe on God, the immortality of his soul, and the existence of God and other spiritual beings. He has a firm grasp of these truths, though he may have only a slight understanding of them. Yet this much at least he does understand, that reality includes much more than

[16] For a fuller development of this point, see G. P. Klubertanz, S.J., "Metaphysics and Theistic Convictions," to be published in *Proceedings of the 1962 Workshop On Teaching Thomism Today* (Washington, Catholic Univ. of America Press).

is contained in the narrow limits of his own sense experience. Because of his firm acceptance of truths about nonsensible reality he does not find it hard to raise scientific questions about the nature of the real or to follow a purely intellectual argument whose conclusions go beyond the limitations of immediate sense experience. But what a Christian young man or woman accepts and can understand with a measure of fullness, it may take an unbeliever years of experience and study to grasp. Even with the best will in the world, it is the hard work of years to arrive at a full understanding of being, of the existence of God as a nonmaterial and unlimited being, and so forth. For this reason, Aristotle has said, "Young men have no [intellectual] conviction about [the objects and principles of wisdom], but only use the proper language" (*Ethics*, Bk. VI, 1142a19).

But this by no means implies a formal dependence of philosophy upon revelation and faith. Both the Christian and the unbeliever philosophize in the light of rational evidence; both, though with varying degress of difficulty, can arrive at an intellectual understanding of being and its principles and can acquire rational convictions about them.

Unbelievers sometimes imagine that they alone are real philosophers, for they think that they are the only ones who can call everything into question. Now, no one can question anything except from some starting point, for, as we shall see more clearly as we go along, man is a being-in-a-situation, not an absolute and isolated being. If the situation from which one questions is part of the reality which could be called into question, then one's questioning in principle cannot be complete. The contemporary unbeliever raises his questions in the context of this historical moment of human culture, a moment that has as much need of being questioned—and in just the same way—as anything else that he does question. But the believer who wishes to philosophize situates himself in the context of his faith. From here he can raise questions about any and *every* being accessible to reason. Because the believer has an other than merely rational security, he can question more completely as well as more serenely. He is never in a position to yield to panic, nor need he ever be dishonest about a problem. This, however, does not mean that it is easy for a Christian to be authentically rational, but only that he is in a better position to attain complete authenticity.

St. Thomas Aquinas has explained the relation between reason and revelation very satisfactorily in the fourth chapter of the first book of the *Contra Gentiles,* and a careful reading of this fourth chapter will be most rewarding.

7. Thomistic philosophy

As we shall see much more fully in later chapters, there are many ways of considering reality. Every grown person has an outlook on life (sometimes called a *Weltanschauung*) that involves an implicit metaphysics. Philosophers explicitly state and develop their philosophical view of reality—and come to differing conclusions. Some of these philosophers are wrong, as we shall also try to see; but most often it is a question of how adequate a philosophy is to express the totality of the real.

Moreover, we have seen that what is most characteristic of a demonstrative knowledge is the formal intelligibility which it seeks. This formal intelligibility is concretely specified by the principles and the methods which are used. Thus, what we try to do in philosophy is partly determined by what we think it means "to understand something philosophically" and partly by what we think we have to do to reach that understanding. Here, too, there are differences. We can hardly speak of "errors" of aim and method, except when they would be obviously inept, and this is not likely to be the case very often.

As beginners in philosophy, we are not yet in a position to judge all the various philosophers. It is foolish not to try to make use of the help we can get from a good philosopher, and it is impossible to start out entirely without any metaphysics—a normal eight-year-old is already developing an outlook on life. But because our knowledge of reality as such is still on the every-day level, it is likely to be mixed with much error. For practical purposes, therefore, in order to get started in philosophy with some hope of developing a reasonably good philosophy of our own, we must take someone's lead. What kind of criterion can we use to pick a guide? (*a*) He must know that he is building a metaphysics; if he has only an implicit metaphysics, he will not be of much help to us. For this reason, many thinkers who deal explicitly only with specialized problems (for example, with logic or ethics or theory of knowledge or philosophy of science) will not be practical guides. (*b*) He must know the various kinds of philosophies that have been constructed and have seen their advantages and shortcomings through their historical development. (*c*) His philosophy must violate no evidence; it must be in harmony with all the evidence and certitudes that are available. These conditions are excellently fulfilled by St. Thomas Aquinas.[17] (Note that we are not going to take his philosophy as true *because* he said it. To do this would be to acquire not a philosophy but an opinion.)

This temporary procedure, however, should be replaced at the end of our entire philosophy course by our own personal understanding of the truth and adequacy of our philosophy. In judging the adequacy of a philosophy, we must measure the correctness and adequacy of definitions, principles, and conclusions in relation to the proper matter of the demonstrative knowledge within which they function. To some extent we can be doing this even as we go through the course, especially when we have completed a unit.

8. Definitions[18]

The matter (subject matter) of a knowledge designates indeterminately and in its entirety that which a knowledge is about. Concretely, it comprises the "things" that are studied; for example, the matter of geometry is the lines, surfaces, solids, and angles. Abstractly, the matter designates what is common to all these "things"; in plane geometry, this would be "figures drawn on a surface."

The formal intelligibility pertaining to a kind of knowledge is what is specifically knowable about the matter, and this involves the way or ways it is known and the principles that are used. For

---

[17] For a fuller discussion, see below, secs. 122 and 125.

[18] This first set of definitions of terms is simply a vocabulary or glossary, giving the meanings of these terms. These definitions settle no philosophical problems; they only make it possible to talk about such problems. Italicized terms are the ones that will be used most frequently and therefore ought to be memorized.

example, the formal intelligibility of geometry is the construction, measurement, and investigation of the properties and relations of its matter. Note: most "things" of our experience can be known under more than one formal intelligibility.

The proper matter of a knowledge is its subject matter as specified by the formal intelligibility. For example, the proper subject matter of plane geometry is the construction, measurement, and investigation of the properties and relations of figures on a surface (which concretely are the lines, bounded surfaces, angles).

Demonstrative (or scientific) knowledge is an exactly stated knowledge with a single proper matter, organized through self-coherent definitions and, especially, by a single set of principles and shown to be accurate and true by some kind of reasoning process which lead to a certain assent or at least to a well-founded assent. For example, physics, philosophy, geometry and history are scientific knowledges.

Science is a kind of demonstrative knowledge concerned with the observation of facts, the establishment of general laws, and the explanation of these facts by means of general concepts logically constructed and deductively verified. Only the natural sciences are sciences in this strict sense.

Philosophy, descriptively speaking, is the collective name of metaphysics, philosophy of nature, epistemology, and ethics, taken together. Defined according to its abstract subject matter, philosophy is a (quasi-) genus of demonstrative knowledge about reality and the major kinds of reality taken as inclusively as possible. Defined according to its general formal intelligibility, philosophy is a (quasi-) genus of demonstrative knowledge that seeks (to draw from experience by means of direct insights, ontological concepts, and causal analysis) as complete and coherent an explanation of its matter as is possible.[19]

[19] To define "philosophy" essentially is a very difficult task. Many so-called definitions really define metaphysics; dictionary definitions are not of much help. The third definition given above will not be understood by the beginning student; it will, it is hoped, become clear by the time he finishes this book. Note, in the meantime, two things: (a) philosophy is only one among all the demonstrative knowledges; (b) philosophy draws from ordinary natural experience, and so does not in principle exclude faith and

Metaphysics is that "part" of philosophy whose proper matter is the real as real.

Experience is our direct encounter with and knowledge of the persons and things in our world.

Reasoning, in general, is any process of knowledge by which definitions and judgments are reached which are (1) not simply perceptual judgments, or simple essences reached by total abstraction, (2) nor simple insights. Briefly, reasoning is all mediate knowledge.

Total abstraction is the consideration of the nature or quiddity of a thing without consideration of its individual determinants.

Formal abstraction is the consideration of the formal determinants of a thing apart from other determinants of that same thing.

A univocal concept is one which is true of many individuals in exactly the same sense.

Abstraction is the act of considering one intelligibility of a thing without considering others with which it is associated in the real order.

Intelligibility is a characteristic, trait, or aspect (of a thing) which can be understood by the intellect (*ratio*).

Thing is a whole or a complete individual (as opposed to something that is merely a part, as for example, a hand; or to a collection, as a heap of stones). For example, a tree, a dog, a man.

Sensible thing is a thing capable of directly affecting our senses and therefore something capable of being immediately perceived in external experience. The three examples given of *thing* are also sensible things.

Material thing is a thing among whose intrinsic properties are (*a*) that it is capable of being measured and (*b*) that it is able to undergo gradual change; it is not necessary that we be able to sense it. (This is merely a descriptive definition; an essential definition will be given later.) For example, the air 50 miles above ground, a free electron, all sensible things.

---

revealed theology nor necessarily conflict with them. In consequence, philosophy is not *the* explanation of everything, nor the highest wisdom, nor a doctrine of salvation.

special intelligibility of being inasmuch as it does not depend on matter and motion.

> Commentary on the Third
> Book of the Sentences, dis. 27,
> q. 2, art. 4, qa. 2.

Metaphysics . . . considers all things inasmuch as they are beings, not coming down to a proper knowledge of morality or nature. For the intelligibility, "being," since it is different in different things, is not sufficient for the specific knowledge of things.

> Commentary on the First
> Book of the Sentences, pro-
> logue, q. 1, art. 2.

3. The Certitude of Metaphysics

The more a scientific knowledge is prior in nature, the more certain it is. This can be seen in that those sciences whose object can be said to be an addition to that of other sciences are less certain than the sciences which take fewer things into consideration. For example, arithmetic is more certain than geometry, for the objects of geometry have something more than those of arithmetic. This is clear if we look at what each of these sciences takes as its first principle; namely, the unit and the point. For the point adds location to the unit. For the intelligibility of the unit is constituted by undivided being. This notion, when it is taken as a measure, is the principle of number. But the point adds location to this.

The particular sciences are posterior in nature to the universal sciences, because the subject of the former adds to the subject of the latter. For example, "being as changeable," with which the scientific knowledge of nature deals, adds to "being (without qualification)" which is the subject of metaphysics and adds to "quantified being" which is the subject of mathematics. Therefore that scientific knowledge which is about being and the most universal objects is the most certain. Nor is it to be objected that metaphysics is here said to be about fewer things, though it was said above [earlier in the same section, not quoted here] that it knows all things. For the universal comprehends fewer things in act, but more in potency. And a science is the more certain the fewer actual considerations are necessary for the consideration of its subject. Wherefore, practical sciences are the most uncertain, because they must consider the many circumstances of singular operables.

> Commentary on Aristotle's
> Metaphysics, Bk. I, lect. 2
> (ed. Cathala, No. 47).

II

The Meaning of "Being"

10. Various senses of the word *real*

We have seen that metaphysics can be described briefly as the demonstrative (scientific) knowledge of the real inasmuch as it is real, and that therefore its basic question is, "What is it to be *real?*" Before we can go further into this question, we must distinguish the various senses of the word "real."

In the proper sense of the word, a real being is an actual being, one which is not merely an object of the mind or merely possible, but *is* actually in itself. This preliminary description will be made more exact later on. The best way to clarify the proper meaning of *real* is by contrast: an existing airplane is a real machine, an interplanetary spaceship is not real (not in 1962 at least); Carry Back is a real horse, Pegasus is not; Sir Winston Churchill is a real human being, Ichabod Crane is not; microbes are real beings, leprechauns are not; an orange is a real being, a perfect sphere is only an object of thought.

Sometimes the word "real" is used in an extended sense, for example, in logic and epistemology, to designate not only what is actually now but also whatever has existed, will exist, or can exist independently of thought. In this extended sense, a dinosaur is a real animal, but a centaur is not; Hamlet is a real character, Pogo is not; the battles of the Greeks and Trojans were real, the quarrels of Jupiter and Juno were not. This extended meaning of *real* is used to make a distinction among objects of thought: real objects are those that actually exist or could exist; unreal objects are those that cannot exist.[1]

Henceforward, *real* (and forms derived from it) will be used only in its proper sense; that is, to designate the actual things which are now. Thus, when we speak of "knowledge of the real" we will mean "knowledge of things which are here and now actual," and when we speak of "the real order," we will mean "the order (or totality) of things which are actual here and now." If we want to use the extended sense of the word "real," we will always attach the qualification, "in the wide sense."

Since metaphysics is the demonstrative knowledge of the real inasmuch as it is real, and since we can know and talk about things that are not real, obviously our first question must be, What is it to be real? The question, "What is it to be a real thing?" is not a question about our knowledge[2] but about the thing known.

---

[1] For example, a man can think about a dog he used to own which died last year; the dog is no longer part of the real world in which he lives today. A man can think of a purely fictional character; again, no actual, properly real being corresponds to his thought. But the one who thinks about these things can recognize that in the case of the dog there *was* an actual real thing to which, if it were now, his thought would conform; he can likewise recognize that in the case of the purely fictional character there *could be* an actual thing to which, if it were actual, his thought would also conform. In both cases, absolutely speaking, there is no actual real thing of which he is thinking; in both cases there is simply no-thing in the real order. Nevertheless, the word "real" has been extended to designate objects of thought such as these in order to mark off a distinction between them and still other objects of thought to which *no* real thing *can* correspond: for example, the internally inconsistent objects mentioned in the earlier paragraphs of this section (leprechauns, centaurs, Pogo, the world of Greek mythology) or such objects as necessarily involve purely mental objectivity, such as logical genera and species ("the species, man"; "the genus, animal"). A diagram may help to show the relationships of these terms:

$$\left\{\begin{array}{l}\text{real in the wide sense} \ldots\ldots \\ \qquad \textit{as opposed to} \\ \text{the mere object of thought}\end{array}\right. \left\{\begin{array}{l}\text{the properly real, the actual} \\ \qquad \textit{as opposed to} \\ \text{the past, the future, the possible}\end{array}\right.$$

For a further explanation of this, see below, sec. 88.

[2] Questions about our knowledge of the real are questions like, "How do we know real things?" and, "How can we tell, from looking at our knowledge, whether an object of knowledge is real or not?" These questions can-

11. Phenomenalism and the meaning of *being*

To help ourselves see the meaning of this question and the basic importance of the answer, we will look at some historical answers before we look at reality itself.[3] Our purpose is to understand these philosophical positions, not to refute them.[4] But to help ourselves to see that these are not things that one could affirm or deny without any change in his basic outlook on life, we will point out some consequences that are logically connected with them.

A first answer to the question is: A thing is real because, and inasmuch as, it acts or does something. A philosophy which answers the question of the meaning of reality in this way is called "phenomenalism" (from the Greek word meaning "appearance"). Phenomenalism, or "actualism," does not mean, "Every real thing acts in some way" or "We know that something is real because we find it acting" or "We can tell what kind of thing

---

not be answered or even considered now, for the answers to them depend at least in part on the philosophy of human nature.

[3] To make these different answers more concrete, we will refer to various historical positions. We are, however, not studying the history of philosophy, and so we are not bound to an adequate exposition of the thought of the great philosophers or to a refutation of their systems as wholes. We are interested only in clarifying the question and seeing what is involved in it. If a reader should desire further information on some of these basic positions, he can find a full introduction and a guide to further reading in the following books. James Collins, *A History of Modern European Philosophy* (Milwaukee, Bruce, 1954), pp. 109–117 (on Hobbes and materialism); pp. 204–207, 226–228 (on Spinoza and the relation between reason and reality); pp. 267–277, 279–281 (Leibniz and the world of intelligible essence); pp. 707–710 (on Comte and positivism); pp. 408–409, 415, 433–436 (on Hume and phenomenalism); pp. 509–512 (on Kant and the possibility of metaphysics; a highly recommended section). Etienne Gilson, *Being and Some Philosophers*, 2d ed. (Toronto, Pontifical Institute of Mediaeval Studies, 1952), pp. 83–96 (on Scotism and the particular); pp. 51–73 (on Averroës); pp. 74–82 (on Avicenna, another kind of essentialist).

[4] It is unfair to attack something which a person does not understand. Moreover, instead of refuting the position, one is likely to miss the point entirely. So the first requisite is to understand both our own position and those of the philosophers who hold different positions. And once we have a thorough understanding both of our own philosophy and of other philosophies in their historical context, it is usually unnecessary to engage in a refutation of them. To some this proposition may seem a paradox; the only answer is a real study of the history of philosophy.

something is by seeing what sort of actions it performs." These three propositions are perfectly true, but they are not the basic statement of actualism. Actualism holds that action is the reality of the thing. According to this doctrine, for example, "I" am real, in the sense that there are some thoughts, desires, movements, and so forth, which in some inexplicable way belong together. The sources of this doctrine are an incorrect understanding of substance and accident and a misuse of the ability of our mind to consider an action without considering the agent and thus to consider the action as if it were a thing.[5]

To assess the value of phenomenalism we need only to consider attentively the whole real things which are actual. How does an actual real thing manifest itself to us in our experience; for example, a human person? A human person manifests himself to us as something real which acts; a person can act precisely because he is real. A thing is not real in consequence of its action; rather, it can act because it is real. We will have to investigate the relation between a being and its action later on,[6] but for the time being it is sufficiently clear that acting is not the very meaning of being real.

If reality essentially consists in activity, and if activity is in continual change, there can be no permanent personality and no immortality for the human soul. Further, if in such an explanation of reality a philosopher still talks about God, this will not be the transcendent, creative God of Christian thought but perhaps some ideal action or complexus of actions.

12. Materialism and the meaning of *being*

A second answer to the question, What is it to be real? is the answer given by materialism. As a preliminary approach to the materialistic view, we can ask ourselves what the difference is between an architect's idea of a house and the real house which is the result of that plan. It is that the plan has been "realized" in the material components of lumber, cement, stone, clay, and so forth. According to the materialistic view, a plan, order, or structure is not real of itself; matter is the principle of reality.

[5] See below, secs. 39, 96, 103, 108, 109.
[6] See below, secs. 39 and 109.

Superficially, we may think of materialism as an explanation of reality based on human productive activity.

Materialism can take several forms. The most extreme sort of materialism holds that only matter exists and simply denies that anything else is or can be real. Dogmatic behaviorism, for example, denied that men really had thoughts and feelings; general semantics, today, admits that men have sensible feelings but persists in the denial of thought.

A more moderate sort of materialism admits that there are some realities, such as ideas, which are not simply material. But it is still a materialism, for it holds that these nonmaterial realities arise from matter, depend entirely on matter, and vanish completely when they are separated from matter. This moderate materialism is professed by some who call themselves "modern materialists," as well as by the Marxists, who call their system "dialectical materialism."

According to all materialists, all the things we see are material, and the differences between them arise from various combinations of simpler material elements. The ultimate elements are then the principle of reality for them. The older materialists and the Marxists think of these principles as material, substantial particles which always existed by themselves. Others, trying to bring philosophy more into line with what they consider to be the best scientific views, think of ultimate reality as a large amount of "free energy" which can be either structured into things or left "free," "unattached" (for example, in the form of radiation).

For the moment, we are going to consider only one point: the meaning of *real* as given by materialism, "To be real is to be material or in matter." It is true that the things which we experience are material. Why should we even question the identification of reality with matter? We question it for the simple reason that we have equally immediate experience of our own conscious activity, especially that of intellectual knowledge and of choice. These activities have as much claim to be called real as any activities of the things we find that are distinct from us. If we wish to respect the evidence, we must admit that both the activities of physical things and our own conscious activities are truly real. If we look attentively at our own acts of knowledge, they do not present themselves as sensible. They have no directly discoverable relation *as actions* to any material characteristic. Intellectual understanding has no sensible qualities; it presents itself as simply different from, and not describable in terms of, mass and motion, chemical action, electromagnetic activity, or in one phrase, any activities of nonhuman things. Take the act of understanding what a square is (or what justice is or that a given syllogism is valid). Examine that act. It is real; you do understand. Yet that act remains indescribable except in its own supersensible terms.

Hence, it is good to ask: "Is matter *identically* reality?" "Is matter the principle of reality in all real things?"[7]

Matter, as the extreme materialists talk about it, is not something which we can experience. Matter is "in itself" always determin*able*. It becomes this or that, it acquires this or that structure. *Real* matter is always some *kind* of matter. As far as direct sense experience is concerned, we experience minerals, plants, animals, men, air, the planets, and so forth. But the determinability of "matter in itself" is more strikingly seen in the case of the supposedly ultimate particles or energy: these ultimate particles have definite electrical characteristics and a definite size;[8] energy is always of some definite kind and quantity; a particle is always an electron or a proton or some other kind of particle (or "wave packet" or whatever other term scientists may find better). In other words, the "matter in itself," which is alleged to be the principle of reality, is itself a determinable genus that is determined by some other principle.

But to be real is to be fully determinate. Why? Because to be determin*able* has a double implication: (1) to be *able* to be

---

[7] The first of these two questions implies the position of extreme materialism, the second, of moderate materialism.

[8] At the present time (1962), physicists hold that the electron (and other subatomic particles as well) does not have a completely determined position. Without going into an explanation of the nature of scientific theory (see Chap. XIV, sec. 115), this much at least is clear: subatomic particles have a definite quantum and kind of energy; their size is not completely indefinite but can be known within some limits; their location cannot be determined at the same time as their velocity, but it also is not completely indefinite.

something or other and (2) at the present moment *not* to be it. We must then ask the question, Does it make sense to say, "That in virtue of which a real thing is determinable, and consequently *not* yet a definite reality, is simultaneously that in virtue of which every real thing *is* real"? Recall again the precise point of the present discussion. It is not to determine whether there is or is not an individual existing thing which is purely spiritual (without any matter at all); it is simply this, Is a real thing (material or not, as the case may be) real in virtue of some indeterminate "matter in itself"? In other words, Is there something even about a material thing which is not merely "matter in itself"?

If matter is not the whole of reality, is it at least the principle of reality? Another way of putting the question is, Is matter the reason for all reality? Modern materialists and dialectical materialists say that it is; at one time, they contend, there was only matter. Through the course of millions of years, this matter acted and reacted with itself, and so plants, animals, and men came about. But in the last analysis, the simple elemental particles of matter are the self-sufficient cause of all reality; they are eternal, indestructible, active, as we gather from the statements of these philosophers. This position will need to be examined from several different points of view as we go on.

Materialism involves a number of consequences which we are not going to take up here, but which it will be useful to point out. It involves (*a*) the denial of any spiritual reality or person; (*b*) at least logically, the denial of any essential differences in the activities of things; (*c*) the explanation of life and consciousness in terms of the nonliving and the nonconscious. The first of these consequences is evident. The second follows from the admission by the materialist that matter is an undifferentiated principle. Differences can therefore be only accidental. Those materialists who hold that consciousness, desire, and so forth, are really different from nonconscious activities do so at the cost of logical consistency. For—and this is the third consequence—if matter is the principle of reality, then real activities are material, and the activities of nonliving things are the constitutent elements of all activity. It is fine rhetoric but poor logic to insist that materialism fully respects the evidence of life and knowledge.

THE DIALECTIC OF DISAGREEING POSITIONS

We have noticed a disagreement about the reality and significance of material things. Materialism is one of the recurring parties to the dispute; it has a special attraction because of its direct appeal to the reality of the body and because it gives a reason for dedication to a program of action in this world. Idealism, on the other hand, appeals to reflective and intellectual people; it gives a reason for discounting the errors and excesses of sense. Both systems must contain a truth, else they would have no interest for thinkers; they are in conflict because each sees its partial truth as the whole.

The truth in materialism should be evident to each one of us, because man has a body. Yet there are those who deny this aspect of their experience, doubt it, or relegate it to some insignificant corner as being merely practical, biological experience, not to be even mentioned by an intellectual. Yet what we see, taste, and touch—this food, that car, that television set, this boy, that girl— are real even in their materiality. They are real in that they are independently existing subjects, and their independence of us is manifest to us in that they are spatially exterior to us and act upon us or undergo our action.

Yet idealism and essentialism have a point to make: the sensible is not the real without qualification. If we were only animals, we could not even be materialists. Idealism and essentialism assert that the intelligible is the real and that the intellect is the proper judge of reality, not the senses. Being, after all, is known. Yet what is material and sensible is to that extent changeable and subjective— it is not so much "what is" as "what seems for a fleeting instant to be." Being, as we find it in ourselves, is both knowing and known, and this is as it should be. For any being worthy of the name should be present to itself, with itself, in possession of itself, and these are the marks of a knower. Matter—that sheer extended, barely qualified, senseless reality—thus appears as entirely impossible (Berkeley), as a projection from subjective sensation (idealism), as irrelevant to intelligibility (essentialism). An exaggeration, no doubt; yet essentialism can point to the history of science: as long as science established itself on the basis of sensible qualities it made little progress; after it abandoned these qualities in favor of purely intelligible mathematical relations it made great progress, both in understanding and in its successful creative effort to deal with things. If physics deals with anything real (atoms, forces, etc.) it deals with something intelligible, not something sensible.

Existentialists in their turn admit that man must rise above the limiting and confining biological interests before he reaches his stature as a man, who can know being. Thus, they have no intention of becoming materialists. Against essentialism they object to the lifeless and heartless abstractions with which science deals, but think that this is a necessary result of all ordinary scientific knowledge. They wish to find reality, too; and they find it in human personality, known not scientifically but "subjectively," as personal, in a personal dealing with the world, especially in the person-to-person encounter.

The values of these three positions lie then in these points: material things are real; the real is the intelligible, and in understanding we must in some way grasp an essence, yet the intelligible and the essential are *in* the things which we sense in the first instance; abstraction is useful and necessary, but it is not the way by which we arrive at the real as real; only judgmental knowledge is sufficient; but judgmental knowledge can be the basis of a scientific metaphysics.

DIRECT CONFRONTATION OF THE EVIDENCE

With these lines of thought in mind to help us keep our attention on significant points, we need to look again at some real thing.[12] We should—each one of us—take some really existing singular immediately present to us (not something imagined, not merely some words describing something which was present to someone else). Let us take ourselves in our immediate situation,

[12] The discussion of three basic philosophical positions in the preceding section was not a proof of the Thomistic answer nor a full philosophical refutation of the opposing positions. The discussion was intended to clarify the meaning of the question about the real and to direct our attention to the various factors which should be considered.

As for starting with the real itself, rather than with some a priori notion we might concoct in withdrawing from reality—the reason we do this will become clear as we proceed. See also below, sec. 116.

or some person here and now present to us. This person is performing *actions* by which we become aware of him; even in our own case, our awareness of ourselves arises from something we do or undergo. A person—ourselves also—is something which has at least something about him that is *material* and sensible. A person is some *kind* of reality; he has a human nature and not some other kind of nature. Yet a person is also different from the things around him; he is free and *self-determining;* he is the one *for* whom things are; and things for their part are related to his knowledge because they are knowable.

These propositions are true, and the evidence for them is precisely the acting material existents, some of whom, but not all, are persons. Yet all of these truths are just as intelligible when we consider them abstractly—the relation of action to the agent, materiality, nature, and the relation of knower to known can be intelligibly signified without saying that they are actual. Only when we say that they *are* do we signify them as actual. My reality is my actually existing as a free knowing being, and so too the reality of other persons around me is their actuality as knowing and free; finally, the reality of the things in my world which are variously related to me is their actually existing as such things.

Our being expresses itself in action; it is limited by materiality, by the nature which we have, and by the situation in which we find ourselves. Yet when we reflect on our own awareness of ourselves, each one of us sees immediately in his own highly personal experience: I am not simply any one of my actions (much less a collection of or sequence of actions). I am material, but that *I am* is not what I mean by materiality or vice versa. The same evidence will appear, though in a different way, if we attentively consider another person or thing.

On the other hand, when we say, "I am," "you are," "it is," we are not speaking equivocally. Whenever we apprehend some real thing which we sense, at the same time we also perceive ourselves as knowing and as reacting in various ways to the thing we know. Our own actuality is involved with our world, including nonpersonal things, and our world's actuality cannot be perceived by us except in an act by which we also perceive ourselves. This world is sensed and not only understood to be real. In our "being

together with people in the world," we have at once the evidence
that "to be real" is primarily "*to be*," and at the same time that
"to be" is neither to be material nor to be some particular essence.

Confirmatory consideration

An indirect reflection may clarify this proper meaning of
"real." Suppose we compare a real human person here and now
present in our experience with a fictional character, for example,
Sherlock Holmes, and a real thing or animal with the Hound of
the Baskervilles. The real person and thing as well as Holmes and
the Hound are singular or individual; all have an intelligible essence—Holmes and the man even have the same intelligible essence, that of humanity; all have the sensible qualities by which
we know matter; all have particular actions of their own, and the
qualities and actions of all of them are described by the same
words. Yet the difference between them is more important than
all the similarities: the person and the thing we are experiencing
are real, Holmes and the Hound are mere objects of thought. And
the statement that precisely shows this difference is this: the person and the thing *are*, exist, whereas the fictional character and the
fictional animal do not exist, do not have their own proper act of
existing.

Grammatical analysis

From the statement, "The properly real is that which is," we
get its proper technical name, being. The verb *is* has as its infini-
tive *to be* (for which the variant form *being* is sometimes used[13]),
as its participle, *being* (note that the participle implicitly includes
some subject for the verb), and as its corresponding verbal noun,
also *being*. Hence, the verbal noun, *being*, in its first sense means
"that which is" or "something having an act of existing."[14] For

[13] In other verbs, the formation is somewhat different: run, to run, running, runner. The context will usually determine which form is to be
understood; in ambiguous cases we will shift to a nonambiguous form or
to an equivalent phrase.

[14] The term "something" means "an individual object, known and expressed in an unspecified way." A real thing can be called "something";
so can fictional and mathematical objects. Hence, we can say technically,
"something" directly signifies an indeterminately known essence and usually
connotes existence. See above, sec. 8 on the definition of "thing" and
below, secs. 16 and 86; see also *Summa Theologiae*, Pt. I, q. 30, art. 4.

the phrase "act of existing" we will sometimes use the noun "esse"; for example, we might define "being" as "something having esse."

Since the properly real is that which *is*, and since metaphysics is the demonstrative knowledge of the real as real, we can express the object of metaphysics fully and accurately by the phrase "being as being" or, in the fuller form, "whatever has an act of existing (esse) inasmuch as it is." That is why we call metaphysics the "philosophy of being."[15]

This grammatical analysis looks easy enough, but there are many problems concealed in it. How have we done this? What sort of knowledge of being do we have?[16]

16. The primitive notion of being

We must approach the problem of our knowledge of being in two stages, for there are two knowledges of being. There is, first, the primitive notion of being, "something which is as the things of my experience are" (which St. Thomas mentions in the expression, *ens primum cognitum*), and, second, the being which is the object of metaphysics, namely, being as being.

We noticed in our grammatical analysis that we move from a statement (or statements) to a verbal noun which no longer contains a definite subject. Have we therefore made use of an abstraction?[17] First of all, abstraction, even total abstraction, always

[15] This point is treated in Selected Passages, No. 4.

[16] See also below, sec. 24; the treatment of our knowledge of the being even of sensible things will not be completed until sec. 43.

[17] See above, sec. 1.

The subsequent discussion is a straightforward phenomenological analysis of experience. For those who approach this problem with preconceptions (philosophical or otherwise), the following points may be made. (*a*) The human *intellect* (not just the human knower) does know singulars. (See G. P. Klubertanz, S.J., "St. Thomas and the Knowledge of the Singular," *The New Scholasticism*, XXVI [1952], 135–166). (*b*). The doctrine of the three degrees of abstraction is not a complete analysis of *all* knowledge, but only of scientific knowledge; it ignores perceptual knowledge. (*c*) The metaphysician, the philosophical psychologist, and the epistemologist will see that the "commonness" of metaphysical conceptions, principles, and propositions is not arrived at by abstraction (properly so called) but by separation and related processes. The logician (who ignores processes and meanings and considers only terms) calls all nonsingular terms abstract and measures their "distance" from sensation in terms of degrees. Hence, since

leaves some part of our initial reality out of consideration. Now, if we were to say that "being" is reached by abstraction from a real being, we would imply that there is in the real thing some not-being, which is left out of consideration; but since not-being is nothing, nothing can be left out of consideration. Second, abstraction pertains to the first operation of the mind (simple apprehension), for according to its definition it is a "nonconsideration of . . . ," and so it concerns only essences.[18] But, as we saw above, an essentialist view of reality is not adequate. There is "more" to being than essence, and that "more" is its act of existing. Thus, to be is other than and different from the definite essence in the being. Hence, we can consider the essence by itself, and such a consideration is properly an abstraction. But the thing with its act of existing cannot be the object of an abstraction (nor can the act of existing by itself be the object of an abstraction, either, as we shall see later); and unless the act of existing is included in being, we do not have being in the proper sense of the word. Hence, for both of the reasons advanced above, being cannot be reached by abstraction. In other words, the knowledge of being is not a simple concept (apprehension) of an essence.

There are, however, other forms of intellectual knowledge, namely, judgment and reasoning. Judgment is that act of the mind by which we assert (or deny) that something is, or is modified in some way or other. Judgment, therefore, directly reaches the esse of a thing, for in the judgment we know that a thing is. The judgment, it is true, virtually[19] contains an apprehension of an essence. We cannot assert "is" without at least implicitly under-

---

metaphysics can conclude to beings which cannot be sensed at all, the logician will consider it the "most abstract" of all sciences, in the "third degree of abstraction." For a person to insist on doing metaphysics as if it were logic is to doom the whole metaphysical enterprise to ruin from the start. See also sec. 120.

[18] By the term "essence" we mean that which we name, describe, or define (that is, as what it is). The term "quiddity" is an unfamiliar term for "essence." The statement in the text is not meant to imply that all the objects of apprehension are simple concepts; there are some very complicated objects which we will consider below briefly in sec. 88.

[19] The term "virtually" means here: "does not actually contain an apprehension as a distinct act but has a function equivalent to that of an apprehension."

standing "something" ("this," "it," and so on) as a subject for that
verb. But what is special and peculiar to the judgment is that a
direct perceptual judgment is a knowledge that some existent is.

The things that we directly and immediately assert to exist are
the sensible things of our experience, as we have seen above, and
the judgments that we make about immediately experienced
things are called perceptual judgments. The act of existing thus
attained is the esse of a material, singular thing.

At some time in our lives we can explicitly realize that many
things are and that we have said, "This is," "That is," and so on.
The second thing we notice and assert *to be* makes us realize that
the "is" is not identical with either the "this" or the "that"; the
"somethings" are many; the "is" is somehow general, since it is
truly applied to two different individuals, and so also meaningful
in itself. When we have done this, we have denied that "is" is
identical with any one of the singulars we have experienced,
though we have also implicity affirmed that "is" has a common
intelligibility in all cases. Yet we have not denied that there is a
subject; we have only denied that the subject of "is" must be this
or that in particular. The result of this denial coming after an
affirmation is a generalization: we go from (1) "this is," "that is,"
through (2) "neither necessarily this nor that," to (3) "something
is." Thus, we have disengaged a common intelligibility from its
original presentation in the completely singular sensible thing. But
we have not *abstracted* it; we have not left anything out, we have
not failed to consider anything. The term *something* is not strictly
abstract; rather, it is a term which contains the singular implicitly.
It expresses indefinitely a completely determined, singular thing,
or, as is sometimes said, it has an indefinite reference to the singular as such. The denial which is the second term of the process
we have been describing we will call "the negative judgment of
generalization."[20]

In this discussion, we have been assuming that usually a person
will have experienced many beings and asserted the existence of
a number of them before he ever comes to the kind of reflection

[20] Some authors, borrowing an expression from Cajetan, call the process
"abstraction by confusion." A student—at least an English-speaking one—
will be confused by a misleading translation of what was at best an awkward
term.

we have been describing. Certainly, the negative judgment of generalization is considerably facilitated by the experience of two or more beings. But we might suppose a person skilled in logical analysis, who has seen that whenever we have a direct concept, whatever we can express in a single concept is strictly one, and when we cannot do this, then we are dealing with two really distinct factors. He would, for example, realize that "white man" cannot be reduced to a single concept, and that therefore "white" is not a constituent of "man," but really distinct from it. Next, if he had sufficient grasp of the object, he could see that "white" is not a logical property of man, but a contingent attribute. He could therefore come to see that man is not necessarily white and that white things are not necessarily men. Now, in making the judgment, "This is," he could similarly see that this cannot be turned into a simple concept of an essence; that "is" is not a logical property of any finite thing. From this it does not follow that other things exist; our logician could not even infer that other things are really possible. He would be limited to this: since "this is," and since "is" is neither a constituent nor a logical property of "this," then there is no reason deriving from "this" or from "is" that this be unique. But even this very limited negation would enable him to proceed to the generalization, "Something is."

From the judgment "Something is," we can form a complex apprehension[21] of "something which is," "something having esse." This complex apprehension implicitly contains a real judgment, and so properly is expressed by the participial noun, "a being." However, we can also stress its noun function; in that case, it is expressed by the noun used absolutely: *being;* and if we wish to make this emphasis clear, we will use a hyphenated expression, "that-which-is," "something-which-is."

[21] A simple apprehension or concept is an act by which the mind grasps a nature or quiddity without affirming or denying, but simply considering it absolutely in itself. In addition to this sort of understanding, there is another type of conception, which, although not an explicit judgment, has arisen from a preceding judgment in such a way that the judgmental function of knowledge of esse remains. Cf. Klubertanz, *The Philosophy of Human Nature*, pp. 178–180.

17. The metaphysical knowledge of being

But the being that we derive from sensible things by direct perceptual judgments and the negative judgment of generalization is precisely the being of *sensible* things, not being as being. Though we have not explicitly said so, what we experience is not an unqualified being; sensible things as sensible do not merely have a sensible essence but a sensible mode of being (the reason for saying this will become clearer later). We could say, "This man is-sensibly," "This dog is-in-matter-and-motion." Hence, we have not yet reached the being of metaphysics. Can we move from being as sensible to the being of metaphysics by abstraction? If we suppose that we do, we would imply either (1) that a sensible thing contains both sensible being and being as being, so that we can abstract from the former to have only the latter, or (2) that the "sensible" part of *sensible being* is nonbeing and so can be abstracted from to leave only pure being. Both of these alternatives have no basis in our experience: we directly see a sensible thing which is, and that-which-is in a sensible thing is-sensibly. Moreover, the second of the two alternatives is self-defeating once we have arrived at the conception of being as that which *is*. Hence, the supposition that we reach being as being by abstraction is false.[22]

Let us re-examine the process we used when we tried to determine what it means to be real.[23] We used the reflections of many philosophers to illuminate our own experience, and with their help examined the beings that we immediately know. We saw that these beings are sensible and material. Yet being is not merely material, for among beings are persons, who are intellectual and free. We therefore carefully examined a being (or many beings), and we noticed that a being (mere thing or person) is (1) some particular kind of thing, which is (2) acting or being acted on, (3) knowing or being known, (4) singular, and (5) sensible and material. We examined each one of these aspects of a sensible thing, and saw that either singly or taken together they are real—provided that the thing in question truly *is*. But, upon reflection

[22] One of the reasons for this is mentioned in Selected Passages, No. 7.
[23] See above, secs. 11 and 15.

and analysis, it became equally clear that although the thing which we immediately experience as a matter of fact (1) always is a particular kind of thing, it is not real because of its essence, for there are many different kinds of essence, essences are sometimes merely possible and merely understood, and things with essences change. (2) Action and being acted on are found in all beings of our experience, and are the immediate reason why we experience them; but action presupposes the reality of the agent and (in our experience) also of the patient; action changes; and there are many different kinds of action. (3) Things are known; persons know and are known, and a thing is not real *for us* except to the extent that it is known; and if we wish to say that the possibility of knowing and being known belongs ultimately to the constitution of persons and things, we can truly say so; yet, as far as human knowledge is concerned, it ultimately presupposes the reality of both knower and known, and the possibility of knowing and being known must ultimately be grounded on some actuality, if it is to be a real possibility and not merely a logical relationship. (4) Things and persons are singular, but so also are mere objects of the mind; moreover, there are many singulars, so that reality cannot be the same as singularity. (5) Things are sensible and material, and so, too, to an extent, are persons; yet, in the last analysis, sensibility and materiality are fundamental traits in the order of essence (for they belong generically to *what* things are); they do not account for the possibility of the things' knowing or being known; they are ultimately the root of the continuous change of things, and so are fundamentally mut*able* and determin*able;* hence, materiality cannot be the ultimate actuality by which things are real.

The discovery that "is" asserts the actuality of all of these and not their nature—what they are, including, as we must, action and materiality in the order of essence—leads to the discovery of the act of existing as not identical with any of them. And this discovery of the act of existing—esse—is the moment of discovery of metaphysics. In other words, after the direct perceptual judgment, "This is," we make a negative judgment, "And its actuality is not identically its materiality, and so forth." This special negative judgment we will call the "judgment of separation,"[24] for by it we separate the intelligibility of what it means *to be* from the intelligibility of what a sensible, material quiddity or essence is.[25]

Perhaps it will help us to understand the judgment of separation if we consider it as a summary negation including a series of specific negations which are probably not made all at once. Most likely, the first of these negations is the understanding that reality is not a "property" of any particular thing or due to any form of singularity. Next, we may come to realize that activity is not identical with reality when we learn that things remain real even when we do not experience their action. Then, we come to understand that sensibility is not identical with reality, for even popular science tells us of realities that we cannot sensibly experience. As we come closer to a philosophical grasp of being, we see that matter is not simply the whole of reality or the principle of reality, even in a material thing; this we see when we come to understand that matter is potential and determinable. Finally, by a still more difficult reflection, we come to understand that essence is not identical with reality and being, and this we do partly by reflection on the many, widely differing kinds of things that exist and partly by reflection on essences that are mere objects of thought.[26]

In the formation, therefore, of the complex intelligibility of "being as being," we make two judgments.[27] (1) "This (sensible) thing is," and (2) "Even for this sensible thing *to be* is not the same as for it to be a particular sensible or material thing with a definite essence." This judgment does not imply that we know that an immaterial being exists or that we think that such a being

[24] Some authors call separation "abstraction in the wide sense" or the "third degree of abstraction." This latter expression is confusing (see above, n. 17); it could even lead to abstractionism and essentialism.

[25] This point is discussed in Selected Passages, No. 5.

[26] This consideration is clinched by a detailed investigation of real change, for if "to be an essence" were identical with "to be or to exist" change would be impossible; see below, sec. 43.

[27] Two judgments are necessary, not three, because the judgment of separation can do all that the judgment of generalization does and more. However, someone may take this in three steps: (1) the perceptual judgment; (2) the judgment of generalization; (3) the judgment of separation.

is possible.[28] At the present stage of our investigation, we do not know demonstratively that there are immaterial beings. The second of these two judgments—the judgment of separation—may sometimes be only implicit, in the way in which it is implied, for example, in the explanatory phrase, "Being as being is something which is *inasmuch as it is.*"

In this analysis of the beings of our experience and of our knowledge of them, we have been dealing throughout with sensible, material existents. The point of our consideration has been to establish a scientific knowledge of the properly real. We have seen that a real thing which exists, is material, has a singular essence, and acts is *real* precisely because it exists; and that in such a thing, that in virtue of which it *is* is an act—its act of existing. The scientific understanding[29] of the properly real, "being as being," is formed through an implicitly double judgment, in which we have our first explicit knowledge of existence.

18. The first principles of knowledge

A principle of knowledge is some knowledge from which some other knowledge follows or flows. In reasoning, the premises are the principles of the conclusion. But not all principles are *first* principles, for some principles are themselves conclusions from some other premises. A first principle is one that is not proved from or developed from some other, prior principle. There are first principles in every demonstrative knowledge, though it can often happen that some of the first principles of some science (for

[28] It is extremely important to note that just as a material being is not a being because it is material, but because it *is*, so, too, an immaterial being (if such there be) is not a being because it is immaterial, but because it is. In general, the *kind* of essence a being has does not make it a being; whatever its essence, it is a being because and inasmuch as it is.

Hence, it is illusory to attempt to base a knowledge of being as being on the demonstrated existence of immaterial things. Either "is" is freed from its sensible and changing context (prior to the proof of the existence of immaterial being, and thus is meaningful when we conclude to the existence of such being) or "is" remains as we first find it immersed in sensibility and change. In the latter case, "is" means "is sensible, material and changeable," and to assert that "An *immaterial, immobile* thing is *sensible, material and changeable*" is a contradiction.

[29] See also below, sec. 25, on the "unity" of the knowledge of being.

example, physics) are developed in another science (for example, mathematics). If we want to speak of first principles, we must therefore distinguish between first principles in some particular order and absolutely first principles. In the absolute sense of first principles, sense experience is a first principle of human knowledge.

In the order of intellectual knowledge, there are two types of knowledge, apprehension and judgment, and each of these should have its own first principle. When we began this chapter, we noticed that there are various senses of the word *real*. We noticed there that metaphysics deals with the real in the proper, or strict, sense of that word. But there is a wide sense, which is about the same as that of the word *possible*. The *real*, in the wide sense, or the *possible*, is whatever can be, whether it ever was or not, or whether it ever will be. To this there corresponds also a concept of being—not the being of metaphysics, nor the primitive notion of being, but that "being" which is the simplest of all, which all other notions presuppose, and which itself presupposes no other intellectual knowledge. But then, by definition, this is the first principle of all apprehension, and so we can truly say that being (in the sense of whatever can be) is the first principle of knowledge. In the philosophy of human nature, we will see that being in this sense is the proper object of the intellect and that every concept other than being is understood in some relation to, or as an elaboration or determination of, being. Moreover, since human knowledge begins from sensation and from sensible things, we can also define "being (as first principle)" as the quiddity of sensible things.

Judgments, for their part, implicitly contain apprehensions; therefore, to that extent, being is also the implicit first principle of all judgments. But judgment, in addition, is an affirmation (or negation), and so its proper first principle will be concerned with this characteristic. We can state it this way: "Affirmation is not the same as negation," or, in a fuller and more usual formula: "It is impossible to affirm and deny the same thing of the same subject at the same time." We can also state it in terms of being: "A thing cannot both be and not be at the same time."[30] This principle is called "the principle of contradiction."

Because metaphysics is the demonstrative knowledge of the real as real, we must briefly consider, in a preliminary way, a question that has been asked by various philosophers throughout the whole history of philosophy, namely, "Can there be a reality which cannot be known by us?" If we are working with a concept of essence or with the primitive notion of being, then we will not be able to answer the question at this point, and perhaps we would have to give an affirmative answer. But if we are working with being as being, then we can say immediately, "Any alleged or proved reality, since it will be, in some sense of the word, *something*, and since it will *be*, can be known by us as being."[31] And in the same way the principle of contradiction will be applicable to any present or proved or alleged reality.

The truth, as well as the absolute applicability, of the principle of contradiction is known simply in understanding that principle. We discover that a thing cannot both be and not be at the same time when we experience something which is, understand it, and reflect and compare it with its opposite. If we ask, "Where and how do we find the principle of contradiction?" the clear answer is: "Inductively, in experience." If we ask, "How or where do we know the truth and universality of that judgment?" the answer is "In itself, that is, in what we understand when we affirm that a thing cannot both be and not be at the same time." In other words, when we experience a being and understand the act of existing, it is precisely that act and our insight into it that grounds our judgment. For this reason, a principle like this is called "per se known" or "analytic."[32]

[30] Per se known principles are mentioned briefly in Selected Passages, No. 6.

[31] This point will be taken up again in secs. 78 and 88.

[32] An analytic principle is one which can be discovered to be true from an analysis of what it says. When the term "analytic" is used as here defined, it is correct to call *first* principles analytic. But there are other meanings of the term which are not suitable. (1) The Kantian meaning ("An analytic proposition is one in which the predicate is drawn out of the subject by analysis") cannot be applied to any of the principles of metaphysics. (2) There is another meaning which implies that both of the terms which compose the proposition are first known separately by two distinct simple

Sometimes it helps our understanding of a per se known proposition to take a negative and dialectical approach to it, in other words, to try to see whether we can suppose it to be false. Suppose a man were to say, "It is true that affirming and denying the same thing can be done at the same time." In that case, his affirmation itself is affected by what he says, so that the affirmation does not exclude a simultaneous negation—in other words, his affirmation turns out to be meaningless. In other words, no man can really *think* the opposite of the principle of contradiction, although he can form a meaningless string of words which looks like a denial of that principle.

19. Definitions

A *real* thing, in the proper sense of the word, is an actually existing thing, one which exists in itself and is not merely an object of thought.

A real thing, in the wide sense of the word, is something which is, was, will be, or at least can be.

Materialism is the philosophical doctrine that things are real inasmuch as they are material.

Essentialism is the philosophical doctrine that things are real inasmuch as they are or have an essence or quiddity.

Being is something having esse (an act of existing).

Being as being is something having esse inasmuch as it is, exists.

Judgment is that act of the mind by which we assert (or deny) that a thing is (was, will be), or that it is modified in some way.

Simple apprehension is the simple and absolute grasp of *what* a thing is (concept).

Complex apprehension is an intellectual grasp of an intelligibility by way of or through a judgment.

Separation is a negative judgment: a judgment by which we deny that one (thing or intelligibility) is another.

---

apprehensions, then the content of each apprehension is analyzed, and finally the judgment is made. Such a process is possible in some per se known propositions (for example, in the proposition, "Incorporeal things do not occupy space"), but certainly it is not possible with the principle of contradiction or with many other principles, such as the principle of causality.

20. Summary of the argument

A. The real is properly being.

The real things of our immediate experience, though they are sensible and therefore material, are real, not because they are material or because they are what they are or because they are singular but because they are, exist.

Comment. To be real does not mean to be material, because matter in itself is determinable and is not the principle of actuality and determination; nor does it mean to be acting, because acting follows being; nor does it mean to have an essence or to be singular, because quiddity and essence do not serve to distinguish the properly real from the real in the wide sense and so cannot be the principle of the properly real.

B. Being as being is not reached by abstraction but by separation.

The act of abstraction belongs to the first operation of the mind, which concerns quiddities or essences and leaves something out of consideration. But being is not merely a quiddity, and there is nothing outside of being which could be left out. Yet being as being is not the same as being material, and this denial or negative judgment is called separation.

21. Readings

St. Thomas Aquinas, *On the Power of God,* q. 7, art. 2, ad 9 (that is, the seventh question, the second article, answer to the ninth argument; this answer is a very condensed but comprehensive expression of the primacy of esse); *Contra Gentiles,* Bk. II, Chap. 54 (especially the paragraphs beginning "First" and "Secondly"; this passage explains that the *whole* thing is that-which-is); *Summa Theologiae,* Pt. I, q. 5, art. 1, ad 1 (the meaning of "being," in comparison with the meaning of "good"); Pt. I, q. 16, art. 4 ad 2 (things are known before one knows one's self); Pt. I, q. 29, art. 1, art. 3; q. 30, art. 4; and q. 98, art. 1 (on the meaning of "person" and the metaphysical status of persons); Pt. I, q. 40, art. 3; *Compendium of Theology,* Chap. 62 (these two passages speak of the two types of abstraction); *Commentary on the Metaphysics of Aristotle,* Bk. VI, lesson 2, Nos. 1171–1190, pp. 465–470 (on the meaning of being).

Max Charlsworth, "The Meaning of Existentialism," *Thomist*, vol. XVI (1953), 472–496; a good introductory article.

W. Norris Clarke, S.J., "What is Really Real?" in *Progress in Philosophy*, ed. James A. McWilliams, S.J. (Milwaukee, Bruce Pub. Co., 1955), pp. 61–90; argues that the possibles are not the primary objects of metaphysics.

Etienne Gilson, *Being and Some Philosophers*, 2d ed. (Toronto, Pontifical Institute of Mediaeval Studies, 1952), pp. 203–205, on the difference between the simple concept and the judgment, and on our knowledge of esse; *The Christian Philosophy of St. Thomas Aquinas* (New York, Random House, 1956), pp. 29–45, on the meaning of "being."

Robert J. Henle, S.J., "Existentialism and the Judgment," *Proceedings of the American Catholic Philosophical Association*, Vol. XXVI (1946), pp. 40–53. This is a detailed and very penetrating analysis of the importance of the act of existing in the philosophy of being and of the judgment as our only adequate knowledge of esse; "A Thomist on An Experimentalist on Being," *The Modern Schoolman*, vol. 35 (1958), 133–141; an enlightening rejoinder.

Jacques Maritain, *Existence and the Existent*, trans. L. Galantiere and G. Phelan (Garden City, Doubleday, 1956), pp. 20–55, on the notion of being.

Oliver Martin, "An Examination of Contemporary Naturalism and Materialism," *Return to Reason*, ed. John Wild (Chicago, Regnery, 1953), pp. 68–91; an excellent study of the inadequacy of materialism.

Van Cleve Morris, "An Experimentalist on Being," *The Modern Schoolman*, vol. 35 (1958), 125–133; a pragmatist critique of the Thomistic notion of being.

Elizabeth Salmon, "What is Being?" *Review of Metaphysics*, vol. VII (1954), 613–631.

Kenneth Schmitz, "Toward a Metaphysical Restoration of Natural Things," *An Etienne Gilson Tribute*, ed. Charles J. O'Neill (Milwaukee, Marquette Univ. Press, 1959), pp. 245–262; a very fine treatment of what the metaphysician discovers in directly experienced reality.

Erwin Schrödinger, *Mind and Matter* (Cambridge, Cambridge Univ. Press, 1959); brief, somewhat difficult reading, but can be helpful in overcoming materialistic monism.

Wilmon H. Sheldon, "Critique of Naturalism," *Journal of Philosophy*, XLII (1945), 253–270; pertinent to our present interest is the critique of naturalism as a form of materialism.

Gerard Smith, S.J., "Before You Start Talking about God," *The Modern Schoolman*, XXIII (1945), 31–32; the importance of a properly metaphysical understanding of being.

Paul Tournier, *The Meaning of Persons*, trans. Edwin Hudson

(New York, Harper and Bros., 1957), pp. 179–198; on the differences between the world of persons and the world of things.

John Wild, "What is Realism?" *Journal of Philosophy*, XLIV (1947), 148–158, discusses the meaning of "real"; the main stress of this article is on the opposition to various more or less mitigated forms of idealism.

SELECTED PASSAGES FROM ST. THOMAS AQUINAS

4. *What Is the Subject of Metaphysics?*

. . . [Aristotle] says, first, that there is a demonstrative knowledge, which considers being as being, as its subject, and considers also "those things which of themselves [per se] are in being," that is, the per se properties of being.

But he says, "as being," because other demonstrative knowledges, which deal with particular beings, do indeed consider being—for all the subjects of knowledge are beings—yet do not consider being as being, but as it is some kind of being, that is "number," or "line" or "fire" or something of this sort.

He says also, "which of themselves are in this," and not simply, which are in this, to show that it does not belong to this demonstrative knowledge to consider those things which accidentally are in its subject, but only those things which of themselves are in it. . . . This demonstrative knowledge, whose subject is being, should not consider all the things which accidentally are in being, because thus it would consider everything which is considered in all kinds of knowledge, for everything is in some sense being, but not inasmuch as it is being. . . . The necessity of this knowledge which considers being and its per se properties, is clear from this, that these things should not remain unknown, since the knowledge of other things depends on them, as the knowledge of proper objects depends on common ones. . . .

Here he shows that this knowledge is not one of the particular knowledges, from this consideration. No particular knowledge considers being universally as such, but only some part of being divided from other parts. And about this part it considers the per se properties. . . . But the common knowledge considers universal being as being, and so it is not the same as any of the particular knowledges. . . .

Here he shows that this demonstrative knowledge, which we have before us, has being as its subject, this way. Every principle is of itself the principle and cause of some nature. But we are seeking the first principles of things, and the highest causes (as was said in the first book); and these are of themselves causes of some nature. But this is only the nature of being. And this is clear from this, that all philosophers, investigating the elements inasmuch as they are beings, sought this kind of principles, namely the first and highest. Therefore in this demonstrative knowledge we are seeking the principles of being as being. Therefore being is the subject of this knowledge, for every demonstrative knowledge seeks the proper causes of its subject.

> *Commentary on Aristotle's*
> Metaphysics, Bk. IV, lect.
> 1 (ed. Cathala, Nos. 529–
> 533).

5. Abstraction Contrasted with Separation

The response. It is to be said that for the evidence of this question we must know how the intellect can abstract according to its operation. We must know therefore that according to the Philosopher in the third book of the *De Anima*, there are two operations of the intellect: one which is called "the understanding of indivisibles," by which it knows what anything is; the other, by which it composes and divides, that is, by forming an affirmative or negative proposition. These two operations correspond to two [principles] in the thing. The first operation considers the very nature of the thing, according to which it has a definite place among beings, whether it be a complete thing, like a whole, or an incomplete thing, as a part or an accident. But the second operation considers the very esse of the thing, which follows from the coming together of the principles in a composite thing, or accompanies the simple nature of the thing, as in simple substances. And because the truth of the intellect lies in this, that it is conformed to the thing, it is clear that according to this operation, the intellect cannot truly abstract what is joined together in the thing, because, in abstracting, a separation according to the esse of the thing would be signified, as, if I abstract man from whiteness, saying "man is not white," I mean there is a separation in the thing. Hence, if in the real order man and whiteness are not separated, the understanding will be false. And so according to this operation the intellect cannot truly abstract except such things which are separated in the real order, as in saying, "Man is not an ass." But according to the first operation of the mind, it can abstract things which in the real order are not separate, not all indeed, but some. . . .

Thus the intellect distinguishes one from another in different ways according to different operations, because, according to the operation by which it composes and divides, it distinguishes one from another in this, that it understands one not to be in the other. But in the operation by which it understands what everything is, it distinguishes one from another, inasmuch as it understands what this is, understanding nothing about something else, neither that it be with the other, nor separated from it. This latter distinction, therefore, is not properly called separation, but only the former. . . . Since abstraction cannot take place, properly speaking, except of things which are joined together in reality, according to the two modes of conjunction (that is, the way in which the part and the whole are united, or form and matter), there are two kinds of abstraction: one by which form is abstracted from matter, the other by which the whole is abstracted from the parts. . . .

And so there are two abstractions of the intellect: one which corresponds to the union of form and matter or accident and subject, and this is the abstraction of the form from sensible matter; the other, which corresponds to the union of the whole and the part, and to this there corresponds the abstraction of the universal from the particular, which is an abstraction of the whole, in which some absolute nature is considered according to its essential intelligibility. . . . But in such things which can be divided according to their esse, we rather have separation than abstraction.

Thus, in the operation of the intellect there is a threefold distinction. There is one according to the operation of the intellect composing and dividing, which is properly called separation, and this belongs to the divine knowledge or metaphysics. There is another according to the operation by which the quiddities of things are formed, which is the abstraction of a form from sensible matter, and this belongs to mathematics. There is a third, according to the same operation, of the universal from the particular, and this belongs also to physics, and is [in some way] common to all knowledges, for in every demonstrative knowledge we omit what is accidental and take what is per se.

> *Commentary on Boethius's*
> De Trinitate, q. 5, art. 3.

6. *Principles Known Per Se*

Those things which are per se known to us, are made known immediately by sense experience, for example, when a whole and a part are seen, we immediately know that every whole is larger than its part, and we know this without any investigation. Therefore the Philosopher says, "We know principles when we know their terms" (*Posterior Analytics*, I).

> *Commentary on the First Book*
> *of the* Sentences, dis. 3, q. 1,
> art. 2.

7. *Abstraction and the Knowledge of Immaterial Substance*

A certain philosopher, called Avempacé, held that through the understanding of material substances, following the true principles of philosophy, we could arrive at an understanding of immaterial substances. For, he contended, our intellect has such a nature that it can abstract the quiddity of a material thing from matter; if there is still something material left in that quiddity, the intellect can abstract once again; and since there cannot be an infinite series of material principles in a quiddity, finally the intellect can arrive at an understanding of some quiddity which is entirely without matter. And this, he maintains, is to understand an immaterial substance.

This reasoning would be effective, if the immaterial substances were the forms and essences of the material things present to us, as the Platonists maintain. If we do not take this position, but rather take the position that immaterial substances are of an entirely different kind than the quiddities of material things, then, however much our intellect abstracts the quiddity of a material thing from matter, it will never obtain anything even similar to an immaterial substance. Therefore through material substances we cannot perfectly know immaterial substance.

. . . immaterial substances cannot be known by us in such a way that we apprehend their quiddities, but we can learn something about them through the way of removal [separation] and of relation to material things.

Summa Theologiae, Pt. I, q. 88, art. 2 and ad 2.

III

The Analogy of Being:
First Approach

22. The fact of knowledge in common

In the preceding chapter, we have begun with the many things of experience, and after a long and complicated analysis have arrived at a conception of being as being, thereby establishing the object of metaphysics. Now, we can consider this as a movement which arises from the broad base of many individuals to the unity of one complex apprehension. In this, we have shown that metaphysics fulfills one of the requirements for an organized, demonstrative (scientific) knowledge, that we can reach some kind of common knowledge of individuals. But, having reached this peak, we must ask ourselves how this common knowledge is related to the many individuals. For, by "common knowledge" we mean a single knowledge that is true of many things. For instance, it is true of any sample of water that water is H_2O. So, too, the law of freely falling bodies is true of any and all such bodies; the laws of learning are verified in their way in every case of learning; the theory of the cellular structure of living things is applicable to a great variety of living things. And similar examples of common knowledge can be drawn from any science, from mathematics, logic, and philosophy. (The individuals to which a common knowledge can be applied are sometimes called the "inferiors" of that knowledge.)

Logicians and grammarians sometimes speak of equivocal terms as common. An equivocal term is one and the same term (same in sound or spelling) that has different senses and signifies different kinds of things. An example of an equivocal term is "bank," which can mean the ground bordering a river or an establishment for the keeping and lending of money. We can speak of an equivocal term if we refer to an external sign. But an equivocal term does not imply common knowledge, because equivocal terms have entirely different meanings.[1]

23. Univocation and its basis

The kind of common knowledge with which we should be most familiar is *univocation*. By univocation we mean the use of one and the same term and its corresponding knowledge to apply to each of many individuals in the same sense. Examples of univocation can be found in the use of everyday terms like "water," "sheep," "tree," as well as in scientific terms like "vertebrate," "triangle," "syllogism." A univocal term is given its name because of the identity of meaning (*uni-* means one; *-vocation* here means naming). Often a univocal term is called a *universal* because it can be applied to all the individuals of a given kind in exactly the same sense.

How can one and the same term rightly be applied to a number of individuals which are different? How can one and the same act of knowledge include (explicitly or implicitly) many different individuals? There must be a double basis for this. We have already seen the basis for univocation when we considered abstraction; because some knowledge abstracts from particularities we can deal with what-things-are univocally. But in order that abstraction be legitimate, there must be some kind of distinction between what-a-thing-is and its particularity. For the present, we are not going to consider what this distinction is or on what it is based. It is enough if there is some kind of distinction between the essence of a thing (*what*-a-thing-is) and its particularity.[2]

24. Is being a universal?

We have already seen that our knowledge of being is not an abstract one. It is nonabstract, because it is rich enough to in-

[1] Kinds of common terms are spoken of in Selected Passages, No. 8.
[2] This distinction is considered in detail in sec. 42.

clude all things and in all their diversity. It is therefore always growing and is able to go on growing indefinitely. But, because it is nonabstract, it cannot have the same kind of community that an abstract knowledge has. We must examine this relationship more closely and also see what its basis is.

First of all, individuals are, or exist. But, we may wonder, do any nonindividual things exist?

Now, a nonindividual is either a *formal* (or reflex) *universal* or a *simple universal* (an absolute nature). A formal universal is defined as that which is known to be common to many and predicated of them (for example, the species "man," the genus "animal"). If a formal universal were to exist as such, as existing it would be not common, but a distinct thing in itself. But it is a contradiction to suppose that one and the same thing should be both common and not common at the same time. Hence, the supposition that "A formal universal exists" is false.

A simple universal or absolute nature is that which is absolutely meant by terms like "man," "horse," "animal," "car," and so forth. It is that which we predicate, a logician would say, whenever we predicate a noun or attribute of a subject. As such, it is not formally universal (else it could not be predicated of singulars) nor explicitly singular (else it could not be predicated of many); it is neither really existing nor a mere object of thought. Now, some thinkers suppose that such absolute natures exist, either in themselves or as distinct elements in things. For example, in the horse Carry Back, there are said to be as many distinct nonindividual elements as there are distinct ways of knowing what Carry Back is (for example, horse, swift, rangy). But this supposition involves a number of unintelligible or contradictory consequences: that something which is potential (can be either singular or universal) is also actual, namely, an actual element of a real thing; that something can be neither singular nor not-singular (that is, not merely be *considered* abstractly, but *be* abstractly), and therefore that contradictory propositions are not completely opposed to each other; that the real thing is composed of distinct elements, each of which taken singly is indifferent or neutral to reality. But any supposition that involves impossible or unreal consequences is not true. Therefore it is not true that an absolute nature or essence exists as such.

Hence, only individuals exist, or, all existents are individuals. Being means that which is, and so it includes the particularity of that which is. But being does not determinately include the particular; in other words, being does not necessarily mean this thing or that thing; it means *any*, or, *a* thing. This special way of signifying the particular as particular we shall call "indefinite reference," because it makes use of the indefinite article to signify a very definite, concrete, singular thing.

Consequently, being is not a univocal nor a universal term. Being is not univocal, for whenever we assert that something *is*, we speak of a unique individual which has an act of existing all its own. Hence, being is not universal, for no two individuals can be exactly alike inasmuch as they exist.

25. "Being" is common to many

Thus far we have seen a number of points which are the data for the problem of the community of being. We will consider them in summary form.

(1) Only concrete individuals exist and can exist in the real order.

(2) An individual real thing is an existent and formally a being because of its act of existing, not because it is material or is what it is.

   Nevertheless, the beings of our experience are material things of a particular kind.

(3) *Being* that is presented to us by the real existents of which we have direct experience includes both a thing-element and esse.

   Being is an intelligibility, the *ratio entis;* it is that which we understand when we know a real thing as a being.

(4) Each existent presents itself as an individual thing distinct from all other things, that is, as a unique subject of esse.

   In other words, each individual thing is a unique way or mode (manner) of having esse.

(5) As the subjects of esse differ from each other, so also do the existential acts.

For example, this dog's existential act is different from that dog's, just as this dog is different from that.

(6) Hence, each individual thing exists with *its* own act of existing.

It would be foolish to imagine that one thing or person could exist with the act of existing of another.

(7) And yet *being* is realized in each existent.

Every real thing is manifestly a singular definite thing having its esse.

Thus, *being* is common to all things.[3]

But the problem is *how* being is common. Being, in any singular existent, cannot be entirely and exactly the same as it is in any other thing. It must in each instance be and be known as a definite singular thing uniquely ordered to its own act of existing. It must in each instance include all that is unique and proper to the singular individual, and so it cannot be an univocal intelligibility. Since, on the other hand, the intelligibility, being, is presented to

[3] Though most Thomists subscribe to the formula of Cajetan, "being is simply many, but one *secundum quid*," they also maintain that it is one concept and is *predicated* analogously. Is there one *concept* of being? Of course, there are all sorts of "concepts of being," from Hegel to Sartre; even some self-styled Thomists have a "concept" which they call "being"—one, unique, confusedly containing all its inferiors, and so on. Such a *concept* is *not* the being which is the subject of metaphysics.

Because beings are analogous, they cannot be correctly understood in any *one concept*. But long familiarity has accustomed us to use the unity (even if it is only partial and derivative) and ignore the multiplicity (even though it is basic).

Most philosophers want to go too rapidly; they overlook the basic importance of the verb *is*. For the first problem of metaphysics is, "What does *is* mean?" "How do we predicate *is* of differing individuals?" The verb-predicate "is" should be investigated before we even ask about the attributive noun, "being." We understand and assert *is* analogously, and this analogy demands our first attention. The failure to realize that *is* can be a verb which expresses existential act is the capital fault of logicism (or essentialism) and distorts both the ordinary spontaneous experience of individuals as well as metaphysics. To substitute a noun and a concept for the verb is a serious error. At best, the problem of metaphysics is poorly expressed as a problem of unity amidst diversity; at worst, *being* is turned into an essence or form in order that it may have a true conceptual unity.

See also below, sec. 86.

us by, and verified in, any singular concrete existent, being cannot be equivocal. (As we have already seen, no intelligibility can be equivocal; only terms can be equivocal.) Being, therefore, is somehow midway between univocation and equivocation, and hence we say it is *analogous*, that is, similar.

Univocal terms signify an absolute nature or, at least, something understood after the manner of an absolute nature. They have a definite meaning by themselves, and so can be used alone; for example, the items in a grocery list are meaningful, clear, and distinct, even though they may be just single words. When univocal terms are used in a proposition, they have exactly the same meaning. This is to be expected, for, since they are abstracted from individuals, their meaning does not change when they are applied now to this individual, now to that.

But being is not an abstract concept. We have seen that when we come to know a thing as a being, we know it in such a way that none of its reality is left out. Therefore, being means the whole being. Now, individual beings differ. Consequently, being, when predicated of one being, cannot have exactly the same meaning as it has when predicated of another. Each time it is used its meaning is *proportioned* to the subject of which it is used. We can express the thought of this paragraph by saying, "Analogy is proportional predication."

Yet we do not call the second being "being" by a mere fiction of the mind or by some kind of extrinsic reference of one to the other. (When we do this, as when, for example, we speak of the "right" or "left" side of the road, we are using what is called "improper predication.") Each one of the two has its own intrinsic act of existing which is its own; consequently, each one of them is properly called a being. Consequently, the analogy of being, when we are talking about real things, is proper predication.

26. The formal structure of analogy

But if we are to use one term to signify two things which are not (logically) identical, then there must be some relation between those things. It is not relevant here to say that the predicate is always related to its subject, for we are asking why the same predicate is applied to two really different things. So there must be some foundation in the things themselves.

The unity of univocal predication—to start with the simplest and most easily understood kind of unity—lies in this, that *in* each one of the "inferiors" there is a "part" which, at least abstractly considered, is formally the same. This kind of unity is the strongest of the logical unities—the logical identity of the "part." But the various "inferiors" of an analogous conception— the so-called analogates—cannot be unified in this way. Nor can we have recourse to various strictly ontological unities, such as the unity of an undivided being (the unity of a single person, for example)—these are irrelevant, since we are concerned with individuals which are ontologically many as beings.

There is left, for our purposes, only the unity of relation. Now, relations among things can fall into three, and only three, patterns. First, one of the things may be directly related to the other; we will refer to this as a "one-to-one" relationship. Second, the things may not be directly related to each other, but they may be variously related to a common third; this is the "many-to-one" relationship. Third, the things may not be directly related to each other (either as wholes or in their parts), but they may have internal relationships which are related; this is the "many-to-many" relationship. And this enumeration is exhaustive: "many" and "one" can be combined in only these three ways, while more elaborate combinations will easily reduce to these simpler ones.

For a better understanding of what is meant here, we can look at some examples. A traditional example is that of "health"; the relationships are extrinsic, but this is not important here, since what we want to see is the *pattern* they form. First, an animal is healthy, and various other things are correctly called healthy, for example, food as preserving health, complexion as manifesting it, and so on. Food is directly related to the health of the animal as its partial cause, and thus stands in a one-to-one relationship. Second, in this same example, we can compare the predication of the term *healthy* to the food and to the complexion. There is no direct relation between the food as health-producing and the complexion as health-showing, except through the animal which is healthy.[4] Therefore, food and complexion do not stand in a one-to-one relation to each other, but in a many-to-one relationship, where the "one" is outside the many, and yet is the reason for the common attribution. Third, we can consider the predication of the term *good* to a wine and to a ballplayer. There is no direct relationship between the one and the other; there is no common third. There is no common quality, no common action. Is then the term merely equivocal? Not at all. For in each case the term designates a relationship. A wine is good when it is such as to be well adapted to human taste and digestion. A ballplayer is good when his actions are well adapted to his function in the game. The two relationships, however, are not identical, since the very meaning of "adaptation" differs in the two cases. But they are still proportioned, or similar. We can view this pair of relationships as a proportional comparison:

$$\text{wine : taste : : ballplayer : his function}$$

For this reason, the many-to-many analogy is usually called "the analogy of proportionality."[5]

After this analysis we can examine the analogy of being to see where and how it can best be expressed.

[4] There apparently *are* direct relationships between the food and the complexion. But the precise point is: as far as *health* is concerned. The complexion may be ruddy, smooth, oily, and so on, and these qualities may be directly connected with the diet. But they are not the qualities of a healthy skin except in reference to the health of the animal itself, and this is relative to the animal, not to the intrinsic qualities of the complexion considered in itself. So the "health" example remains a valid one.

It is not amiss to point out that it does have two defects. As we have noted above, the act or perfection, health, is found only in one of the analogates, and so the analogy is improper or extrinsic. Secondly, health is first of all a univocal term in relation to a number of individuals, the healthy animals, and is only afterwards applied analogously; we can call it a "secondarily analogous term." But being is analogous from the start; it has no original univocal sense. We can therefore, by contrast, call it a "primarily analogous term." This is a very important difference.

[5] A "relation of relationships" or "a proportion of proportions" can just as well be univocal as analogous. Take the proportionality, 2 : 4 :: 3 : 6; here the relation "double" is obviously univocal. Or, if this seems too simple, consider this one: 2 : 4 :: 3 : 12 :: 4 : 32 :: 5 : 80; the rule of this progression is absolutely univocal.

27. Analogy of individual beings

Being is never presented by any two beings as *exactly* the same. In other words, *being*, as presented by one existent, is always and necessarily and intrinsically different from the being presented by another. From one existent I derive one definite intelligibility; from another, another; and so on.[6] So it is clear that we are not dealing with a univocal term but with a proportional predication; moreover, since each existent is by its own intrinsic perfection a being, the predication is proper or intrinsic. Hence, there must be some sort of relation between beings.

Our predicating of being must, of course, be based upon what we find in the real order. The question, then, is, Which of the three patterns is verified on the basis of what we have already found? for we do so predicate being on the basis of what we have found. Is there a direct relation of an individual being, as such, to another individual being? Obviously there are all sorts of relationships in our world: father and son, twins, builder and building, equally big automobiles, better rockets. But these are not relationships *of* and *in being*. My next door neighbor is another being, and it makes no difference to his character of being another being that he be my brother or a total stranger. Thus, we cannot find a one-to-one relationship between the beings of our experience simply as beings.

In fact, the individuals of our experience seem to be so unrelated directly that we might well be inclined to think that the many-to-many relationship is most likely to be the one. But is it? Remember that we are now considering two beings, explicitly taking into account only this, that they are *two beings*. We might think this way: a thing is a being inasmuch as it has an act of existing; one being is to its own act of existing as the second is to its own act, and so on; hence, individual beings are analogous with the analogy of proper proportionality. The only difficulty is this: if we only know that we are confronted with two beings, we cannot determine the meaning of the "similarity" expressed by the word "as" in our proportionality above.[7] We cannot

---

[6] See above, n. 3, and below, sec. 86.

[7] See above, n. 5. The fact that proportionalities *can* be univocal as well as analogous is clear from the mathematical examples given in note 5. It is

determine *how* a given being is related to its act of existing unless we know what kind of being it is. So we must rule out the possibility of a many-to-many relationship as relevant in *all* cases of the analogy of individual beings among themselves.

What about the many-to-one relationship? We can find some help by comparing this predication with univocal predication. Let us take the relationship of *man* to Peter, James, and John. *Man* as absolute nature is in the mind, and so not identical with the three men; it is therefore a many-to-one pattern. But because *man* arises by abstraction, it is a single concept, with exactly the same relationship to each of the three, so we have, not analogy, but univocation. Now, take three beings, *x*, *y*, and *z*, of which we only know that they are actually existing things, three in number; therefore, they are related to the common conception of being as it is in the mind. But, unlike the case of the univocal term, being is not predicated in the same way, for it is predicated proportionally to the subject. Moreover, being is not a single concept but is at most a kind of ideal unity, which, in developing, transcends any individual being we may find. There is then, a kind of communication of *x*, *y*, and *z* as individuals in the ideal unity, which fits into the many-to-one pattern of relationship. We will call this the "analogy of individual communication."

This answers our immediate question, but at the price of raising a new one: How is it that individuals are thus understood? Can beings which are not directly related be truthfully understood in reference to one conception? To say that they *are* so understood is true enough but insufficient. The question cannot be answered with what we have already discovered; it can only be answered when we are ready to examine some of the real relations between beings, in Chapters VII, VIII, and IX.

---

the common teaching of Thomists that every proportionality in being is analogous. But consider a proportionality like this one: this man : his act of existing :: that man : his act of existing. In what sense can we say that this man is differently related to his own esse than that man is? He has exactly the same kind of nature, and nature (or essence) is just the capacity for existing in a certain way. Hence, we cannot at the same time assert the analogy of proper proportionality between two individuals of the same species and the univocation of the term that denotes their nature. For a fuller discussion, see G. P. Klubertanz, S.J., *St. Thomas Aquinas on Analogy* (Chicago, Loyola Univ. Press, 1960), pp. 136–140.

28. Person and thing as beings

From the very start, we have recognized two very different sorts of beings: persons and things. We have noted that whenever we know a thing, we also necessarily know ourselves as beings and precisely as the subject or agent of knowledge. Conversely, we cannot know another person without contacting a thing-aspect of him, namely, his body. In ordinary experience, we do not even experience ourselves as pure subjectivity. My body is myself, in some way, and yet ordinarily it is simultaneously perceived as thing (object, facticity), even if only by kinaesthetic (internal) touch. In this sense, subjectivity and thinghood are equally immediate (that is, one is not in terms of the other), and both are independently known as beings of two different kinds. (To prevent misunderstanding, it is necessary to point out that all reflective analysis of subjectivity and personality must take place through analogies with things as sensibly experienced, so that being as sensible retains a priority in the order of objective intelligibility; in the causal order, our mind is first actuated by the intelligibility received through the senses before [not in time, but in causality] it can be conscious of its own activity, and so it is first conscious of itself as understanding a sensible thing.)

Being as thing and being as subject each has its own intelligibility. These intelligibilities are alike only inasmuch as each is proportionally similar to the other. That is to say, we can and do recognize that as a thing is to its act of existing, so a person is to his.[8] But this comparison is not an equality. For a thing *has* an act of existing, in the sense that it has received it, and is now actuated by it; its act is in it, and in no other. On the other hand, a person has an act of existing, in the sense that he possesses it through the self-consciousness of intelligence and the self-determination of freedom. A thing is present only to some other than itself; a person is present to himself. A thing is self-identical only in a very imperfect way, in that its actuality is dispersed both in space and in time. A person's self-identity is only partially

[8] This "relation" is not a predicamental but a "transcendental" relation; see below, sec. 108.

spatialized and temporalized and in its peak of self-consciousness is both aspatial and atemporal.

Yet these similarities and differences cannot be parceled out into two groups, one group containing univocally common perfections, the other listing simply diverse ones. The possession, presence, actuation of the being by its esse is just that which is both similar and unlike. Not only is the essence of a person not the same as the essence of a thing, nor a person's act of existing not a thing's act; the very way (mode, manner) the being is related to its own proper act is different. Hence, in this case, there is an analogy of proportionality, properly so called. (After we learn that there are more that just these two levels or "grades" of being, then we shall see that the analogy of proper proportionality applies to these grades also.)

In both of these analogies, the analogates are the things of our real world as they are presented to us in our experience. Each analogate is a whole individual existent, formally understood as a being. These analogies of being are therefore primarily and basically analogies between *beings*—between two or more real beings each having its own act of existing.[9]

Later on, we shall see that there are relationships and analogies within beings, that is, between the various internal principles of being. We shall also discover still other analogies among beings, especially between some effects and their causes, and finally a different kind of analogy between God and all other beings.

In summary, then, *being* is analogous. It cannot be applied to any two beings with exactly the same meaning. It is not a

---

[9] At this point it is traditional to treat of metaphor, and it is frequently said that metaphor is "the analogy of extrinsic proportionality." Thomists point to texts like *Summa Theologiae*, Pt. I, q. 13, art. 6. It should be noted that *metaphora* is a Greek term, translated into Latin as *translatio*, and means nothing more than "figure of speech" (as a proof of this, note that St. Thomas instances causal attribution as well as what is commonly recognized as metaphor in the passage cited). At the first level of analysis, metaphor is the extrinsic attribution of an alien nature; see Robert R. Boyle, S.J., "The Nature of Metaphor," *The Modern Schoolman*, XXXI (1954), 267–280. For a suggestion about an underlying analogy in metaphor, see below, Chap. IX, secs. 77, 81.

univocal intelligibility, for every being, inasmuch as it is a being, is unique. Being is not obtained by any kind of abstraction, properly so called. On the other hand, the term "being" is not equivocal. One being is simply diverse from any and every other being, but it is also similar to any and every other being of our experience. Between beings as individuals we find the analogy of individual communication. In addition, we find that persons and things are similar as beings, but also different, in that each possesses its own act of existing in its own way, as intrinsically proportioned to the kind of nature it has. Beings, as persons and things, are therefore analogous by an analogy of proper proportionality.

29. Definitions

A *univocal* term (and knowledge) is one that is applied to many individuals in wholly the same sense.

An equivocal term is a term that has the same external sign (same in sound or spelling) but entirely different meanings.

An *analogous* term (and knowledge) is one whose meaning is is not exactly the same; nor is it entirely different; it is not merely a combination of a univocal and an equivocal element but that which is the same is somehow also different.

Analogy of proportionality is a many-to-many relationship, consisting in a similarity (proportion) of proportions between pairs of diverse parts, principles, and so forth, though the analogates which are constituted by these principles have no direct relationship to each other.

Analogy of individual communication is a many-to-one relationship, consisting in a similarity of the relationship of each of the analogates to a "one" which is distinct from the analogates singly as well as taken together; the analogates have no direct relationship to each other.

An analogue, or analogate, is one of the things, terms, principles, and so forth, to which an analogous term is applied or of which an analogous knowledge is true.

30. Summary

A. Only individuals exist.

Nonindividuals are either formal universals or absolute natures (simple, or direct, universals).

But: neither formal universals nor absolute natures exist (*a*) because formal universals must be *one* in order to be what they are, and that which is one is not-many and therefore not-common, yet an existing formal universal should also be common to many; and (*b*) because absolute natures, which *can* be either singular or universal, cannot simultaneously be fully actual. Absolute natures cannot exist as such in singulars, because a real thing cannot be composed of elements each of which is indifferent to reality.

Therefore: no nonindividuals exist, or only individuals exist.

B. Being is not a universal.

A universal is an abstract and univocal term.

But: being is not abstract, for it includes the whole real thing; nor is it univocal, for it includes all real differences.

Therefore: being is not a universal.

C. Particular beings are analogous with the analogy of individual communication.

The analogy of individual communication is found whenever there are many analogates which are not directly related to each other, but are similarly related to a "one" which is distinct from the analogates singly as well as taken together.

But: particular beings, considered merely as individual beings, are *as such* not directly related to each other, but are similarly related to "being," and "being" itself is neither one of these analogates nor their sum.

Therefore; particular beings, as individuals, are analogous with the analogy of individual communication.

D. Some beings are analogous with the analogy of proportionality.

The analogy of proportionality is found wherever there are

similar wholes, which, although they are simply and really different, have a similar relationship of diverse parts.

But: some beings, although simply different, have a similar relationship of diverse parts because each of them is something having its own proper act of existing, not in the same way, but only in similar ways.

Therefore: some beings are analogous with the analogy of proportionality.

31. Readings

St. Thomas Aquinas, *Summa Theologiae*, Pt. I, q. 13, arts. 1, 2, 3, 4, 5 (a penetrating, detailed discussion of analogy and our knowledge of God); Pt. I, q. 30, art. 4 (on common terms); *On the Power of God*, q. 7, art. 7 (analogy between God and Creatures); *Contra Gentiles*, Bk. I, chap. 34 (same point).

Etienne Gilson, *The Spirit of Mediaeval Philosophy* (New York, Scribner's, 1940), pp. 477–448, n. 14; an excellent presentation of the role of analogy.

George P. Klubertanz, S.J., *Saint Thomas Aquinas on Analogy* (Chicago, Loyola Univ. Press, 1960), pp. 111–155.

Joseph Owens, C.SS.R., "Diversity and Community of Being in St. Thomas Aquinas," *Mediaeval Studies*, vol. XXII (1960), 257–302.

Kenneth Schmitz, "Toward a Metaphysical Restoration of Natural Things," *An Etienne Gilson Tribute*, ed. Charles J. O'Neil (Milwaukee, Marquette Univ. Press, 1959), 245–262; analogy as found in sensible things.

Paul Tournier, *The Meaning of Persons*, trans. Edwin Hudson (New York, Harper and Bros., 1957); differences between persons and things.

SELECTED PASSAGES FROM ST. THOMAS AQUINAS

8. Kinds of Common Terms

Something can be applied to many things in different senses, and this can happen in two ways. In one way, something can be said about many things according to intelligibilities which are entirely different and do not have any relationship to unity. These are called "purely equivocal" terms, for by chance it happens that one man names a thing by one name, and another a different thing by the same name; this is particularly evident in different men who have the same name. In another way, one name can be given to many things according to intelligibilities which do not differ totally, but agree to some extent.

. . . Sometimes this agreement . . . is according to one proportion of different subjects. For sight has the same proportion to the body as the intellect has to the soul. Hence, as sight is a power of a corporeal organ, so also the intellect is a power of the soul alone without a body.

> Commentary on Aristotle's
> Ethics, Bk. I, lect. 7 (ed.
> Pirotta, No. 95).

9. Examples and Kinds of Analogy

Things are one by proportion or analogy which are alike in this, that this has itself to that as another to another. Such a relation can be taken in two ways: either some two things have diverse relations to one thing, as "healthy" applied to urine means a "sign of health," and to medicine, means "the relationship of cause with respect to the same health." Or, there is the same proportion of two things to different objects, as tranquillity to the sea and serenity to the air; for tranquillity is the quiet of the sea, and serenity, the quiet of the air.

> Commentary on Aristotle's
> Metaphysics, Bk. V, lect. 8
> (ed. Cathala, No. 879).

The act of existing of a man and a horse is not the same, nor of this man and that man.

> Summa Theologiae,
> Pt. I, q. 3, art. 5.

IV

Becoming—Change—Motion

32. The problem of change

We have just engaged in a detailed consideration of the fact that things are. That things change is a fact which is also directly known, and the investigation of what change is will occupy us for the next three chapters. This chapter is introductory. We do not intend to prove any particular changes, nor whether there are different kinds of change. There is a prior problem of what we mean by change in general. Therefore we will begin with the ordinary idea of change, which admittedly is a rather vague one, and only gradually arrive at more accurate notions.

Some philosophers have found difficulty in admitting both being and change at one and the same time. Some of the essentialists, in defining reality as that-which-is-*what*-it-is, have combined permanence with this self-identity so much so that they consider the changing to be unreal. Some have even gone so far as to assert that all change is an illusion. We can take as a simple example of this kind of position the argument of Parmenides, an Italo-Greek who flourished in the early fifth century before Christ. According to this Greek philosopher, the real or being is that-which-is-what-it-is. If the real were to change, it would have to be what-it-is (by definition) and at the same time what-it-is-not (on the supposition that it changes). But this consequence is a contradiction, and so the supposition is false. Again, we can consider this position from another point of view. To change is to become other than what one was. Now, the real is what-it-is, and that which is other than (or opposite to) the real is nothing. So, change would be possible only if the opposite of the real were also real; but this is false, and so change is impossible. This is a very simple position, but more elaborate forms of it have been held at various times.

A position which is almost the direct contrary of Parmenides' view is that of Heraclitus, an Ionian Greek of about the end of the sixth century B.C. He was impressed by the unity of the universe and by its ceaseless activity and change. It seemed to him that if change is real, then everything which is real is change. And so Heraclitus not only asserted that change is real, he denied that anything is permanent in being. Everything is in flux, in process; he found the best example of his notion in the restless, ever changing fire. An elaborated form of this opinion has been held at various times and is relatively popular at the present time. Many modern philosophers express their notion of it by saying that there is no substance, no *thing* which acts; there is only activity without an agent. They deny the reality of the things and persons which we immediately perceive, not because their perception is any different than ours but because they cannot see how they can admit the reality of both change and being.

Are we really forced to choose between change and being? It is easy to see that those who chose being and denied change did so because for them "to be" was "to be an essence"; to be real was to be *what* a thing is. But the strange thing is the same faulty understanding of being led others to the opposite position of denying being in favor of change. Accepting the notion that "to be" is "to be unchangeably and permanently what a thing is," they have also accepted the immediate evidence that the things of our experience are in constant, more or less perceptible change. Because they are empiricists, they prefer facts to theories. In their minds, the fact is that change is going on; the theory is the notion of being as "that which remains what it is." Rightly questioning this notion of being, they have failed to ask a more fundamental question: "What is it to be real?"

Hence, since we have seen that to be is to exercise an act of existing, and since we have direct and undeniable evidence that change is going on, it is necessary to ask whether change is incompatible with being when being is understood as that-which-is.

By change, we understand "becoming different." We must therefore investigate what is meant by "sameness" and "difference."

33. Identity, distinction, and difference

Identity is sameness, oneness of a thing with itself. We say that a thing is identical with itself when it is the same at two points of time, or under several considerations, and so forth. Identity is absolute when all the characteristics, traits, and so forth of a thing are the same. Identity is partial, limited, or qualified, if some of the characteristics, traits, and so forth are the same, and others are not the same. Several types of limited identity may be pointed out as examples. Numerical identity is the basic sameness of one and the same individual along with various minor changes; we speak, for example, of the numerical (personal) identity of one and the same person throughout his life. We speak of specific identity when we have two individuals which belong to exactly the same *kind* of reality; for example, in geometry we speak of identical triangles. We speak of the material or real identity of a thing which we are thinking of in several ways; for example, John Doe as father of a family is materially identical with the same John Doe as a business man, but he is being considered now with one set of relations, now with another.

Distinction is lack of identity. It always implies plurality and division of some sort or other, for wherever there is a distinction, there must be more than one thing or part or aspect. Distinctions are basically of two types: real and of reason. A real distinction is found wherever there are really several things, parts, elements, and the like, independently of any act of the mind. A real distinction and a real identity are opposed as contradictories: that is, a real identity denies a real distinction, and vice versa. A common sign of a real distinction is separability: wherever two things or parts can be separated, such that one can exist without the other, those things or parts are really distinct. But not every real distinction implies the separability of those things or parts which are distinct. When the distinction is between complete things or beings, we speak of a major real distinction. When the distinction is between the parts (elements, principles) of one thing, we call it a minor real distinction (for example, the distinction between a man's hand and his foot; or the distinction between his color and his shape).

A distinction of reason is not a distinction within the thing itself but a lack of identity between two ways of understanding one and the same real thing. A typical example of the distinction of reason can be found in the parts of a definition: "rational animal," which is the essential definition of man, is composed of two parts. What we understand when we say "animal" is different from what we understand when we say "rational"; but the thing we understand in these two incomplete ways is one and the same. When at least one of the two concepts (between which there is a distinction of reason) does not imply the other, the distinction of reason is a major one. For example, though "rational" does imply "animal," yet "animal" does not imply "rational," and this we can find as well from an inspection of these two concepts as from the fact that there are animals which are not rational. On the other hand, when both concepts imply each other, we speak of a minor distinction of reason; an example of such a distinction we will find later on is the distinction between "one" and "being."

Difference can mean the same as distinction in some of its uses, but often the term "difference" is used to express the reason for a distinction. In our usage, the term "distinction" will more commonly be used to indicate that one thing (part, element) is not another; the term "difference" will be used to indicate the way in which things differ or, sometimes, that by which things differ. Of the differences between things two will be mentioned frequently in the material which will be considered next. A "numerical difference" is that between two individuals which belong to the same species or kind; for example, there is a numerical difference between Peter and Paul, between two shepherd dogs, two trees, two chairs. An "essential difference" is the difference between two things, which, in addition to being individually different, also are of different kinds or species. In logic, we learn that a definition is composed of a genus and a difference and that things are said to be specifically different when, having a common genus, each has some attribute proper to itself by which it differs from the others (this proper attribute is called the "difference").[1] But in logic any common notion suffices for a genus, and any less common one for a difference. In metaphysics and the philosophy of nature we do not work with such arbitrary classifications. Rather, we try to determine as accurately as possible *what* things are according to their intrinsic constituents. When this has been done, and we find that the intrinsic constituents of one are different from those of another thing, then we say that the things differ essentially. These steps necessary for the determination of an essential difference cannot be omitted, and there is no short-cut.[2] The finding of essential differences is not so important directly in the philosophy of being, but it is of major significance in the philosophy of human nature.

Now, it is obvious from our own past experience that we cannot simply look at a thing and know at once, immediately, what it essentially is. We have to learn what things are, and we discover this by seeing directly what they do. Thus, we often cannot tell by looking at a thing whether it is alive or dead. But we watch it act, and so we learn what it is. Briefly, we learn the

[1] Sometimes the "differences" are opposed as contradictories, as "sensitive" and "nonsensitive" are the differences of the common genus, "living." This essential difference is sometimes said to be "according to possession and privation" (*secundum habitum et privationem*); it is the easiest to discover; it is a greater difference than the one to be mentioned next. Sometimes the "differences" are two (or more) positive, diverse attributes, as "sensitive in the mode of touch alone" and "sensitive in the mode of many external senses." It is usually hard to prove that such positive, differing attributes are really essentially diverse in themselves, and it is often equally hard to prove that they are the differences of some real things.

[2] Note that essential definitions and essential differences can be known only if we have some knowledge of things as they are in themselves (see below, sec. 115). This knowledge includes two points: (1) a theory of knowledge in general which allows us to say that we know things which exist independently of our knowledge and (2) a method of knowledge which enables us to know at least some things in distinct detail. Obviously there are very many things of which we cannot give a *specific* essential definition, and which therefore we cannot distinguish specifically. In these cases we can still give a *generic* definition (perhaps only according to a remote genus), and then we could still find some essential differences, that is, according to generic differences.

essence or specific nature of a thing from its activities or operations.

This must also be the method by which we discover specific or essential differences. For example, two things are known to be essentially different if one of them has some operations which the other does not have. Thus, living things have some activities (nutrition, growth, reproduction) which other material things simply do not have. Hence, living things are essentially different from nonliving things.

34. The correct way to talk about change

We began this chapter with a problem urged by many philosophers that there is some kind of incompatibilitiy between being and change. For clarity's sake, we decided to obtain a clear understanding of the terms involved in considering change. We saw that change means "to become other than something was." So we undertook an examination of difference, distinction, and identity. Now we are ready to look at change as it actually happens, and our purpose is ultimately to discover the relation between change and being. In order to keep our discussion concrete and in touch with reality, we shall use as an example the change of a seed into a tree.

What do we mean when we say that a seed changes into a tree? We mean that there was first an initial stage in which there was a seed with a definite size, shape, and structure; secondly that there was some kind of process; and thirdly that there is a terminal stage at which the process arrives, in which the tree has a quite different size, shape, and structure.[3] (Note that the initial and terminal stages are not absolutely initial and terminal but are such relatively to each other and the process.) Moreover, there must be some continuity between initial stage, process, and terminal stage. If, after the seed was planted, some one came, replaced the seed with a seedling, then with a very small tree, then with a larger tree, and finally with a very large one, we would not have an instance of real change in one and the same tree (but an illusion of change if we did not know the difference, and a mere succession of different things if we did).

[3] For the relation of succession to change, see Selected Passages, No. 11.

Let us examine this analysis more closely. For something to change is to *become* other (different) than it was: the seed (A) becomes something different, a tree (B). To become is to come-to-be; in other words, becoming is a process which terminates in being—here, a tree (B). Because there must be a continuity throughout the process, and because the differences of the initial and terminal stages, which are not common to the whole process but precisely restricted to one stage, cannot themselves be the basis of that continuity, there must be something common in addition to the differences, namely, a subject which undergoes that process.[4] For convenience and brevity, we will make some use of the following symbols:

ac—the initial stage, the subject with its characteristics as it is before the change takes place (e.g., the seed A).

bc—the terminal stage, the subject with the characteristics it has after the change (e.g., the tree B).

P—the process itself

c—the common subject, not considered as determined by either the initial or the terminal differences

c is therefore both ac and bc, but this is not a contradiction, since it is not both of them simultaneously. Before c changes, it *can* be what it will be after the change is completed. Hence, at the point at which c is ac, c is said to be *in potency* to bc. After the process, when c has become bc, it actually has the trait, characteristic, or perfection to which the process was originally directed. Hence, after the change, c is now bc *in act*.[5] We can summarize this by saying, "c is both ac and bc; when c is ac in act, it is in potency to bc; when it is bc in act, it is no longer in potency to bc, but, if the process is reversible, when c is bc in act, it is in potency to ac." As an example of a reversible process, we can take heating and cooling; when a thing is hot

---

[4] On the common subject in change, see Selected Passages, No. 10.

[5] Note that we are here dealing with two conditions of a being: "to be in potency" and "to be in act." These two conditions are related to, but by no means identical with, the principles of potency and act which will be studied in Chap. VI. To discover the principles of act and potency is much more difficult than the analysis which is being made here. Moreover, an attempt to pass from the present consideration to the principles of act and potency will result in univocal concepts of act and potency—a consequence that will vitiate the whole understanding of metaphysics.

in act, it is in potency to being cold; when it is cold in act, it is in potency to being hot.

This distinction between "being in potency" and "being in act" enables us to see that change and being are not mutually exclusive as Heraclitus and Parmenides thought. It is not a profound distinction at all; it is primarily finding an accurate way to express the fact of change, and so it is a solution at the level of our language about a fact, just as, to some extent, the ancient Greek problem was at least partly a language confusion. Similarly, this distinction can give us a sharper, more accurate way to define what we mean by change: for a thing to change is for it to become in act what it was in potency.

35. A changing thing is composed

But the fact of change can be used to tell us something about the thing which changes. This will no longer be a linguistic analysis, but a real analysis of the thing itself, and of the conditions which must necessarily be true if change is even to be possible. Thus we will be able to relate change to the being of the changing thing.

We have seen that, first of all, a real change involves a subject which is present throughout the change, and this subject we have designated c. Second, after a real change has taken place, the thing which changed is different—ac is different from bc. Schematically:

$$ac\text{————}P\text{————}bc$$

to show more clearly how the common subject continues throughout the change, we can diagram it thus:

initial stage	process	terminal stage
$\dfrac{a}{c}$	P	$\dfrac{b}{c}$

This process involves two aspects which are present in every physical change, for after the change the special difference of the initial stage is no longer present, and the special difference of the terminal stage is present for the first time. We will call the first aspect "passing-away" and the second, "coming-to-be." All physical changes seem to contain both aspects, and to stress the double aspect, we can call them "interchanges." (The gaining of knowledge seems to be a pure case of "coming-to-be" without any passing-away; there does not seem to be any case of a pure "passing-away."[6]) Schematically:

$$\text{every interchange}$$
$$\frac{a}{c} \text{———} P \text{———} \frac{b}{c}$$

$$\text{involves both:}$$

$$\text{passing away} \qquad \text{and} \qquad \text{coming-to-be}$$
$$\frac{a}{c} \text{———} P \text{———} \frac{\text{not-}a}{c} \qquad \frac{\text{not-}b}{c} \text{———} P \text{———} \frac{b}{c}$$

The subject of change must ordinarily have *both* lost something which it had in act at the beginning of the change and acquired something which it did not have in act but only in potency.[7]

Can the (one or) two positive perfections which (are gained or) interchanged be really identical with the common subject which changes? Clearly, *a*, *b*, and *c* cannot be identical, and we are here on the rock bottom basis of the principle of contradiction. If we suppose that they are really identical, then either there is nothing really common (really no *c*)—and so there is no change, but removal of one whole thing and the substitution of another whole thing (Heraclitus)—or there is nothing really gained or lost (really no *a* or *b*), if we choose to say that the

[6] We have *names* for processes which single out one or the other aspect; for example, death is the loss of life (but this is not purely a loss, for the soul is replaced by other form[s]); conception is the beginning of life (but there is not purely a gain, for the soul replaces other form[s]); so, too, amputation is not purely a loss, for a new figure is gained. The gain sometimes outweighs the loss, sometimes is outweighed by it, and this accounts for our emphasis of one or the other aspect. As for the special case of coming-to-know as a coming-to-be without any passing-away, see G. P. Klubertanz, S.J., *The Philosophy of Human Nature* (New York, Appleton-Century-Crofts, 1953), pp. 72–77.

[7] There are some subtle difficulties of language involved when we want to talk about the temporal interrelations of the elements of a change. Selected Passages, No. 11, deals with these; for a fuller analysis, see G. P. Klubertanz, S.J., "Causality in the Philosophy of Nature," *The Modern Schoolman*, XIX (1942), 29–32.

common element which is identical in all its stages is the whole thing (Parmenides). Therefore, in a real change, at least one of the terms of the change must be composed of two really distinct components.

There are various types of components in a whole being. The term, "part" (although it sometimes is used to mean "any component or constituent") most often means "an equal constituent portion," and in this usual sense it is equivalent to an "integral part." Examples of integral parts are the parts of a human body, the parts into which a line can be divided. Integral parts usually are quantitative parts of an extended (and measurable) whole. There are other types of components which are not quantitative in character, which cannot be discovered by direct sense experience, and which are not capable of existing as distinct beings after the division of the whole. Such components we will call "principles," that is, intrinsic or constituent principles.

In a real change, the components must be really distinct; a distinction of reason cannot account for a real change. If the being which changes is one being, then the component principles will be distinct with a minor real distinction.

Now that we have developed, through an instance of real change, a pattern by which we can understand how change occurs, we are ready, in the following chapter, to look at various kinds of change.

36. Definitions

Change is the process of becoming different or other than something was. (This term stresses the difference between initial and terminal stages.)

Becoming is the transition or process from being in potency to being in act. (This is the technical, scientific definition; the term, "becoming," stresses the relation of process to being.)

Motion in the strict sense (local motion) is change of place or position.

Motion in the wide sense is any change which can be directly measured by time, any change which is continuous or gradual in character.

Motion in the widest (or transferred sense) is any change.

Identity is the sameness of a thing with itself.

Distinction is lack of identity.

Real distinction is a lack of identity independent of any act of the mind.

Distinction of reason is a lack of identity dependent upon an act of the mind.

Being in act is the condition of really possessing some perfection or modification.

Being in potency is the condition of not really having, but being able to acquire, some perfection.

37. Summary

A. Change and being are not incompatible.

Change involves an initial stage, an intermediate process, and a terminal stage. The subject of the change at the beginning is in potency to the determinations which it will have in act at the end.

Hence, change and being are not mutually exclusive or completely incompatible; rather, because change is directed toward being in act, it implies being. Yet, they are not identical either but are related as process and term of the process, as motion and the point of arrival of the motion.

B. Things which change are composite.

Whatever undergoes a real, intrinsic change must be different in its terminal stage from what it was in the initial stage, and yet there must also be a common subject.

But: that by which the initial stage differs from the terminal stage cannot be really identical with the common subject (and this subject is necessary for the continuity of the two terms).

Therefore: that which changes must be composed of a common principle which is in potency and (at least in one of the stages) a principle by which the stages differ.

38. Readings

Aristotle, *Metaphysics*, Bk. IV, chaps. 5, 6 (1010a15 ff. 1011b34), Bk. VIII, chap. 1 (1042a32); *Physics*, Bk. I, chaps. 7-9 (190a32–192b2), on change; Bk. III, chaps. 1-3 (200b12–202b29), on motion.

Jacques Maritain, *Introduction to Philosophy*, trans. E. I. Watkin (New York, Sheed and Ward, 1933), pp. 50–51, 60–63, 239–246.

John Wild, *Introduction to Realistic Philosophy* (New York, Harper, 1948), pp. 277–295, on change.

SELECTED PASSAGES FROM ST. THOMAS AQUINAS

10. A Common Subject in Change

Because every change is from one contrary to another, it is necessary that a subject underlie them, which subject can be changed from contrary to contrary. This the Philosopher proves in two ways. First, because one contrary does not change into another: for blackness itself does not become whiteness. Therefore, if there is to be a change from black to white, there must be something besides blackness which can become white.

The same thing he proves in another way, from this consideration that in every change something remains. For example, in a change from black to white a body remains, but the other thing, namely, one of the contraries—black, for example—does not remain.

> *Commentary on Aristotle's* Metaphysics, Bk. XII, lect. 2 (ed. Cathala, Nos. 2429-2430).

Everything which is changed remains with regard to some element of it and with regard to some other element ceases to be. For example, that which is changed from whiteness to blackness remains with regard to its substance. Thus, in everything which is changed, some composition is to be found.

> *Summa Theologiae*, Pt. I, q. 9, art. 1.

11. Change Implies Succession

Since every change has two terms which cannot be together . . . in every change or motion there must be succession, for this reason that the two terms cannot be together. Hence, there must also be time, which is the measure of that which is before and after, and this latter is the essential note of succession. But succession occurs differently in different cases. For sometimes the end of the motion is remote from its beginning. Between beginning and end there may be the medium of dimensive quantity, as in the local motion of bodies, or in the motion of growth and shrinking. There may be the medium of virtual quantity, whose division is related to the intensity and remission of some form, as in the alteration of sensible qualities. In both of these cases, time directly measures the motion itself, because there is a successive progress to the term, for it is divisible.

Sometimes, however, the term of the change is not remote from the beginning, as in those changes which are from a privation to a form or vice versa, as in generation and corruption, and illumination, and all things of a like nature. Even in these changes, time is involved, since it is evident that matter is not simultaneously under a form and the privation of that form, nor is the air at once subject to darkness and light. However, time is not involved, in the sense that the going forth or passage from one extreme to the other takes place in time. But to one of the extremes (that one, namely, which is first lost in the change) there is joined a motion or alteration (as in generation and corruption), or the local motion of the sun (as in illumination), and at the term of that motion there is also the term of the change. Yet that change is said to be sudden, or in an instant, for this reason that in the last instant of the time which measured the preceding motion, there is acquired that form or privation of which formerly nothing was present. And in that instant we say that something has been generated, but not properly that it is being generated. . . . Consequently, all such instantaneous changes are the terms of some motion.

Commentary on the First Book of the Sentences, dis. 37, q. 4, art. 3.
Cf. *S.T.* I–II, q. 113, art. 7 ad 5

V

The Intrinsic Principles
of Change and Being:
I. In Particular

39. Accidental change and the substance-accident composition of being

GENERAL CONSIDERATION OF THE EVIDENCE

We must now take up the study of change more in particular. The first thing that we will need to reflect on is that, at least descriptively speaking, there are different kinds of change. For example, there is the kind of change that is typified by the various changes that one and the same person goes through in the course of his life. There are changes in size, in bodily appearance, in knowledge and character acquired, in activity, in relations with others. Then there is another type of change most strikingly exemplified in the death of living things; a dead dog, for example, is just not a dog any more.

CLARIFICATION AND DEFINITION

In our general discussion of change in the preceding chapter, we noticed that in every change there must be a *common subject*, and this means that the subject must be the same subject throughout the change, that is, it must keep some kind of identity.[1] But

[1] See above, sec. 33.

there are several kinds of identity. Total, or complete, identity would not allow for any change at all. Numerical, specific, and generic identity are all partial identities which allow for some change.

Unity, on the other hand, is similar to identity, but does not imply a comparison of the thing with itself (as at some other time, and so on).[2] By unity we mean the actual undividedness of something. A thing may be of such a kind as not to have any parts at all; such a thing, which we call *simple*, is not only undivided, but indivisible. All other things which are unified are composed of parts and are therefore divisible. They are units if their parts are actually undivided, no matter how easy or difficult such division may be.

Unity may be intrinsic to the unified thing, or it may be extrinsic. It is intrinsic if the parts belong together of themselves; it is extrinsic if the unity is brought about by something else than the parts. For example, the unity of the parts of an animal is intrinsic; that of a bushel of apples is extrinsic, namely, that of the bushel basket.

But we also say that the parts of an animal naturally belong together. In this case, we mean that the parts of animals are such that when they are together in one unit, they make up a special kind of thing which has its own specific essence.[3] A thing has one essence if all the parts when undivided make up a distinct kind of reality, as all the members of a dog belong to the same kind of animal. Such an essence is also called a nature when we consider it as the source of activities. A natural individual is an actually undivided instance of a certain specific essence, complete in itself and able to carry on the activities of that nature.

But because we can define these notions and give some instance of what we mean by them does not mean of itself that they are legitimate concepts of the real things of the world, nor that we

[2] On unity, see below, sec. 89.
It is also useful to recall that we could not observe change unless we could remember the thing as it was before the change.

[3] On the meaning of species, see above, sec. 33. See also G. P. Klubertanz, S.J., *The Philosophy of Human Nature* (New York: Appleton-Century-Crofts, 1953), pp. 417–420.

know how to use them. So we need to consider these problems also.

Are there natural individuals in the real world, and if so, what are they? The first and most obvious instance is that of one's own self: I am aware of myself as an actually undivided unit. And I know that I am the same individual, with the same specific essence capable of carrying out the same activities, throughout a number of changes which I can remember. Similarly, I know that other people are natural individuals. Most animals and plants can be distinguished as independent and complete sources of activity, but not all. Nonliving individuals are quite difficult to distinguish. Is a piece of iron one individual (as one man is one individual) or many similar individuals having the same sort of nature (like a line of men forming a "living chain" to pull a drowning person out of a lake)? For our present purposes, we can say that it makes no difference: if a piece of iron is not one individual, then it is many, but whatever the last actually undivided whole is, it will be an individual.

A similar problem concerns the kinds of change mentioned above. True enough, we can tell the difference between catching a cold and dying. But we said that a nature is the principle of a certain sort of activity. We know, for example, that living things can generate offspring of the same kind; suppose a man becomes sterile—has he undergone a change of nature? Or, to take a more striking case, suppose he "loses his mind"—does he still have the same nature? Here, we need to point out again that because we can tell some changes from others, it does not follow that we can correctly classify all of them. There have been people who wondered whether imbeciles are human beings, who thought that insanity proved the presence of a foreign nature—"spirit possession"; even people who get confused about their own identity. The difficulty is that often we do not know clearly what happened, and we cannot expect that simple day-to-day experience will reveal it without any effort on our part. In many cases, advanced scientific knowledge will enable us to tell what happened, and then the problem ceases. But there remain many instances which no one yet clearly understands.

If we were studying the philosophy of nature, where we would be concerned with natures for their own sake, then we would be obliged to find at least the principles of a solution. But in metaphysics we are interested in understanding how beings are, not in determining which one is which; in understanding how change takes place and how it is related to being; in getting to see the major sorts of change, not in determining all the fine points of difference. (This is somewhat like the problem of species; a biologist wants to know exactly how many species of plants there are; a philosopher of nature is more interested in seeing how species of plants are determined; the metaphysician finds the material for his reflection in this: that some individuals differ only individually within the same species, and others differ also specifically.)

DETAILED CONSIDERATION OF THE EVIDENCE AND ANALYSIS

We will take for our first consideration that sort of change in which we know that the same individual is the common subject of change, in the way in which I know that I am the same person even though I move around, talk, study, read, and so forth. We will begin with a number of examples. A baby frog has no legs, a full-grown frog has legs and has lost its tail. A scraggly tree may be trimmed into a regular shape. Birds fly from one tree to another. Some things change in size, particularly living things; a giant redwood, hundreds of feet tall and with a trunk many feet in diameter, was once a little seed. Some things change in activity; trees grow during spring and summer, and show no signs of such activity during winter; animals sleep, run, eat, and some hibernate during the winter months; men also change activities in much the same way as other animals (eating, sleeping, moving about), and they also change in their thoughts and desires, they grow in knowledge and acquire virtues or vices.

Now, each one of these beings undergoes a real change; the changes we have been speaking of are not like the changes of clothes on a show-window dummy; they are changes within being. The being, considered as a whole, is different after the change from what it was before. Yet there is also in some way an identity. The frog or tree that grows is the same frog or tree; the adult, mature man is the same human person that he was as a baby, a child, a young man. We know this because the changed thing does basically the same *kind* of activity before the change as after. We know what kind of thing a being is by seeing what kind of activities it has. We can sum up all these examples this way: in the kind of changes described above, the being that changes is the same *kind* of thing that it was before the change, and it is the same individual. In other words, there is a subject that at one time existed under one modification and then later on under another.

In the preceding chapter, we saw that there must be a real distinction between the subject of the change, the common element, and the determinations or qualifications which are gained or lost. But the components of a changing thing are not themselves whole beings but principles or parts. Hence, the distinction between these components is a minor real distinction.

What can we say about these various components and their relations to each other? First, in the kind of change we are considering here, the subject remains what it was, in the sense that it retains the same nature and individuality. But in itself this subject can, and often must, receive further determinations; for example, a man must be in *some* position, but he need not be sitting or standing or lying down in order to be a man. Because this subject remains the same "under" the change, and so "is under" ("sub-stands") the various determinations that it has, it is called a "substance."

Second, though a substance can receive further determinations, the substances which we experience as changing themselves exist, or are, in their own right, in themselves. As subjects of the determinations, they have various qualities, and so forth; substances possess their added and changing differences.

Third, the determinations which come and go "happen to" a substance; hence, they are called "accidents"[4] (*ac-cidens*, that

---

[4] The term "accident" is also used in a logical sense, and in logic it means "that which is not necessarily connected with the essence of some thing." It is also used in a popular sense, "something (usually something harmful), which was unforeseen, unintended, and so on." We can call the meaning of *accident* used in the body of the text the "metaphysical accident."

which happens to). In "happening to" a substance, the accidents further determine, or modify it. We can therefore think of them most accurately as modifiers.

Both substance and accident are principles of being, for they are found *within being;* they are components of a whole, not complete things in themselves. But the whole thing which is the modified substance (we could well say, the "accidentalized substance") is not a natural unit with only one specific essence, since the specific essence remains through the change. We will call it a "per accidens unit."[5] Moreover, substance and accident are not equal principles, for the nature of accident is to modify substance, and in this sense to be "in" a substance. Hence, philosophers often say that accidents *inhere* in substance.

How do we derive the distinct notions of substance and accident? Is "substance" an abstraction? If we look back at the way in which we arrived at substance and accident, it will be noticed that through an analysis of change we proved that one is not the other. But this is again a negative judgment. Substance is therefore a real principle, as real and concrete as the whole being of which it is a part; accidents, too, in their own way, are also real principles. (Substance and accident will be treated more for their own sake in Chapters XI–XIII.)

40. Substance and accident as beings by analogy

We have seen in the second chapter that the properly real thing, or the being, is the entire thing which is. In our analysis of accidental change we found substance and accident, as principles of being, each in its own way. Are substance and accident to be considered beings in the same sense as the individuals of our experience? They do not present themselves this way. Moreover, we could not legitimately conclude that they are beings simply and properly, for our original evidence begins with a single complete being. Now, granted that a changing being is composite, its components cannot themselves be complete beings, on the score that "one" cannot at the same time be "two." It is therefore impossible that a principle of being should itself be *something* which is.

[5] On the kinds of unity, see below, sec. 89.

Nevertheless, if substance and accident are the principles of the real, they must also be real themselves in the real thing, since the real is not made up of unrealities. How then are they real? Since substance and its accidents together make up the whole real thing—and the whole real thing is that which properly is—they themselves are real with a many-to-one analogy. The "many" are the constitutive principles of substance and accident, and the "one" is the whole made up of them. This analogy of the constitutive principles to the whole composite which they make up we can call briefly the "analogy of composition."

In addition, substance and accident are directly related to each other: substance is the "basis" for accidents, and accidents are the modifiers of substance. Can this direct relationship be analyzed in terms of being? Substance is the (more or less) permanent nature of the thing and is that in the thing by which an existent has esse in itself; the act of existing pertains, within the being, most closely to substance. In other words, substance is not a being by itself; but the esse of the whole being is also the esse of all the principles of that being (many-to-one analogy); yet it is also true that this esse is not the esse of all the principles equally but in proportion to the way in which the principles constitute that being. Now, substance is the essential nature of that which is, and so we can properly and directly say that a substance exists. Hence, substance is directly ordered to the act of existing; we can say directly and without qualification, "A man, a cat, a dog, a tiger exists."

Accident, on the other hand, is related to that which is, not of itself, but through substance. The nature of an accident is to modify the substance in which it is. In other words, accident, according to its nature, is not in itself but in another.[6] Since accident naturally depends on substance for its being, we can say that accidents *are*, not directly but by inherence. For example, we can say, "Whiteness exists—in white things." Here then we have a one-to-one analogy of the constitutive principles of being, based on the relationship of these principles to each other. This relationship makes it possible for us, more or less properly, to

[6] See below, Chap. XII, especially secs. 103 and 105.

call both substance and accident beings.[7] Briefly, substance is
being in its own right, since it is that in the being *by which* the
being has an act of existing *in itself*. Accident is being by its
proportion to substance in which it inheres, for when an accident
modifies the substance of a being, the *whole* being *exists, by* that
accident, *in a modified way;* so we will call this analogy an
"analogy of proportion." For a concrete example, when we
say, "A dog is," we mean, "Some individual existent is, having
the nature of a dog as the principle by which it has esse-in-itself."
When we say, "Whiteness is," we mean, "Some individual existent
is, having in itself as one of its modifying principles the quality
of whiteness," or, more simply, "Whiteness does truly modify the
substance of some being," "Whiteness truly inheres in the substance of some being."

41. Substantial change and the matter-form composition of substance

EVIDENCE

In the discussion of accidental change, we considered those
changes in which the changing being remained the same kind of
thing and the same individual that it was. However, there are
also other changes in which the thing after the change is of a
different nature than the thing before the change. The clearest
examples of essential change can be found in the death of living
things. A live animal has a certain nature, which is shown by the
fact that it can perform certain kinds of activities. When the
animal dies, the dead body of the animal is simply incapable of
vital activities, and so is essentially or specifically different from
the living thing. A very similar example can be found in the
nourishment of living things. In nourishment, some nonliving
material is changed into and becomes a part of a single living
thing. In this case, two beings of different kinds become one
being.

Our experience shows us that there are some accidental changes
which prepare for and are the means of bringing about the
change of nature. And there are still other accidental changes

[7] See also, Selected Passages, No. 13. See below, sec. 124.

which are necessarily consequent upon the specific change. To illustrate this from the examples given above, we know that whether death is violent or natural, in either case some dispositions or qualities are changed by force or disease or simply by the wearing out of the organism. And we know also that properties of a nature are necessarily connected with the nature, so that when the first nature is present, these properties are present, and they go with the nature, while the new nature which is the term of the change brings with it its own properties. But over and above these accidental changes, there is a change of the nature itself, which is made known to us from the kinds of activities that the two beings in question perform.[8] Hence, there is a change in the very substance of the thing changing.

ANALYSIS

By applying our analysis of change to these changes of substance from living to nonliving, we get the diagram:

(1) Living substance — changes to $\longrightarrow$ nonliving substance

$$\frac{l}{c} \xrightarrow{\hspace{6cm}} \frac{n}{c}$$

(2) Living + nonliving — change to $\longrightarrow$ one living substance

$$\frac{l}{c} + \frac{n}{c} \xrightarrow{\hspace{6cm}} \frac{l}{c}$$

Hence, all substances which undergo substantial change are composed of two intrinsic principles. One of these principles is that by which a substance is of a definite kind: living, nonliving, and so forth. This principle has received the name of "substantial form"—*substantial*, because it is the determining principle of substance; *form*, because it has the same relation to its coprinciple as shape or structure has to the materials used. Substantial form is the principle *by which* a substance is the kind of substance it is; therefore, it is not itself a substance, much less a being, and so it is not a reality which we could possibly find in our direct sense

---

[8] To establish this fact we are using knowledge at the subscientific level. In the philosophy of nature, substantial or specific changes and specific differences are considered and proved at the level of demonstrative knowledge.

experience or by any instrument. Note that in metaphysics we deal only with substantial form as a principle of substance and being without qualification; in the philosophy of nature we shall discover that there are different kinds of substantial form and that one kind of form (the human soul) is not only a substantial form but also a principle of operation and of being.

The second of the two coprinciples of substantial change and composition cannot of itself have any particular nature, since it is precisely the common element in the change of nature or kind. It is of itself merely a subject of change, and for this reason it is called "primary matter" or "first matter." It is called primary matter because it is the first principle of the most basic type of change and is determin*able* to any nature which material things can have. Since substantial form is not a thing or a being or a substance properly so called, much less is primary matter a thing or a being. Of itself, primary matter is not actually any kind of thing; nor does it have quantity or any kind of qualities or other accidents. Hence, primary matter cannot exist in itself; it cannot be found as such in direct or indirect sense experience; it cannot even be understood separately from substance or substantial form. It is an intelligible *co*principle and so is real as a principle of substance and can be understood only in the same way.[9]

Are primary matter and substantial form really distinct? Since the changes which are explained by these coprinciples are real changes, matter and form must be distinct with a minor real distinction. In a way, matter and form are like substance and accident, yet there are also many differences. One of these differences is that accidental change can be gradual because the subject of accidental change (namely, substance itself) is the actual principle by which an individual is in itself. But substantial change must be instantaneous since the subject of substantial change (namely, primary matter) is purely determinable. Substantial changes seem to take time because of the accidental changes which are the means of substantial change.[10]

[9] See also, Selected Passages, No. 12.
[10] That continuous change implies primary matter is established by St. Thomas in his *Commentary on Aristotle's* Metaphysics, Bk. VIII, lect. 1 (ed. Cathala, No. 1686). But this consideration seems to belong to the philosophy of nature rather than to metaphysics.

Another approach to the composition of sensible things is derived from a consideration of the various ways in which accidents are related to their subjects. On the one hand, we find that there are specific qualities and properties which indicate different kinds of things. What one thing is is different from what other things are; what each thing is is characterized by determination, actuality, and some kind of fixity. Hence, substance, which is the proper subject of accidents, must itself have these characteristics. On the other hand, we also find that some modifications are common to all material things—chief among them being quantity and the continuous way in which their contingent accidents vary. Thus, we find two sorts of modifications of substance: one characterized by being proper (that is, not common) and relatively fixed, the other by being common and fluid or relatively "formless." But this distinction of accidents cannot be based on a simple, indivisible substance, for a simple subject cannot be the source of contrary dispositions. Hence, material substances are composite, made up of two principles, one of which is determining and specific (substantial form), the other, common to all material things and in itself indeterminate (primary matter).

Primary matter and substantial form are not things or beings; they are not each, properly speaking, a substance. But they are principles of substance; *by them* a substance is respectively capable of substantial change, relatively indeterminate, and like other material substances, and, at the same time, actually of a given kind or species, determinate, and different from other kinds of material things. Hence, these two principles can be called substances—not in the primary sense of that term but by an analogy of proportion, inasmuch as they are proportioned to each other and to the substance which they constitute. They are reducible to the category of substance.

42. Individuals in a species and matter-form composition

So far we have been considering material substances with regard to their real changes and real internal constitution. There is another important consideration of material substances whose point of departure is our knowledge of them.

THE PROBLEM

We have already noted, as a fact, that in material things there are many individuals having one and the same specific nature. We have also noted that a specific identity is not a total identity, but a partial one. We have observed, as a fact, that we have universal knowledge, and that this universal knowledge is true of individuals, though each individual is distinct and different from each other. This fact of universal knowledge is indeed striking, and it is one of the perennial starting points of philosophical reflection from Plato's time on. As metaphysicians, we are interested in seeing whether these various facts show us anything about the structures of being and, to a lesser extent, anything about the structure of knowledge.

A simple parallel between our knowledge and the structure of reality might appear an appealing solution, and because the first of such solutions was attempted by Plato, similar efforts are usually dubbed "Platonic." The basic principle is that universals are real by themselves, and they are to be found either in a "world" all their own (Plato's version) or somehow in singulars, yet still not merely mentally distinct from singulars. Aristotle pointed out one difficulty with this solution: it creates a new problem of the relation of the universals to the sensible singulars. Moreover, the metaphysical status of these distinct universals is difficult indeed: we have seen above that universals canot exist, and if they do not, how can they account for the nature of the sensibles and for our knowledge?

A second solution eliminates the problem by denying universal knowledge, the "solution" offered by nominalism. Only words (and perhaps also concepts) are universal, but the universality of knowledge is just a fiction. To this attempted solution, we can first retort that universal knowledge cannot be just a fiction of the human mind.[11] That which we know in our universal knowl-

[11] We are here appealing to many evidences for a moderate realism. First of all, we do have true knowledge of a world of sensible beings distinct from ourselves, and we know the existence of these beings by our intellect but through sense perception. This evidence cannot be proved, first, because it is an evidence; secondly, because sense perception is a principle of all our knowledge, as will become clear from the philosophy of human nature.

edge is somehow found in the real order. Comparing our knowledge to reality we find the situation which can be diagrammed in this way:

The real being, Peter, who   *is known*   { man
is individual throughout   *by means of*   { Petreity

Therefore, if our knowledge is true, there must be some reason or foundation in things for our knowing them universally and particularly, and yet this foundation cannot be a common nature as common really distinguished from particularity.

THE SOLUTION

The solution has three steps. The first may be called the epistemological; it consists in clarifying the relation between the universals of knowledge and the singulars of sensation and being. First, it is not to be thought that universal knowledge is a complete and adequate knowledge; it is only partial. It may be a very important part, yet it does not substitute for the direct experience of singulars; it simply does not include in any way the real individuality of the singular things. Second, when we say that universal knowledge is a knowledge of singulars, we mean this with a distinction: it is true with regard to what it says and with regard to what things are; it is not true with regard either to the mode of the knowledge (its universality, abstractness, "timelessness," necessity) or to the mode of the singular (its singularity, concreteness, temporality, contingency).

The second step may be called the psychological, and consists in examining the origin of our universal knowledge. We will here

---

Secondly, there are many considerations which particularly concern universal knowledge. Pragmatically speaking, universal knowledge can be used as a means to deal with real singulars. More deeply, when we mentally construct fictions we are aware of our activity in that construction and can trace the process, but in knowing singulars by direct universal knowledge we do not find ourselves constructing a fiction. Ultimately, we can see that our universal knowledge is a knowledge of the thing which exists. It is not a complete knowledge but one which abstracts from singularity. However, to abstract is not to deny. It would be false to deny that things are singular; we have a true but incomplete knowledge when we know a singular thing without knowing its singularity. To develop these brief considerations is the task of an epistemology or theory of knowledge.

present only a sketch of what is found and proved in the philosophy of human nature. The human intellect receives its knowledge of reality through sense from sensible things. First, then, sensible things act on us; action arises from form (substantial and accidental), not from matter, and therefore does not principally bear the imprint of individuality but of nature and form. Second, sense knows according to formal intelligibilities (color, sound, and so on), even though it knows them only in a singular. The repeated fleeting experiences of sense are conserved in the imagination; the complex image thus developed is already partly disengaged from absolute singularity as found in external sense. Third, the absolute nature is received in the intellect; the intellect, as knowing subject, contributes no temporality or individual limitation of its own, and is affected only by the formal intelligible attributes of what is contained in the image. (The precise causalities of this process need not concern us here.)

The third step is the metaphysical, and consists in elaborating what we already know about material things, together with some additional reflection on these things.

We have in the immediately preceding section found that material things are composed of primary matter and substantial form. Substantial form is that principle by which a substance is *what* it is, that is, has such a nature or essence. Primary matter is that principle by which a thing is capable of substantial change and which therefore is the subject or recipient of substantial form. The possibilities opened up by this very composition are suggested by a simple comparison with accidental form and substance: accidental forms are multiplied (as in the mass production of artifacts) insofar as there are a number of substances to receive them (there are as many pins as there is metal to be cut into pieces). Similarly—and very much in general—primary matter is a recipient for substantial form, and as recipient is the ontological basis for the possibility of there being many individuals (for example, many men) in the same species, whereas the (abstract) unity of the substantial form is the basis of our knowledge of these many individuals in a single concept, the universal. But this parallel has only a heuristic value; we need to look at the things, not merely at some parallel from which we would atempt to deduce the structure of reality.

What then do we find in the real order? We find individuals differing a great deal. Among men, for example, there are both seven-foot Watusi and the five-foot Pygmy; the fragile Japanese dancer and the beetle-browed Neanderthal man.[12] We find some individuals whom we can easily describe by means of relatively distinctive qualities, and others who are alike as identical twins. But even though an individual has apparently unique qualities, these qualities alone do not, absolutely speaking, "identify" him; any quality or any combination of qualities can, at least in principle, be found in another individual. Consider, for example, how qualitatively "identical" two crystals can be. Things can still be two even if these two have no discoverable qualitative differences. But two material beings cannot be two beings unless their temporally determined locations are different.[13] In other words, we can always certainly identify an individual if we know where he is and when.

Now, qualitative differences are differences of accidental form, and so suppose the substantial individual already constituted. Moreover, qualities flow from substantial form—in various ways, as properties, as contingent attributes, as possibilities of modification by external agents.

The substantial individual, who is one of many in a species, is therefore exactly our problem. If all these individuals belong to the same species, then their forms as such cannot be the source of their differing as individuals. What about primary matter?

[12] It must be stated very emphatically that the notions of both "individual" and "species" are analogous. Moreover, such problems as the variability of species and the origin of particular species (speciation), the possibility of varieties and families within species, evolution, degeneration (as in parasitism), hybridization, isotopes—just samples of problems occurring in particular sciences and in the philosophy of nature—these are simply not capable of being treated by a metaphysician. As a wise philosopher remarked centuries ago: metaphysics bakes no bread.

[13] This is not meant to deny "compenetration" or the possibility of a subatomic particle "passing through a solid"; if such events do happen, they are nevertheless explained by means of differences in the "here" and "now."

Since primary matter is the subject or recipient of substantial form, it could, by division, account for the plurality of individuals. But this seems impossible. Primary matter cannot be divided in itself, since in itself it is purely indeterminate, and division implies distinction, difference, and so some kind of determination. True enough. But so far, we have not yet made use of the ultimate criterion of the individual—his being here and now. *Here* and *now* are functions of quantity, as we shall see more clearly later on. Quantity or extension is such that it has parts outside of itself and of itself is divisible. Hence, primary matter with quantity or dimensions[14] is that which is the principle of individuation[15] of a material thing. There are many individuals in a species inasmuch as the recipients of specifically the same substantial form are divided from each other in relation to tri-dimensional extension.

It will help us if we compare the order of logical composition (common nature + individuality) with the quite different order of real composition (substantial form + primary matter + quantity).

(1) *In the order of logical composition,*

Peter	James	John
$\left\{ \begin{array}{c} \text{man} \\ + \\ \text{Petreity} \end{array} \right\}$	$\left\{ \begin{array}{c} \text{man} \\ + \\ \text{Jamesness} \end{array} \right\}$	$\left\{ \begin{array}{c} \text{man} \\ + \\ \text{Johnness} \end{array} \right\}$

[14] At any given moment, the dimensions in question are the actual three dimensions of the particular individual limited by the external surface; these are called "determinate dimensions." But because in some individuals (living things) the dimensions change—between limits—during their lives, we must consider their dimensions with their variable limits; these are called "indeterminate dimensions." By indeterminate dimensions we mean the tri-directional quantity of an individual, with variable limits, as it were, "at the center."

[15] The principle of individuation is that in the particular thing by which that thing has its particular part or share of the specific perfection and so is only one of many in the species. Distinguish this term from "individuality." Individuality is the sum total of positive perfections pertaining to this individual as *this* individual. Individuation is the quasi-negative, limiting principle; individuality is the correlative, positive perfection.

(2) *In the order of real composition*,[16]

$$
\text{Peter} \qquad\qquad \text{James} \qquad\qquad \text{John}
$$

$$
\left\{ \frac{f}{p_x + x} \right\} \qquad\qquad \left\{ \frac{f}{p_y + y} \right\} \qquad\qquad \left\{ \frac{f}{p_z + z} \right\}
$$

f = substantial form by which each individual is a man.
p = the primary matter.
x, y, z = the diverse quantities.
The subscript letters indicate the determination [designation] of matter by diverse quantities.

Once this has been understood, we can easily come to see how new individuals arise by the division of previously existing ones. This is basically the way in which new living beings arise; we can see it most simply in the origin of new unicellular organisms. Many of these organisms are multiplied by simple division (fission); one individual divides into two individuals which are numerically distinct from each other, and yet each of the new individuals has the undivided perfection of the species or kind of living thing. Diagrammatically:

$$
\frac{\text{form}}{\text{matter}_{qu} + \text{quantity}} \longrightarrow \left\{ \begin{array}{l} \dfrac{\text{form}}{\text{matter }_{qu}{}^1 + qu^1} \\[2ex] \dfrac{\text{form}}{\text{matter}_{qu}{}^2 + qu^2} \end{array} \right.
$$

From our consideration of individuation, we arrive at a fuller understanding of the relationship between matter and form. Form of itself as form is simply what-it-is; it is the principle of determination, actualization of specific or substantial perfection. But matter, as divided recipient or capacity, is the principle of multiplication and limitation as well as of substantial change. No individual has the full perfection of what-it-is-by-nature (that is, through its form), because each form is concretely limited by

---

[16] Because the diagram is somewhat complicated, here is how it should be read: "In the real order, Peter, as *this* man, is composed of a substantial form (principle of specific perfection) and of a primary matter distinguished in function of a particular quantity plus the quantity which has the function of designating primary matter as this (principle of individuation)."

the matter in which it is received.[17] Some of these perfections actually are mutually exclusive; if it belongs to a nature to have one of several colors, a given individual can have only one, and thereby cannot have the others. In many subtle ways similar alternative possibilities are found at the levels of the higher qualities of sense and intellect. Thus, no man has the full perfection of the human nature which he possesses through his form (his soul), because each man's soul is concretely limited by the body (in the sense of primary matter) in which that soul is received. As a result, we can derive some understanding of a species by coming to know one individual, for we will find in that individual (supposing it to be mature and otherwise capable of manifesting its nature) all the properties of that nature, at least in their minimal form. But only after knowing many individuals can we learn the full range of the possibility even of the properties, and much more of the contingent actualizations of that nature.

This relationship of form and matter may perhaps be better understood by a consideration of a kind of being about which various philosophers have spoken, namely, the separated substances, also called "angels," "pure spirits," "pure intelligences," and so forth. There are a number of very subtle and difficult arguments by which the existence of such beings is suggested and proved. Neither the time nor the background is available to us here, so we will speak of such beings hypothetically. If such

---

[17] Some students are bothered by the pseudo problem, What keeps a separated soul from either ballooning up to be a universal or being identified with all other human souls? All existents are singular; if the soul exists after death, it exists as a singular and with the singularity and existence it had before. Along these lines, there are only two reasonable questions that can be asked. (1) How can separated souls, which are singular forms, be known by universal knowledge? (2) In what sense can a separated soul be said to be the "soul of Peter"? The answer to both questions is the same: because each separated soul has been the soul of a given individual and permanently retains a relation to that individual's body.

Other students are confused because it seems to them that geometrical figures, though pure forms (abstract, it is true, instead of real), are multiplied by themselves without composition. Careful reflection will show that such abstract forms are not multiplied by themselves *qua* forms, but by "intelligible matter." In simpler terms, such abstract forms are multiplied positionally, that is, by reference to a hypostasized extension which serves as a receptive background. This substantialized quantity is quality-less, and therefore individuates only numerically, i.e., without other distinctions.

beings exist, their substance is not composite; they are not substantially determinable and so cannot undergo substantial
change.[18] Furthermore, their substance is entirely determinate;
they are entirely what they are. There is nothing else in their
substance except their specific pefection. Hence this substance
is entirely expressed in a single individual, and consequently
there cannot be many of these beings in a single species. Each
one differs specifically from every other (and so in a kind of
way also "numerically"). Because they are pure forms, the formal
perfection of such beings is incapable of multiplication; by a
somewhat improper use of language, we could say that each individual pure form is its own species (for there are really no
species among such beings).

43. That-which-is and the act of existing (esse)

THE PROBLEM

So far we have found composition and distinction of principles
at the level of accident and activity and at the level of substance.
Because we can know *what* is by simple apprehension (concept),
but whether a thing *is* only in a judgment (affirmation or negation), we are led to inquire into the relations between what is and
its act of existing (esse). It is quite clear that the questions, "What
is it?" and, "Is it?" are two quite different questions. It is also clear
that as far as all the things in our direct experience are concerned,
the act of existing is not a specific perfection, not a further determination of what the thing is. As Kant said, a hundred real dollars
are not a penny more than a hundred possible dollars.

If we attentively reflect upon an existent as it is given to us in
immediate experience, we see first of all that the meanings of
to be and *what-is* are different. As we progressively understand
this difference between what-is and its act of existing, we form
the primitive understanding of being, "some (sensible) thing
which is"; then, on the level of the scientific knowledge of metaphysics, we are led to make the judgment of separation, and so
come to understand being as *that which is.* Now, however, we
need to study being still more closely.

[18] See also, Selected Passages, No. 14.

Let us consider a being, for example, a person, present to us in immediate experience. What that person is (namely, this concrete human nature with all his accidental modifications) can be grasped in a series of concepts and is analyzable into the principles of matter and form, substance and accident. These principles are principles of an existent, but their immediate role is that of constituting the essence.[19] These are the principles by which the being is what it is, is limited, is capable of change in various ways. But a being must *be* before[20] it is determined, limited, modified, capable of changes. *To be*, as we have seen, is the ultimate actuality of all principles—essence and form among them. To be limited and capable of change is thus the correlative opposite of being: a person is limited in the sense that he does not have some perfection; he is capable of change only if he does not yet have the perfection. The principles of limitation and change cannot as such also play the role of intrinsic actualization. What then makes a thing to *be?* Precisely, the act of existing (esse), that real principle in the thing that corresponds to the "is" of the judgment.

Again, the actuality of being is found in many things, each of which as an individual is different from all the others, many of which differ also specifically from some others. *If* being were an abstraction, a remote genus like "sensible substance," we could be tempted to think that the "generality" of being is merely an ab-

---

[19] On essence, see sec. 16, n. 18. Historically, the term "essence" is used in the strict sense to mean "the specific constitution of a thing." In this sense, *essence* is that "part" or "aspect" of the substance of a thing which constitutes it in its species. In the secondary sense, we can speak of the *essence* of an accident as "that specific intelligibility of the accident according to its kind, abstracting from its individual and contingent circumstances."

In a wide sense, the term "essence" has been used to mean "what a thing is." In this sense, we can speak of an individual essence. Nevertheless, in the direct phenomenological analysis of concrete being, we first find *essence* in the wide sense, as the *thing-principle* of that which is.

On this broad sense of "essence," see *Summa Theologiae*, Pt. I, q. 29, art. 4 ad 2.

[20] "Before," in this sentence, does not mean a priority of time, but a priority of nature and intelligibility. In other words, determinations and so on presuppose an existent and depend on the act of existing of the existent in order to be real.

straction, merely the real conceived in the most vague and potential way. But, since being is not an abstraction; since, in fact, it is opposite to the vague potentiality of a common genus, because it expresses the ultimate actuality of the concrete real, the community of being must be based on a principle that is real and intrinsic in each being. This is the same reason that we considered above when we were forced to accept the *analogy* of being, though it is here used in a different context. In somewhat the same way as specific unity is accounted for by substantial form, and numerical individuality by primary matter, so the analogous unity of being must be referred to one real principle, and the multiple and limited individual beings must derive their multiplicity from another real principle, really distinct from its correlate.[21] It is clear that distinction and limitation are connected with the essence of things, by which each is *what* it is. The act of existing, then, which is common to all of these many things, must be really distinct from the essence, as a correlative constituent principle.

Thus, direct experience and analysis of the real show us that essence and the act of existing are really distinct. These principles, of course, are not spatial or integral parts (like the trunk and members of a living body) nor essential parts (like matter and form). They are purely intelligible principles, not observable as distinct but understood to be distinct with a minor real distinction. (It will be noted that essence-esse as a being is precisely that which is and is analogously.)

CONFIRMATION

The fact of change can be used to support the conclusion that essence and esse are really distinct.[22] We experience a thing com-

[21] This point is explained more fully in Selected Passages, Nos. 15 and 16. See, in addition, sec. 64, where the relation of essence and esse is still further clarified.

[22] There are some philosophers, and even some Thomists, who think that this proof is inadequate. They hold that (a) an explanation of change can be given by means of the principles of substance and accident, matter and form; (b) that the composition of these two principles is a sufficient basis for the proof of the existence of God. Both of these statements are true enough. One can give some explanation of change without going into the question of the distinction between essence and esse. But if one remains entirely on that plane, one is reasoning within the philosophy of nature, and

ing to be and ceasing to be. But neither essence nor form (which is the determining principle of essence) can change—*horse* cannot become cow or carrion. A horse can die; but what-it-is-to-be-horse cannot die or change in any way in itself. The unchangeableness of an essence is simply a particular expression of the principle of contradiction: "horse is horse and cannot be not-horse." If what-a-thing-is and its act of existing were really identical, then the horse-which-is would exist as necessarily as horse-is-horse. But living things do die; things do change. Hence, what-a-thing-is and its act of existing are distinct, with a minor real distinction.

Hence, what-a-thing-is and its act of existing are two really distinct principles of a being. What-something-is, because it is immediately related to esse (the act of existing), is often called essence.[23] Sometimes also that principle is called quiddity (from the Latin *quid,* meaning "what").[24]

44. The agent and his activity

In our first approach to the intrinsic composition of beings, we discovered the two principles, substance and accident. At that point, we were looking at being from the point of view of change and what was necessary for change to take place. From this point of view, accidents include the activities of the thing. After discussing matter and form, we turned to what is and the act of

---

therefore should not expect to find anything about being as the metaphysician considers being. The distinction between essence and esse is implied in any metaphysical solution of the problem of change. If this distinction remains only implicit (as it did in Aristotle), the solution is good as far as it goes, but it is incomplete. If, however, essence and esse are thought to be identical in the real order, then each one of the components of a thing, such as substance and accident, which are essences, must be identically also acts of existing. But that which is its act of existing cannot lose it. All that could happen would be to move the necessarily existing components around, and such an interpretation of change is the denial of all *intrinsic* change. But intrinsic change evidently happens, and therefore essence and the act of existing cannot be identical in the real order.

[23] "Essence" implies that we are considering what a thing is as a principle of its being. "Quiddity" implies rather an absolute consideration of what it is, as a pure intelligibility. Strictly speaking, therefore, metaphysics is interested in essences but not in quiddities.

[24] See also, Selected Passages, No. 17.

existing, and from this point of view, we saw that both substance and accident belong to what is. If we stopped here, we would have a static and formal notion of activity which could be very misleading, and at least would be very incomplete.

EVIDENCE

At least some activities are distinct from substance and the act of existing of a being, and this is clear from experience, without much analysis. For example, most living things have one or more activities[25] which are sometimes interrupted—by sleep, by climatic changes, by development from immature offspring to senility, and so on. For example, consider the conscious activities of a human being: he has certain kinds of activities like seeing and thinking, and these change from one act to another throughout the waking day; when he is sound asleep, these activities cease altogether. Here, obviously, the activity is distinct from the rest of the being, for it comes and goes and varies, although the being itself continues in existence.

In all the things of experience, we find activity. There is no existent which is absolutely deprived of all action. Even the most passive-looking, apparently inert being is also active, as the investigations of physicists have abundantly proved. Activity is a consequence, an overflowing into the order of action, of the dynamism of the act of existing.

ANALYSIS

What is the relation of activity (action, operation) to the thing which acts? First, a thing acts only if it exists; a nonbeing cannot do anything; a mere concept cannot perform real actions. Second, a thing acts according to its nature. In fact, we learn the nature of a thing first and foremost from its activities. Not only is this true in fact; it is necessarily true. For action comes from an agent; it is the fullness, the complement of that agent's being. The substance is that which receives the other accidents and at the

---

[25] How we distinguish one activity from another and one power of activity from another will be considered in another part of philosophy; cf. G. P. Klubertanz, *Philosophy of Human Nature* (New York, Appleton-Century-Crofts, Inc., 1953), pp. 86–102.

same time is the ultimate principle of activity. Now, as we have seen, a substance in our experience is what it is because of its substantial form, and, likewise, the same substantial form specifies the kind of activity which a given kind of being has. Hence, activity and nature must necessarily correspond.

Third, in the things of our experience, being is *for* its activity.[26] This is most obvious in the things we know best, persons and living things. Inactivity is felt as a loss and a restriction; successful activity as an expansion, a fulfillment of capacities and tendencies. These three relationships are all stated implicity in a common axiom, "Action follows being."

But these relationships, particularly the third, raise a question. There seems to be a double line of actuality: esse and activity. How can this be? How are they related to each other and to being? These questions cannot be answered here, because, though the evidence that raises them is direct enough, we have not yet elaborated the tools of analysis.

45. Definitions

Accident is that principle of being whose nature it is to be in another.

Substance is that principle of being which is modified or determined by accidents (nominal definition).

Substance is that principle of being whose nature it is to be directly ordered to esse in itself (real definition).

Essence in the strict sense is substance considered as being of a certain kind of species and being capable of receiving an act of existing.

Essence in the wide sense is what a thing is. It may include substance and accidents (together as subject of esse); it may be used of principles, of objects of knowledge, of operations, relations, and so forth.

Nature is substance or essence in relation to activities.

Analogy of composition is that many-to-one analogy in which the "one" is the whole made up of the "many," and the "many" are the constitutive principles of the whole, in such a way that

---

[26] One important distinction between two kinds of activity, immanent and transient, will be made from the viewpoint of teleology; see below, sec. 69.

they are not univocally of the same nature as the whole nor of a different kind.

Analogy of proportion is that one-to-one analogy which is based on definite direct relationships between two of the analogates.

Substantial form is the determining and specifying principle of essence or substance.

Primary (first) matter is the determinable and limiting principle of substance in material things and, thereby, is also the common subject of substantial change.[27]

Individuation is the limitation of a nature to a particular individual.

Individuality is the sum total of positive perfections, or the fundamental positive perfection, peculiar and proper to some individual.

That-which-is is the essence in the wide sense.

Act of existing (or, *esse*) is the principle by which ultimately a thing is or exists.

46. Summary of the argumentation

A. Beings that change accidentally are composed of substance and accidents.

It is a fact of experience that at least some beings change in some characteristics while remaining of the same nature as they were.

But: this change is not possible unless the accidentally changing being is composed of a principle which is of itself and others which are in the former as in a subject.

Therefore: accidentally changing being is composed of substance and accident.

[27] Aristotle gives two classic definitions of primary matter. It is "the primary substratum of each thing, from which it comes to be without qualification, and which persists in the result" (*Physics*, I, 192a31, tr. by Hardie and Gaye), and "By matter I mean that which in itself is neither a particular thing nor of a certain quantity nor assigned to any other of the categories by which being is determined" (*Metaphysics*, Bk. VI, 1029a20, trans. Ross).

B. Beings that change substantially are composed of primary matter and substantial form.

It is a fact of experience that one kind of thing changes into another.

But: this kind of change implies that each of the beings is composed of a principle by which it is specifically what it is and a principle which is common to both terms and receives the determining principles.

Therefore: things which undergo substantial change are composed of substantial form and primary matter.

C. Individuals in the same species are composed of matter and form.

It is a fact of experience that material things belong to a limited number of kinds of things yet differ among themselves.

But: identity and difference in nature cannot flow from one and the same principle but require two distinct principles.

Therefore: individuals in a species are composed of a principle of specific perfection (substantial form) and a principle of individuation (primary matter with quantity).

D. That which is and the act of existing are distinct in all limited beings.

The beings of our experience manifest themselves as subjects having or exercising an act of existing.

The beings of our experience manifest themselves as many, and as each limited in its being.

But: multiplicity and limitation cannot come from the same principle which constitutes the analogical unity of beings in their being.

Therefore: multiple and limited beings are composed of a principle in virtue of which they are what they are and a principle by which they are (act of existing, esse).

47. Readings

St. Thomas Aquinas, *On Being and Essence*, trans. Armand Maurer, chap. 2, pp. 30–34 (on essence, matter and form, on essence and individuation); *Summa Theologiae*, Pt. I, q. 3, art. 2 (no matter and form in God), art. 4 (no distinction of essence and esse in God), art. 6 (no accidents in God); q. 12, art. 4 ad 3 (on our knowledge of the act of existing); q. 14, art. 6 (the act of existing is not the only perfection); q. 50, art. 2 (angels are pure forms); q. 76, art. 1 (the human soul is the form of a body), art. 2 (and is individuated by the body); q. 77, art. 6 (on the relations between accident and substance); *On Spiritual Creatures*, art. 1 ad 9 (individuals in a species), art. 3 (is there a medium which joins form to matter?); *Commentary on the Metaphysics of Aristotle*, Bk. VIII, lesson 2, Nos. 1691–1702, pp. 627–630 (on form and matter).

Leonard J. Eslick, "The Real Distinction: Reply to Professor Reese [see below]," *The Modern Schoolman*, vol. 38 (1961), 149–160, excellent for understanding some of the more subtle difficulties.

Etienne Gilson, *Being and Some Philosophers* (Toronto, Pontifical Institute of Mediaeval Studies, 1949), pp. 169–170, 175, 184–185, on essence and the act of existing.

Etienne Gilson, *The Christian Philosophy of St. Thomas Aquinas* (New York, Random House, 1956), pp. 84–95, on the real distinction and the proper meaning of the act of existing.

J. Quentin Lauer, S.J., "Determination of Substance by Accidents in the Philosophy of St. Thomas," *The Modern Schoolman*, XVIII (1941), 31–35, on substance and accident.

Bernard J. Lonergan, S.J., "The Concept of *Verbum* in the Writings of St. Thomas Aquinas," Part III, "Procession and Related Notions," *Theological Studies*, vol. VIII (1947), pp. 408–413, esp. p. 412, activity is more than existence or form.

Jacques Maritain, *Introduction to Philosophy*, trans. E. I. Watkin (New York, Sheed and Ward, 1933), pp. 207–210, 217–227, on substance and accident, matter and form.

Armand Maurer, C.S.B., "Form and Essence in the Philosophy of St. Thomas," *Mediaeval Studies*, XIII (1951), 174–176; form, essence, and the act of existing.

William L. Reese, "Concerning the Real Distinction of Essence and Existence," *The Modern Schoolman*, vol. 38 (1961), 142–148, some difficulties with the real distinction.

William A. Van Roo, S.J., "Matter as a Principle of Being," *The Modern Schoolman*, XIX (1942), 47–50; the relation of matter to form and to the act of existing.

William M. Walton, "Being, Essence, and Existence," *Review of Metaphysics*, III (1950), 339–365.

SELECTED PASSAGES FROM ST. THOMAS AQUINAS

12. Change, Matter, and Form

He says that it is necessary to posit matter in sensible substances as substance and subject. For in every change there must be a subject common to the terms of the change in changes which involve contraries. For example, in change of place there is some common subject, which now is here, and then, there. And in growth, there is a common subject, which now has this quantity, and then a smaller one (if it is a decrease), or a larger one (if there is an increase). And in alteration there is a subject, which now is healthy, and then sick. And since there is also a change in substance (that is, generation and corruption), there must be a common subject, which lies under contrary changes of generation and corruption, and this involves the positing of terms, which are form and privation—in this way, namely, that at one time the matter is in act by the form, and at another time, it is the subject of the privation of that form.

From this reasoning of Aristotle's, it is clear that substantial generation and corruption are the principle of coming to a knowledge of primary matter. For if primary matter of itself had some proper form, by that form it would be something actual. Thus, when some other form were brought about in addition to the former, matter would not simply be by that form, but would become this or that modified being. And thus there would be some kind of generation, but not generation simply. Hence, all those who posited that the first subject was some body—as, air or water—held that generation was the same as alteration.

From this consideration it is clear how we must take the understanding of primary matter, for it is so related to all forms and the privations of them, as an alterable subject is to contrary qualities.

> *Commentary on Aristotle's*
> Metaphysics, Bk. VIII, lect.
> 1 (ed. Cathala, Nos. 1688–
> 1689).

13. Substance and Accident as Beings by Analogy

Those things which have one predicate in common, which is not univocal, but is predicated of them analogously, belong to the consideration of one demonstrative knowledge. But being is predicated in this way of all beings. Therefore, all beings belong to the consideration of one knowledge which considers being as being, namely, both substance and accidents. . . .

He says, first, that being, or, that which is, is predicated in many ways. But we must know that something is predicated of different things in many ways; sometimes, according to an intelligibility which is entirely the same, and then it is said to be univocally predicated of them, as animal of the horse and the ox. Sometimes the predicate is predicated according to entirely different intelligibilities, and then it is said to be predicated equivocally of them, as dog, of the star and the animal. Sometimes the predicate is predicated according to intelligibilities which are partly different and partly not different; different, that is, inasmuch as they imply different relationships; the same, inasmuch as these different relationships are referred to some one and the same thing. Then they are said to be predicated analogously, that is, proportionally, according as each one, by its own relationship, is referred to that one same thing.

Secondly, we must know that that one thing to which the different relationships are referred in analogates is one in number, and not merely in intelligibility. . . .

Every being is called being, in relation to one first thing. This "one first thing" . . . is the subject. For some things are called being, or are said to be, because of themselves they have *esse*, such as substances, which are principally and primarily called beings. But others are called beings, because they are the passions or properties of substance, such as the per se properties of any substance. Some others are called beings, because they are the way to substance, such as generation and motion. Still others are called beings, because they are the corruptions of substance, for corruption is a way to nonbeing, as generation is the way to substance. And because corruption ends at privation, as generation at form, it is suitable that even the privations of substantial form are said to be. And again, qualities or some other accidents are called beings, because they are active or generative principles of substance, or of such things as are related to substance according to one of the above mentioned relationships, or according to any other relationship. Likewise, the negations of those things which are referred to substance, or even of substance itself, are said to be. Hence, we say, "not-being is not-being." We would not say this, unless "to be" pertained in some way to negation.

> *Commentary on Aristotle's*
> Metaphysics, Bk. IV, lect.
> 1 (ed. Cathala, Nos. 534–
> 536, 539).

14. *Essences: Simple and Composite*

The intelligible nature of quiddity or essence does not require that it is composed or a composite. Consequently, there can be found and understood a simple quiddity, which is not a result of the composition of form and matter. But if we find a quiddity which is not composed of matter and form, that quiddity either is its esse, or it is not. If that quiddity is its esse, it will perforce be the essence of God himself, which is its esse, and it will be entirely simple. But if it is not its esse, it is necessary that it have an esse acquired from another, as is every created quiddity. And because this quiddity is by supposition not subsisting in matter, esse will not be acquired by it in another, as is the case with composite quiddities, but it will acquire esse in itself. And so, this quiddity will be that *which* is, and its esse will be that by which it is. And because everything which does not have a perfection of itself is possible with regard to that perfection, such a quiddity, since it has esse from another, will be possible with regard to that esse and with regard to that principle from which it has esse (in which principle no potency can be found). And thus in such a quiddity there will be found potency and act, inasmuch as the quiddity itself is possible, and its esse is its act. This is the way I understand composition of potency and act in Angels, and of that by which they are and that which they are, and likewise in the soul. Hence, an Angel or the soul can be called a quiddity, or a nature, or a simple form, inasmuch as their quiddity is not composed of diverse principles; and yet they have a composition of these two, that is, of quiddity and esse.

> Commentary on the First Book
> of the Sentences, dis. 8, q. 5,
> art. 2.

15. Multiplicity in a Species

Whenever the essence of some thing is divided by the sharing [of many in it], the same essence is shared according to its intelligible constitution, but not according to the same act of existing. Therefore, it is impossible for that in which essence and esse do not differ to be divided or multiplied by an essential sharing.

> Commentary on the First Book
> of the Sentences, dis. 2, q. 1,
> art. 1, arg. 4

16. Multiplicity and Composition vs. Unity

That which is simply the First can only be one, and this for three reasons. First, from the order of the universe, whose parts are discovered to be ordered to each other, somewhat like the parts of an animal in the whole animal, which parts help each other. There can be no such coordination of many things, unless they are striving for some one end. Therefore there must be one highest and ultimate good, which is striven for by all, and this is the principle. Secondly, this is evident from the very nature of things. For we find in all things the "nature" of being, in some of greater value, and in others of less. And yet the natures of these things are not the esse which they have. If they were, esse would belong to the understanding of any essence, and this is false, for the quiddity of any thing can be understood, without understanding that it is. Therefore, it is necessary that they have esse from some principle, and ultimately we must come to something whose very nature is his own esse, otherwise we would have an infinite regress. This is the principle which gives esse to all things, and it can be only one, since the "nature" of being has one intelligibility according to an analogy. For the unity of what is caused requires unity in its per se cause, and this is the proof of Avicenna. The third reason is the immateriality of God. For it is necessary that the cause which moves the heavens be a power which is not in matter, as is proved in the eighth book of the *Physics*. In those things which are without matter, there can be no diversity, except inasmuch as the nature of one is more complete and more in act than the nature of another. Therefore, it is necessary that that which is perfectly complete and entirely act, is only one, from which proceeds everything that contains potency. For act precedes potency, and the complete precedes the lessened, as is proved in the ninth book of the *Metaphysics*.

> *Commentary on the Second*
> *Book of the* Sentences, dis. 1,
> q. 1, art. 1.

17. *The Meaning of Being*

Since in everything which is, it is possible to consider its quiddity, by which it subsists in a determinate nature, and its esse, by which it is said to be in act, the noun *thing* is given to it from its quiddity, according to Avicenna, but the name, *He Who is,* or *Being,* from the act of being. But since it is the case that in every creature its essence differs from its esse, such a thing is properly named from its quiddity, as "man" from "humanity." But in God his very act of existing in His quiddity, and so the name which is taken from the act of existing properly names Him, and is His proper name.

> *Commentary on the First Book*
> *of the* Sentences, dis. 8, q. 1,
> art. 1.

Our intellect can consider in abstraction [in the broad sense] what it knows as concreted. For, although it knows things having a form in matter, nevertheless it analyzes the composite into the two [principles], and considers the form by itself. And, like our intellect, the intellect of an angel, though naturally it knows esse concreted in some nature, nevertheless separates esse by the intellect, inasmuch as it knows that it itself is one [really distinct principle] and its esse is another.

Since, therefore, the created intellect by its nature is able to apprehend the concreted form and the concreted esse abstractly by way of analysis, it is able to be elevated by grace to know [directly] a separated subsisting substance and a separated subsisting esse.

> *Summa Theologiae,*
> Pt. I, q. 12, art. 4 ad 3.

VI

The Intrinsic Principles
of Being: II. As Analogously One

48. Comparison of the three sets of intrinsic principles

We have seen that the individual beings of our experience are composed of various sets of principles. To sum up the results of our preceding investigation, we can consider a being thus:

being $\begin{cases} \text{act of existing} \\ \text{essence} \end{cases}$ $\begin{cases} \text{accident} \\ \text{substance} \end{cases}$ $\begin{cases} \text{form} \\ \text{matter} \end{cases}$

If we look back at our arguments by which we discovered these principles, we find matter and substance are alike in this: that each is a common subject for a different type of change, and that essence is somewhat similar to matter and substance in that it is the source of possibility in being itself. Hence, we can link these principles in a proportionate series thus:

$$\frac{\text{accident}}{\text{substance}} \quad : \quad \frac{\text{form}}{\text{matter}} \quad : \quad \frac{\text{esse}}{\text{essence}}$$

Considering these principles in this relationship, we can find a corresponding similarity in accident, form, and esse, for each of them determines a subject, making its correlative subject to be respectively such, this kind or species of thing, or simply to exist. Yet there are also differences in the three sets of correlatives. For example, the subject of accidents is a being in itself, whereas the subject of form is a mere possibility of being-determined-to-some-essence, and essence, in turn, receives all its reality in receiving the act of existing. Hence these three sets of principles, being both similar and different in their relationships to each other, are analogous to each other; and the analogy is an analogy of proper proportionality within a being.[1] But inasmuch as they are analogous, their relationships can be summed up in a single relationship, which is called "act and potency," or the "act-potency correlation."

We first discovered act and potency in the preliminary analysis of change,[2] and at that time we saw that that which changes is first *in potency* and later on *in act*. We saw at that time that the stages of being *in* potency and being *in* act exclude each other— that which is in potency is not yet in act, and that which is in act is no longer in potency. But a further analysis of change showed us that the thing which changes is composed, and the still more detailed analysis of change carried on in the preceding chapter (Chapter V) showed us that the changing things of our experience have at least a triple composition of essence and esse, substance and accident, and matter and form. We need therefore to learn a new and different meaning of "act" and "potency," a meaning which is to be developed from a much more advanced knowledge of change.[3]

What is meant by "act"? We need to go back to experience and consider what has been acquired when something has come to be in act. For example, actual knowledge of biology is what the biologist has when he is considering what he has previously learned. Act is, for example, seeing as compared with the in-activity of closed eyes; being awake as compared to the unconsciousness of sleep; what the carpenter does to a piece of wood when he is at work; the way in which a wax candle is molded as compared to the possibility of being thus molded when it was just a roundish lump; the billiard ball rolling as compared to its previous state of rest; the new tissue become human in the living

[1] Note that we do not say, "Accident is to its esse as substance is to its esse," and so forth. Why we cannot do this will be clear from Chap. XII, sec. 103.

[2] See above, Chap. IV.

[3] On the meaning of "act," see Selected Passages, No. 18.

body of a man as compared to the assimilability of the undigested food. Thus, act may mean any sort of activity, immanent or transient, any sort of actuality, determination, or perfection. Hence, act is an intrinsically analogous intelligibility;[4] with what analogy, we shall see later on.

So, too, with potency as a capacity for act. Potency in itself, it is true, is not act. But we must understand potency positively. Take, for example, the knowledge of biology (the information of a certain kind, and competence in using it). A baby, a puppy, and a doll are alike in this: that none of them know biology; they do not have or possess the actual knowledge. But from our experience with human beings we have found out that some adults know biology and that all (normal) adults can learn it. From this we infer that the baby also can learn biology. We also know that puppies and dolls cannot. There is therefore a real difference between them and the baby: the baby has a potency to know biology; the others do not have this potency. Now, such a potency is something real, but it is not something which can be discovered in itself *as potency*. (The potency we have been studying here is an operative potency, a potency to perform an operation or action. Some operative potencies can sometimes be without their acts, but we cannot apply this to other types of potency.)

Another type of potency is commonly called "passive potency." A passive potency is one which merely receives an act or perfection. For example, a piece of wood or wax is in potency to receive another shape than the one it has now. But its potency to receive a shape (which potency is the substance) is almost purely passive —that is, it depends almost entirely on something else outside it. A thing at rest is in potency to local motion, and this potency depends entirely on something outside itself to be actuated. A piece of steak is in potency to become part of a living thing, and in this case the potency is the primary matter. This steak can become living, not by itself but by the activity of a dog or a man, for example. Primary matter, in itself, is a pure potency; that is, of

---

[4] "Act," when used about the things of our immediate experience, is an intelligibility, not a being or even a principle of being. There is no being of our experience which is purely act; and each of the actuating principles of being is some *kind of act:* form, esse, accident, operation. See also below, sec. 88.

itself it has no act and cannot positively contribute to the acquiring of an act. Passive potencies other than primary matter and the capacity for local motion are passive only inasmuch as a subject is capable of receiving a perfection, or determination. Thus, the sense powers, the human intellect, and the will are primarily passive.[5] But they are not *purely* passive; they are also principles of operation. So too, essence is a potency for the act of existing. We never *find* essences in potency—this would be a contradiction—but always as actuated. And yet the facts of change, limitation, and multiplicity show that essence of itself *can* be and that the act of existing is precisely that by which an individual essence *is* in the real order.

49. Theorems of act and potency. I: Act and potency are distinct in their order

Thus it is clear that act and potency are first learned together, in relation to each other. As we find them in immediate experience, neither act nor potency are absolute designations, but correlative intelligibilities: act is the act of a potency, potency is the potency to some act. When we attempt to state the relations between act and potency accurately and inclusively, we state them in exact propositions or formulas which may be called "theorems." These theorems are not obviously self-evident upon casual inspection; neither are they deductively proved; rather, they are the products of an analysis of experiential evidence in the light of being as being.

The act and potency we have been talking about so far are real act and potency, and we have already seen—in the case of substance and accident, matter and form, essence and esse—that these principles are really distinct. By a real distinction, we mean a real absence of identity, independent of any one's consideration of them. Act and potency can also be found in the logical order: the subject of a proposition is potential to the predicate, the genus to the difference. But these are considerations of the mind and, consequently, are distinct with a distinction of reason.[6]

[5] It is important to note that "passivity" should be considered not merely in relation to form or esse or efficient cause but also—and this is a fundamental point often overlooked—in relation to telic cause (purpose, goal).

[6] On distinctions, see above, sec. 33.

We might wonder: granted that in fact, in the cases we have seen, act and potency are distinct in the order in which they are respectively act and potency, must they be distinct? What are act and potency? They are principles which stand in correlative opposition to each other. As intelligibilities of being, they must always have all the characteristics which belong to their own nature. Now, when we understand a *relation*, we understand that it consists in the way in which one (thing) *is* to another (thing), and this necessarily implies that the one is distinct from the other. It would be a contradiction to suppose that there is a relative opposition and that in the same order in which the opposition is found there is at the same time a lack of distinction. Hence, act and potency *must* be distinct in the order in which they are act and potency.

50. What is the potency for activity?

When, in the preceding chapter, we analyzed the various changes of beings, we found in the first three cases a paired set of correlates: substance and accident, matter and form, essence and the act of existing. We had originally included activity as one of the accidents, and thus it follows that in some way substance in changing beings is correlative to activity.[7] Yet, a further consideration of activity showed us that it stands in a special relation to being—action *follows* being, and is the perfection of being to which being is ordered. It seems therefore to be a special kind of act. Can we therefore think of substance and activity as standing in the correlative opposition of potency and act?

On the one hand, substance does seem to be able to have this relation. *Substance*, after all, is the same as *nature*, for nature is just the substance considered as the ultimate intrinsic source of activity. Substance, from one point of view, as essence, is the proper and correlative potency for the act of existing. The same substance, from another point of view, as subsisting subject, is the potency for the various accidents which are its formal modifiers. Why could not substance, from still a third point of view, be the potency for activity?

On the other hand, there are the special characteristics of activ-

[7] See above, sec. 44.

ity. We have already discovered and discussed several points about activity. First, the operation or activity of any limited thing is not and cannot be identical with the act of existing. For (*a*) transient action affects something distinct from the agent, whereas the esse of a thing is its own, and (*b*) immanent actions are interrupted, whereas the esse of the thing continues throughout interruptions and variations.[8] Second, other accidents are modifications or determinations of substance; they confer an added or secondary perfection to the essence-side of being rather than to the existence-principle. Third, activity is by no means the same as substance and certainly is not the substantial form of a being. Fourth, activity is on the side of existence; it presupposes existence. Yet, activity is not the act of the act of existing, for the act of existing cannot be considered as in any way at all a potency, so that the act of existing could be the potential principle which receives activity. *To be* is strictly an ultimate actuality. So, activity is somehow existential without being a further actuation of esse. Fifth, activity in some cases corresponds to inclination; we know that in some of our actions these actions are the realizations of tendencies. When we look at the natural activities, properly so called, of other things, we find that they are present if they are not impeded.[9] We find also that it requires a positive action to impede such activities, and therefore we conclude that there are similar tendencies in other cases and other beings.[10]

There is still another point of view to be taken on activity and

---

[8] This argument is sufficient for all the beings of our immediate experience. If we wish a complete argument which would include even the angels, who are not subject to such variations, we can take the argument of St. Thomas, *Summa Theologiae*, Pt. I, q. 54, art. 3, which is based on the intrinsic and necessary correlation of act to potency. Since activity is a distinct kind of act, its proper potency must be a distinct one, proportioned to the act, and this potency is precisely the accidental operative potency, or power.

[9] Recall that many "activities" of things, especially nonliving things, are not the *natural* activities of those things, but passions which happen to them from other causes. Thus, the movement of the rocket as it rises is not an action *of* the rocket, but rather a passion. In ordinary language we use these terms loosely, but here we must carefully distinguish between the action *of* a thing, and a passion, which is the action of something else *in* that thing.

[10] Tendency will be considered at greater length below, secs. 60 and 69.

the passivity that corresponds to it. The other principles which we have considered earlier are all *intrinsic* principles: they make a being in itself. Some of these principles indeed give grounds for various similarities and comparisons,[11] but just by themselves the relations that follow are purely formal and static. Only through activity and passivity does our world become, not only dynamic, but positively and dynamically interrelated. These dynamic inter-relations are constituted by or are the results of activity. Activity, therefore, in creatures, relates a being to other beings outside itself.[12] From this point of view, also, as outgoing and directed to other beings, activity is a different kind of act from all the other acts.

Must it then have a proper and distinct potency that corre-sponds to it? There are three considerations by which we can answer this question. (1) In some cases, the activity is a property of the nature (for example, reasoning in man). This activity is also sometimes not actually present. But: a property cannot be absent from a nature, since the formal connection between essence and property is necessary, as we know from logic; moreover, properties in creatures are really distinct from the essence. There-fore, if a proper activity is sometimes not actually present, it must be potentially present, formally as such a specific characteristic and as distinct from the essence. This formal, accidental property, which is the operation in potency, is the power of performing the proper operation. (2) The activities of any being are multiple and varied. It is very difficult to see how an essence that is actually one can simultaneously and immediately give rise to multiple and varied activities. But powers as sources of kinds of activities would be fewer in number and more easily ordered to each other and to the essence. Therefore, it would be easier to understand a being by means of powers as mediating between the unique essence and the multiple activities. (3) Potencies must differ from each other in the same way that acts differ, for potency and act are correlative

---

[11] On relation, see below, sec. 108.
[12] Activity can also be directed to the being which acts; for example, we can know not only things distinct from ourselves, but ourselves also. We are not saying, therefore, that *all* activity is directed to something distinct from the agent. We are saying that only through activity and passivity are beings dynamically interrelated.

and define each other. In every creature, however, as we have seen, activity is a distinctive kind of act, different both from the esse of the being and from its form. But, essence (and the formal principles associated with it) are potencies to esse, and conversely, esse is the act of the essence (substance primarily, formal accidents secondarily). Hence, there must be a distinctive and proper potency for activity, and since this potency must be distinct from the substance, it can only be one of the accidents. Therefore, the proper potential principle of activity is a qualitative accident inhering in the substance; this proper potency we will call "power."

51. Theorem II: Act and potency are not strictly beings but principles of being

If act and potency were each a being, they could not be found combined within a single being (1 being + 1 being = 2 beings). In every order, act is that *by which* a being is or is some kind of thing or exists according to some modification; and for its part potency is that *by which* a thing can be or can be some kind of a thing or can exist according to some modification. But because act and potency are precisely principles of being, we can correctly speak of them as being, by the analogies of composition and proportion.

This analogy, however, works out differently in the different analogues of act and potency. The most proper sense of *being* is that which is, or something having esse. The being, properly speaking, is the whole. And only the entire thing perfectly fulfills the intelligibility of "that which is." But, after the whole, and in a derived and less perfect sense, the various principles of a being can be called beings, to the extent and according to the way in which they pertain to being and share in the esse of the whole. Substance and accident are the constitutive principles by which an essence is this essence. Substance, as we saw, is that principle of essence by which an essence has being *in itself*. Within essence, therefore, substance is the more proper subject of the act of existing. Accident is, on the other hand, *by* being *in another* (that is, in substance) as in a subject. According to its nature, therefore, accident is called being inasmuch as it actually inheres in the substance which is in itself. Yet, accident is as act to substance, which is as potency. The substances of the things of our experience could not exist as stripped of their accidents, since in that condition they would be indeterminate within one whole order of essence and yet have their ultimate act, which is esse. Accident, on the contrary, is act in the order of essence, but its relation to esse is naturally indirect, that is, through substance.[13] Matter and form are not directly beings but rather principles of substance, which is being by proportion. By being the principles of substance, form and matter can be called beings by an indirect proportion—form, more properly, inasmuch as it is the actualizing principle of substance; matter, less properly, or more remotely, inasmuch as it is capable of being actualized by form and so made suitable to receive an act of existing. Esse, however, although it is most truly act among all the principles of being and is precisely that by which a being *is*, nevertheless, in the beings of our experience, is precisely distinguished from essence and so is *not a subject* of existing in those beings. Hence, in all such composite beings the act of existing cannot be called a being even by proportion. The act of existing—as a principle of being—is not that which shares in, or is proportioned to, an act, but is precisely the act which is shared, to which there is a proportion.

52. Theorem III: Act, in the order in which it is act, is unlimited in itself and limited by the potency in which it is received

All the beings of our immediate experience are limited, and the acts they have are likewise limited. Act, as we find it, is a principle of being. Acts are found as perfections of some being. They are all limited acts, correlates of some potency. Indeed, all acts of limited beings are necessarily limited. This holds true, whether the act in question is esse, substantial form, accidental form, or activity. Thus, the act of understanding as it really occurs is necessarily limited, as the act of this or that power, of this or that person. The knowledge of biology for instance, as it is to be found in any existing biologist, is limited by his particular capacity. The act of playing a violin by even the most skilled of

---

[13] For the consequences of this special nature of accident, see below, sec. 105.

violinists is in fact limited and determinate. The accident of whiteness, as it is found in any white thing, is a particular grade of whiteness. The circularity of any round thing is just the kind of roundness that a material subject can have.

But none of these acts is a limitation of itself—not the act of understanding, not the act of playing the violin, not the substantial form of man, not the act of seeing. A limited act is this limited act precisely and only because it is received in the potency or proceeds from the potency. Any accident inhering in a substance is limited by the nature of the substance; thus, "roundness," as it really exists, is limited by the nature of the substance which is round. In the order of matter and form, we can also see the limitation of act by potency. For example, a man is a man by his substantial form, which is his soul; but human nature is never found in its complete fullness in any existing man because the soul, in being the act of a particular body, can actuate the potency only as it is in that particular body. Similarly, in the order of knowledge, the relationship between the absolute nature and the individual is a relationship of limitation. What is meant by "man" taken in itself is verified in "Peter" according to the limitations of Petreity. In the judgment, "Peter is a man," "man" is not found according to its full perfection as absolute nature but is limited and particularized by its reference to Peter.

In the orders of accident and substance, we have been speaking of the "limitation" of act by potency. To understand this more clearly, we must recall that some accidents are acts in one order and potencies in another. This situation is especially verified in the case of the powers which as accidental qualities are acts of substances, but as powers are potencies to activity or the undergoing of activity. Take, for example, the human power to see. The power of sight is a qualitative act and, as such, is limited by the potency which receives it: the substance of the person who possesses such a power. On the other hand, the power of sight is an operative potency which limits the act of seeing. When therefore we say, "Accidents are limited by the substances in which they are received," we must understand "accidents inasmuch as they are acts," because accidents, in the order in which they are potency (namely, in the order of operation), are themselves principles of limitation. There is a sense in which we can say that a potency is "unlimited"; for example, my potency to see is unlimited, in the sense that I *can* see all visible things, but my act of seeing is limited at any particular time, in the sense that I actually *see*, not all visible things but only some few. Here, the unlimitedness of potency is precisely an imperfection, for my being able to see is not the act of seeing at all. The unlimitedness of my ability to see is at the opposite pole from act, for the ability to see is no vision at all. This kind of unlimitedness we will call "indetermination." When, on the other hand, we speak of an act being unlimited as act, we mean an unlimitedness in the sense of completeness of perfection. For example, as an act of vision, seeing this white paper is entirely determinate and is completely perfect as act of vision, but *my* act of seeing is in fact limited by the capacity or ability of my eye.

DIFFICULTIES

There are several points which tend to interfere with the perfect understanding of the relationship between act and potency. One of them is that essences seem to be limited to what they are by being themselves and not by any potency. For example, a horse by being a horse is not a cow, and so horseness by being horseness is not cowness. It would thus seem that essence, which is an act, is limited by itself. But this is a confusion. Horseness is not *limited* by being horseness, for cowness is not a limitation of horseness at all in any sense. If cowness were unreal, impossible, and even unthinkable, horseness would not be the more perfect for that. If we stay strictly in the order of essence, then essence is precisely unlimited as essence; one essence is not limited by another or by itself; essence is limited by individuation (horse as horse is complete in itself; it is not lessened by "cow" but is limited in "Man of War"). The source of the confusion is that some philosophers have failed to distinguish between being and essence; they say, "A horse by being a horse is limited, for it is not also a cow." Do they mean, "is limited as a being" or "is limited as a horse"? It is true that a horse, by being a horse, *is* in a limited way; but this is not a limitation of essence by essence but of the act of existing by essence.

A second confusion which sometimes occurs to philosophers is the apparent limitation of a being by its efficient cause. For example, a pail has the potency of holding water, but how full it is seems to depend on how much someone pours into it, and this is a limitation by efficient cause. Two remarks are to be made about this and all similar examples. Firstly, what is limited in the example is not an act but a complete being (the water or whatever else is used as an example). Secondly, the potency in question is not a real potency (for example, an intrinsic potency of the pail), but it can be thought of as a property of the space (which is not a real being). Hence, this kind of example does not illustrate the relationship of potency and act, for it contains neither potency nor act but a number of beings which are composed of potency and act. Another sort of example sometimes used shows merely that an efficient cause is necessary for the production of a limited being. A line, for example, is divisible, but it is actually divided only when an efficient cause makes a division in it. How long a given line is to be depends on the cause which produces the line. but note that we are dealing either with an abstract line (which as abstract is a pure form, and so its precise length is a formal characteristic) or with a line in or on the surface of a real being. In the former case, the line is completely perfect as a line; that is, if it is a five-inch line, it is absolutely and completely perfect as five-inch line, and that it is not a six-inch line is by no means a limitation of a five-inch line. (Line, as genus, of course, is unlimited in the sense of being indeterminate; but in that sense, "five-inch line" doesn't *limit* "line," it determines it formally.) On the other hand, if we are speaking of a line on the surface of an existent being, the perfection of the line is limited by the nature of the surface on which it is, and this kind of limitation the efficient cause can do nothing about. All the examples drawn from quantity and quantified perfection are subject to the same confusion.

We can summarize this analysis thus: a form as form is limited *to* its order, but not limited within its order. A form is self-limited to its order, unlimited within it.

The act of existing transcends all orders. As we have seen, esse is the actuality of all other principles, including forms and essences. But we do not find in our experience an unlimited esse, just as we do not find any other unlimited acts. All the beings of our experience are limited as beings; a being as we find it is always some *kind* of being. So, too, the acts of existing which pertain to limited beings are limited. For example, a tree exists according to the nature of a tree; it *is* by an act of existing proportioned to that nature. A man is, and he *is* in the way in which human nature proportionately has the act of existing. Human existence, the esse of a man, is different from the existence of any and every other kind of being. Is the act of existing limited in and by itself? If we were to say that it is, we would be implicitly contradicting the evidence that the act of existing is that-by-which-a-being exists, simply and absolutely. If the act of existing were limited as act, then things could be only in that one limited way, and other kinds of existents could not be. And so the act of existing, like all other acts, is limited by the potency in which it is received, namely, essence.

53. Theorem IV: Act can be known by itself, potency only through act

This proposition does not mean that in every single case we discover the potency through its act; it does mean that in the first instance of any kind, we can discover potency only through act. If we know something about explosives, we can calculate how strong a particular charge is without setting it off. If we already know something about biology and chemistry, we can sometimes predict what a particular new drug will do. But if we had never heard of radar and knew nothing about electronics, we could not even make an intelligent guess about what a radar set could do if it were turned on. So, too, with living things; to find out whether a grain of wheat is dead or alive we wait to see whether it actually grows or not.

Ultimately, the reason why this is true is that we derive our first knowledge of things from the things themselves. This means that in the first instance things must act upon us before we know them; things do not act inasmuch as they are in potency but in act.[14]

54. Theorem V: Act and potency divide being in general

The things of our experience are neither simply potency nor simply act but composed of potency and act, and that in many ways. In the order of existence, being is divided into potency and act; essence and the act of existing. In this order, potency cannot *be* without its act, for a thing is through its act of existing. Likewise, in this order, a thing either is or is not; there is no other alternative. In the order of essence, that-which-is is divided into substance and accident, and here, too, there is no third alternative; nor can either one of them naturally exist without the other. In the order of substance, material substance is divided into matter and form. Between matter and form there is no third alternative; matter cannot be without any act. In the order of operation, there is potency to act (power) and operation or activity itself. Here, however, some powers can be without their operation. We also find habits, which are acts by comparison with the power of operation itself, but potency in comparison with the operation.

55. Concluding remarks about act and potency

In connection with the order of operation or activity, there are ways of speaking with which we must have some acquaintance. There is, for instance, the term "active power." By an active power, we mean the power which an agent has of influencing something else. It is called "active" by comparison with the thing influenced, but it is called "power" because it is not identical with the action or operation.

Again, there is the term "virtual act," by which we mean that X has the power of producing Y and usually imply that X itself does not have the perfection of Y. For example, in logic it is said that the premises of an argument "virtually" contain the conclusion; this means that the premises bring about the conclusion, but they do not have identically the same perfection.

[14] On the priority of potency to act, and act to potency, see Selected Passages, No. 19.

Finally, there are the expressions "first act" and "second act." For example, if a thing has the nature or essence of man, we say it is human in first act; when it performs the activities proper to man, we say it is human in second act. In general, if we line up the following factors thus:

form	esse	accidents	activity	causality
(*first act*)				(*second act*)

we may lay down this general rule for the use of the terms "first act" and "second act": of any two terms in the above line, the term to the left is first act relatively to the term on the right.[15]

In reflecting on the act-potency correlation and its various analogates, we must be careful to keep in mind our order of approach. First, we found the distinction between substance and accident, matter and form, essence and the act of existing. The arguments for the distinction of substance and accident and of matter and form are very similar and are very closely connected; nevertheless, they are, strictly speaking, independent arguments. The distinction between essence and the act of existing is found without any direct logical dependence upon the previous two arguments. It is only after these sets of principles are each distinctly known that we can see their similarity and formulate this similarity as "the act-potency correlation."

There are two consequences of this approach to act and potency. The first is that we cannot simply *deduce* the existence or distinction of these principles from any of the theorems of act and potency. Nevertheless, we can learn a great deal about each set of principles from our reflections on them as analogously act and potency. One clear case is the discovery of power as an accidental principle of operation in limited beings, which we cannot clearly

---

[15] That which is pure potency is primary matter. "Form" is very often defined as "the first act of matter," for matter cannot receive any other act until it is informed; once informed, it can be, be modified, act, and cause. Of course, this sequence of acts is not a sequence in time. Moreover, we need not take the next term in the series for our comparison of first and second. Thus, when form is called "first act," authors most often are thinking of accident or activity as "second." The series as it is presented above is not something which should be memorized; it is given as a key to help us read St. Thomas and other authors who use the expressions "first act" and "second act."

understand except by reflecting upon activity as an act and reasoning to its corresponding potency. Again, although each set of
constitutive principles has its own unique, independent characteristics, the discovery of the analogical unity of these principles
as act and potency helps us to see the unity, the internal consistency, and the harmony of being.

Secondly, act and potency are analogous conceptions. The pairs
of correlatives—matter and form, substance and accident, essence and esse, the power and activity—are analogous to each
other with the analogy of proper proportionality. But, esse, activity, accident, and substantial form are analogously act. Esse is
the one principle which is act without qualification, for it is the
actuality of any and all principles and the actuality of being. The
other acts are acts by proportion,[16] inasmuch as they are similar
to, and yet not the same kind of act as, esse. Similarly, but in
inverse order, primary matter is pure potency without qualification. All other potencies are potencies by the analogy of proportion, inasmuch as, in relation to their acts, they are determinable
and actuable in a way similar to the potency which is primary
matter.

In every one of the analogates of potency and act, we find a
mutual correlation. Act, as we find it, is always the act of a potency, and potency is that which receives, possesses, and is actuated by act. But potency is always for the sake of act; potency is
ordered to act. We can by no means say that every act is ordered
to its potency. Hence, act and potency are not equal principles.
Potency is an absence of act, yet at the same time it is suited to

[16] The analogy of proportion here is somewhat different from the other
analogies of proportion we have found to hold between the intrinsic constitutive principles of being, essence, and substance. The previously found
instances could be called "intrinsic," since the analogues are directly related
to each other and are denominated from the whole which they intrinsically
constitute. In the analogy of proportion by which esse, activity, and form
are all called "act," we find an extrinsic similarity; none of the principles
are principles of one whole inasmuch as they are acts. Yet there is a
proportion and a dependence of all other acts upon esse, so that esse is the
primary analogue of act. Hence, we would call this an *extrinsic* analogy
of proportion. However, in the order of discovery and knowledge, activity
is found first, and all other acts are discovered through activity; see Selected
Passages, No. 18. On the relation of this analogy and the other analogies
previously discovered, see below, sec. 124.

the act which is its perfection and complement. Perhaps the interlocking of act and potency can be symbolized in the following diagram:

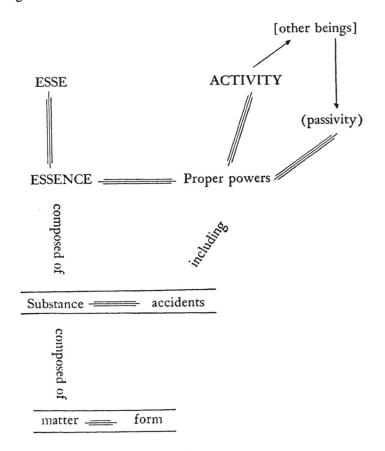

In all these cases, the order of potency to act can be expressed in several ways. "Order" means specification, intelligibility—potency is known and defined by its act; "order" means suitability or conformability—potency and act "fit" each other, though with obvious differences in the various cases.

In the case of power and activity, a very important, special kind of order is to be found. A striking instance of this can be seen in beings which have knowledge. We find that men, for example, can be in three different states with regard to some activity. (1) They can be simply not acting in this particular way. (2) They can be actually engaged in that activity. (3) They can be wanting to act but not doing so for one reason or another. This situation shows us the factor of desire or tendency. Animals likewise have likes, desires, and so on. Plants are not only *able* to grow but tend to; we truly say, for example, that their roots "push" their way—who has not seen a cement sidewalk broken by a tree root seeking water? We even personify nonliving things and say that they "want" this and that, indicating that we discover in them active tendencies. Every power of operation is thus a tendency to that operation.[17] This is so much the case that in nonfree agents that do not undergo structural changes, if the power is present and not externally impeded, the activity is also necessarily there. The very notion of "violence," with its corresponding notions of "active resistance," "reluctance," and so on, testifies to the reality of tendency in things. The tendencies of things flow from the proper nature (substance) and are determined in various ways, depending on the kind of nature and the kind of power. We will have to consider power as active tendency again in the two following chapters.

56. Exercise

Take the three major analogues of act and potency (matter and form, substance and accident, essence and esse), and apply to them the five theorems of the act-potency correlation, pointing out both likenesses and differences between the theorems as stated generally and the particular analogate in question.

57. Readings

St. Thomas Aquinas, *Contra Gentiles*, Bk. I, chap. 22 (the identity of essence and esse in God); Bk. II, chap. 54 (compendious summary

---

[17] In the philosophy of human nature, we find that over and above the tendencies identified with powers of operation (called "natural tendencies" or "natural appetites"), beings with knowledge also have *conscious* tendencies which are distinct powers (sometimes called "animal appetites").

of act and potency in relation to the various analogues); *Summa Theologiae*, Pt. I, q. 84, art. 2 (limitation of form by matter); q. 87, art. 3 (act is known before potency); *Compendium of Theology*, chap. 18, par. 1 (limitation of act by potency); *On Spiritual Creatures*, art. 1 (on the nature of pure forms); *Commentary on the Metaphysics of Aristotle*, Bk. IX, lessons 1, 4, 5, 7, 8, Nos. 1768–1785, 1815–1831, 1844–1866, pp. 654–658, 671–677, 683–689 (on act and potency).

Bernard J. Lonergan, S.J., "The Concept of *Verbum* in the Writings of St. Thomas Aquinas," Part III, "Procession and Related Notions," *Theological Studies*, VIII (1947), pp. 408–413, a striking expression of the distinctive nature of acting, esp. p. 412.

Jacques Maritain, *Introduction to Philosophy*, trans. E. I. Watkin (New York, Sheed and Ward, 1933), pp. 239–256.

A. D. Sertillanges, O.P., *Foundations of Thomistic Philosophy* (St. Louis, B. Herder, 1931), pp. 25–44.

William A. Van Roo, S.J., "Act and Potency," *The Modern Schoolman*, XVIII (1940), 1–5.

John Wild, "Tendency: The Ontological Ground of Ethics," *Journal of Philosophy*, XLIX (1952), 468–472; an excellent presentation of tendency.

Selected Passages from St. Thomas Aquinas

18. Origin and Meaning of the Term "Act"

He shows what it is to be in act, and he says, that this word *act*—which is used to signify the entelechy and perfection (that is, the form), and other things of a like nature, as any operations whatsoever —is derived mainly from motion, as far as the origin of the term is concerned. Since names are the signs of intellectual conceptions, we first impose names on those things which we first understand, even though they may be later according to the order of nature. But among all the acts, motion is the best known and evident, for it is sensibly experienced by us. And so it first of all was given the name of act, and from motion, the term was applied to other things.

Hence, motion is not applied to things which do not exist, although other predicates are applied to non-existents; for we say that non-beings are intelligible, or objects of opinion, or even desirable, but we do not say that they are moved. Since "to be moved" means "to be in act," it would follow that actual non-beings would actually be, and this is evidently false.

> *Commentary on Aristotle's*
> Metaphysics, Bk. IX, lect. 3
> (ed. Cathala, Nos. 1805–
> 1806).

Not only that pertains to perfection in which all creatures communi-cate, namely, esse itself, but also all those [things] by which creatures are distinguished from each other, as to live, to understand, and so forth. . . . For the proper nature of every thing consists in this that it shares in the divine perfection in some way.

> Summa Theologiae,
> Pt. I, q. 14, art. 6.

19. Priority of Act over Potency

Act is naturally prior to potency. And, simply speaking, it is prior in time, for potency is not moved to act except by a being in act, although in one and the same subject which is at one time in potency, at another in act, potency temporally precedes act. Hence, it is clear that form is prior rather than matter, and is also being more than mat-ter is, because "that by reason of which something is such, is itself more such." But matter does not become a being in act except by form. Hence, it is necessary that form is being more than matter is.

> Commentary on Aristotle's
> Metaphysics, Bk. VII, lect. 2
> (ed. Cathala, No. 1278).

First, act is prior to potency in intelligibility. . . . That by which another is necessarily defined, is prior to it in intelligbility, as "ani-mal" is prior to "man," and "subject" to "accident." But potency can-not be defined except by act. For the first intelligibility of the possible consists in this, that it is suitable for it to act or to be in act, as "a builder" is "he who can build," and "a speculator" "one who can specu-late," and "the visible" is "that which can be seen," and so on. Therefore it is necessary that the intelligibility of act precede the in-telligibility of potency, and the knowledge of act the knowledge of potency. Hence, Aristotle earlier manifested potency, defining it by act; but act he could not define by anything else, but only manifested it inductively.

[Secondly] he shows how act is prior to potency in time, and how not prior. . . . Therefore, he says first that act is prior to potency in time, in this sense that in the same species, the agent, or the being in act, is prior to the being in potency; but one and the same numerical subject is in potency temporally before it is in act. . . .

After the Philosopher has shown that act is prior to potency in in-telligibility, and in some sense in time, he shows that it is prior in "sub-stance" . . . that is, in perfection. . . . If perfection and end did not consist in act, there would not seem to be any difference between a wise man . . . and a fool.

> Commentary on Aristotle's
> Metaphysics, Bk. IX, lects. 7,
> 8 (ed. Cathala, Nos. 1846–
> 1847, 1856, 1861).

VII

The Extrinsic Principles
of Being: I. The Agent

58. Principles of change

Change has already been considered from the point of view
of the principles within (intrinsic to) the thing which changes.
These principles we have found to be either matter and form or
substance and accident. Are these principles sufficient to bring
about a change? Or is there something outside the thing to produce the change?

In our experience, we not only find things changing but, in
very many instances, we find within direct experience factors
external to the changing thing which accomplish the change. For
example, we experience a match lighting a cigarette, ourselves
pushing an object to make it move, hitting things and being hit
by them, and so forth.

Sometimes we make mistakes in determining which agent is
the source of a particular change; for example, little children may
think that when they turn on the light switch, they are the agent
which brings about the light. The child is an agent, not directly
of the light but of the local motion of the switch. His action
closes a circuit, removes an impediment to the activity of the dy-
namo. Such an agent which removes an impediment for another
agent is called an *active condition*[1] of the effect of the second

[1] The English word "condition" more commonly means a "passive condition," or disposition, which is in the line of material causality. The verb,

agent. At other times, with regard to causes and effects outside ourselves, we may even confuse an occasion with a cause. By an *occasion* we mean a factor that provides an opportunity for an agent to act. In some cases, we may not be able to distinguish which of the factors present before an effect is the cause, and which are the conditions and occasions; sometimes our failure to distinguish arises from negligence or inattention on our part. There are also many situations in which we do not immediately perceive the change as coming from an agent. For example, before the discovery that lightning is an electrical discharge, it was popularly thought that the damage was caused by the thunder (hence the expression "thunderbolt"). (In O. Henry's classic story, "The Ransom of Red Chief," the kidnaped boy asks his captors, "Do the trees moving make the wind blow?")

But even if we sometimes make mistakes in determining the agent or are unable directly to perceive the agent or sometimes confuse an agent with a condition or even an occasion, it remains true that sometimes we do perceive an agent bringing about a change in some other thing. Hence, a child's perception of his causality can be erroneous to some extent, but his error does not invalidate his perception and direct experience of himself causing something.

Our immediate experience of causality, either as children in the first instance or later on, is a direct and concrete knowledge that a cause is working. We do not have a clear and distinct, abstractive concept of cause, for cause and causality are not essences, nor are they found in the order of essences. Causes are concrete beings which we can experience. That is why even on the level of spontaneous knowledge we have a true and certain (judgmental) knowledge of causes. In the present chapter, we are trying to obtain a scientific knowledge of causality.

As far as terms are concerned, when we use the word "agent," we mean "that which brings about a change in some other thing"; an agent is also called an "efficient cause." The thing which is changed by some agent is called a "patient"; that which is brought about in the patient is called an "effect."

"to condition," is used both in the active sense (bring about a disposition or qualification) and in the intransitive sense (be a disposition).

59. Causal factors

In Chapter V we discussed the intrinsic principles of change (substance and accident, matter and form). Inasmuch as these principles not only are necessary for the explanation of change but also join in the coming-to-be of the effect, we can consider these principles to be intrinsic causal factors. Substance and matter, which are both potency to change, are called the "material factors" or "material causes"; accident and substantial form, which are the acts by which the being is what it is and such as it is, are called the "formal factors" or "formal causes." How and in what sense can these intrinsic principles be called *causal factors*? Because each in its own way concurs in the coming-to-be of the effect. The material cause has its influence in the effect by being the subject and determinable factor in the patient, in other words, by its self-communication to the effect as fully constituted. The formal cause has its influence in the effect by being the act by which the effect is actually what it is, in other words, by its self-communication as the determining and specifying factor.[2]

The agent is distinguished from the intrinsic principles, first, because it is extrinsic to the patient, that is, is not a part of the patient precisely as such, and secondly, because the precise way in which it influences the effect is by its activity, by acting.

There is also a fourth causal factor, the goal (telic cause) which influences the effect by determining the agent to act; we will consider this factor in the next chapter.

[2] Since the intrinsic components of a being are causal factors, and since the act of existing (esse) is an intrinsic principle or component, one might wonder whether it should be included among the causal factors. Most strictly speaking, esse is the very actuality by which the thing is a being, and so is not strictly a causal factor, but rather the very "being made" of the effect. However, in a broader sense of "causal factor," we can say that esse is the principle by which a thing is, and so could be called a causal factor of the being's actuality. What sort of causality would it then have? We could legitimately say that it is somewhat like a formal cause (except that it is not a form in any sense of the word); thus, St. Thomas says that esse is "as it were, the most formal principle in the thing." Or we could say that it is a fifth sort of causal factor. (Or, if we consider the exemplar cause [see below, sec. 63] the fifth kind, then esse would be the sixth. But this whole discussion is more a matter of the propriety of words; what is important is that esse is a distinct internal principle or component of being.)

What precisely does a cause do? In general, it influences the actual being of something; it makes something to be in act. A cause influences the act of existing of some thing. This influence is what we directly designate when we speak of "causality."

60. The causality of the agent or efficient cause

Only a being-in-act can be an efficient cause. A potency, as such, can only be a material cause; that is, it is a cause inasmuch as by receiving the action of a cause according to its capacity it influences the coming-to-be of an effect. From the viewpoint of action, a potency is a principle by which beings can be acted on. We have seen that various principles of being can be considered as "acts." Can we identify the activity of causing with any of the other acts of a being? A careful comparison of each of these acts to causing will not only help to answer this question but will greatly increase our understanding of causality. First, a being is in act when it possesses substantial form, and so substantial form is an act (correlated with primary matter). Is substantial form the act by which immediately a being is an agent? This act is not sufficient to make a being a cause. It is true that an efficient cause actually must be of a certain kind or species and must be a being in itself, but (a) substantial form is of itself the act of a matter, and its direction is toward the internal constitution of a being, and (b) a patient must likewise be of a certain kind and be in itself, so that it can receive an influence. Second, the act of existing is certainly an act—in a sense, it is the ultimate act even of substances, accidents, and forms. And we can go so far as to say that the esse of a thing is the root of all its agency—esse is the dynamism of a thing. Is esse in a limited thing the same as its causality? No, for the actuality of dynamism which is esse is first and foremost an actuation of a being's *own* essence. Third, the formal accidents (quality and quantity) are also acts in relation to substance, and these accidents, too, are necessary for an agent, but as such they are not activity or operation itself. Tri-directionality, expanse, shape, structure, and so on, are indeed related to the activity of material things, as we have seen; they condition and even determine it. These accidents, however, are formal causes of activity rather than acting itself.

The acting of a thing is to all the other acts of that thing as seeing is to the eye, growing to the plant cell, running to the race-horse, thinking to the intellect, and so on. "Acting" is the full internal actuation of a thing; it is the activity in its full concrete actuality as in the agent itself. As such, it not only pre-supposes but in a sense includes the being's actual existence. Hence, "acting" is an analogous perfection, not only because there are different kinds of actions but more directly and immediately because it is an act in the order of existence.[3]

Acting is the actuation of an existing agent *and its power* inas-much as that actuation is in the agent. What is the relation be-tween this act and causality? As a help in making this analysis we can take an example of an artifact, provided we remember that an artifact is not one natural agent, but a number of natural agents grouped together. Let us take the example of a flashlight. It must be a certain kind of substance; it must be structured in a certain way; it must not be worn out; and so on. But merely from the possession of all these acts it does not yet have the full actuality of a flashlight. It exists, it has a formal structure, but as *flashlight* it is still in potency. When the switch is closed, a new act occurs. The flashlight is now *shining*. Is it necessarily *illuminating* any-thing? Suppose the light ray is beamed into a vacuum. The light continues to shine, but nothing happens to any other being. Now, suppose an opaque object is moved into the path of the beam. Immediately that object is illuminated; it is actually visible, and this visibility is caused by the light.

Now, let us see how a natural agent compares with this example. Let us take a man who wants to be a builder (we will not con-sider now that his freedom will come into play, since, in order to carry out his free choice the man will have to make use of his ex-ternal powers). In order to do this work he needs certain abilities and perfections. He must know what a house looks like and how to go about building one. He must decide what he wants to do and, finally, he must carry out his decision by appropriate external activity. That activity is complex, but in the last stages it is a

[3] Note how St. Thomas explains the very notion of act itself through activity; the text is quoted above (see Selected Passages, No. 18).

question of something happening to the bricks, mortar, wood, and so on, of the house that is being built.

In these examples, and others like them, we can mentally distinguish a series of steps in efficient causality (this sequence need not be verified in the form of *really distinct* steps). These distinctions will help us to understand what causality is. First of all, the agent must be in first act. A flashlight without a bulb or with worn-out batteries is still lacking part of its structural perfection, and so there is no activity. Secondly, the agent must not only be complete as a being (first act), it must be in full act as an agent. The flashlight must be actually shining, the builder actually building, and so on. Thirdly, the patient must be actually receiving the action—an opaque object being-illuminated, movable and formable objects being-built, and so on. Thus, there are three steps: a being with its tendencies, its acting, and the reception of its influence. The same three steps can be found in other cases of efficient causality. In the production of a marble statue there are (1) the sculptor with his hammer and chisel; (2) the movements of arm, hammer, and chisel; (3) the being-shaped of the marble. Hence, the causality or influence or action of the agent, considered precisely as such, is in the patient (and not in the agent).

In the patient there is a becoming, motion, or change. Considered as received *in* a subject (from an agent) which changes, the change itself is called a *passion*[4] (that is, an undergoing or being-

---

[4] Let us recall again that potency is by its nature ordered to act. But this by no means implies that every potency is a passive potency, for, as we have seen in sec. 55, there are active potencies. Moreover, it is easily possible to fall into univocation in two ways. One is to imagine that all act is form and that all potency is the capability of being informed by the reception of a specifying form (the basic error of historical essentialistic Aristotelianism). The second is to think that the only cause is the efficient cause and that all passivity is toward an efficient cause (medieval nominalism made this mistake). There is the passivity of matter toward form (and this passivity is reception of a determination); there is the passivity of a passive power toward its corresponding agent (and this passivity is the reception of an influence from an agent); there is the passivity of a tendency toward its goal (and this passivity is not a reception at all—either of a form or of an influence). These remarks are merely a warning against univocation; they cannot be explained at this point. They will be explained partly in the

affected; the abstract term is derived from the same root as the term *patient*). Identically the same change, considered as coming to the patient *from* the agent or cause, is the action or causality.

Distinguish efficient causality in the strict sense, as we have been treating it here, from immanent activity. Immanent acting is the kind of acting or operating that we find in living things; living itself, sensing, thinking, and the like. Immanent acting is the perfection of the being which acts, whereas transient activity or causality as such is the perfection of the patient. Immanent acting will be treated in great detail in the philosophy of human nature; it will be considered only incidentally in this course.[5]

Moreover, a cause, in causing, does not *necessarily lose* anything. For example, a teacher does not lose any knowledge when he teaches someone. An engineer, an inventor, a business executive, and a statesman do not lose that which they contribute; although they expend energy, the energy is not the essential part of the causality. It is true that an agent which is a purely material being, in causing a purely material effect, does lose what it gives. But that is because of the *type* of causality involved. If a man gives money, he no longer has it; if he gives intelligent direction, he does not lose any knowledge or intelligence.

From these two considerations, a very important conclusion follows. (*a*) That which is already in full act does not intrinsically change in becoming a cause, for the action and the change are in the patient. (*b*) An agent as agent does not necessarily lose anything in causing. Hence, an agent, as agent, does not undergo change. If an agent, in our experience, does change, it does so because it is material, because it is dependent upon other causes, and so forth.

From the consideration of what is necessary in order that a being actually be a cause, another important conclusion can be drawn. We have seen in Chapters V and VI that power and activity are related to each other as potency and act. Hence, it follows that causality, which is transient action received from an

___

next two chapters and partly in the treatment of the appetites in the philosophy of human nature.

[5] In metaphysics, the distinction between transient and immanent activity is important mainly from the viewpoint of teleology; see below, sec. 70.

agent in a patient, and passion are identical with each other as well as with action. Hence, the passion, which is the effect in the narrowest sense of that term, is related to the operative power of the agent as act to potency. Now, we also saw that potency and act are proportioned to each other—a potency is specified by its act; an act is precisely the act *of* some potency. Hence, between the agent as agent and the patient as patient there is necessarily a proportion or similarity. Every agent causes something like itself.

A DIFFICULTY

An unreflectively materialistic conception of the origin of our universe offers an opposed view: the cause does not contain the perfection of its effect, and so does not cause something like itself. Many people imagine the story after this fashion. In the beginning, they think, there was a large amount of matter with a huge amount of energy; the matter was either one giant molecule or an undifferentiated mass of elemental particles, depending on the particular theory taken. Simple interactions produced gradually increasing differentiation, with a corresponding loss of energy. After enormous periods of time, the originally undifferentiated cause(s) produced matter in differing structures, though these structures were not precontained in the originating condition. In other words, the laws present-day chemicals obey were themselves produced along with these substances. (This "explanation" contains all sorts of ambiguities; matter and its energy are simply accepted as given; "cause" is probably used in the modern sense of "antecedent"; no distinction is made between partial and total causes; what might be meant by the notion that undifferentiated energy evolves into differentiation with specific laws is rhetorically glossed over. In addition; the explanation is materialistic, and therefore already inadequate, as we have already seen; it denies, usually, all telic causality, which we will consider in the next chapter.)

We can use this difficulty to clarify the theorem that every agent causes something like itself. We will therefore state the supposition in formal, abstract terms, so that its opposition to our theorem is sharp: an effect, as such, is simply unlike the agent as agent, that is, neither univocally the same nor even similar in any way. It would then follow that the agent would not be in act in this particular way at all. But then it further would follow that the active power of the agent would not be proportioned to the act of the patient—which is the same as saying that it is not the power of producing this effect.

From this we can also see that in our universe we have (*a*) agents, with active powers, ordered to, and tending toward, (*b*) patients, with corresponding passive capacities to be acted on and modified. Hence, every such agent capable of transient activity is radically (virtually) related to, or ordered to, any and all other beings which have the capacities to receive such activity.

61. Types of agents: univocal and equivocal causes

The kinds of agents we find in our experience depend upon other agents for both their being and their causality. When we want to express the dependence of an agent upon other agents, we call it a *secondary* cause. In contrast, an agent which does not depend upon other agents is called a first cause.[6] One special aspect of the dependence of a secondary cause upon other causes is that it presupposes a pre-existing patient; in our experience, there must be something for a secondary cause to work on before causality can take place. Consequently, the causal influence of a secondary cause upon the act of existing of another being (patient) does not consist in making something to be where nothing was before (in causing a transition from not-being simply to being) but in bringing about a transition from one kind of thing to another. Hence, we say that a secondary cause does not cause being simply but causes some kind of being. There is a further consequence of this: no thing in our experience is totally dependent upon a single agent. For an effect is dependent upon a cause only in so far as the cause is a cause. For example, a builder is the cause of the coming-to-be of a house, and, conversely, the house is dependent upon the builder for its becoming. But when this coming-to-be has reached its term, and the house is (exists)

---

[6] As we shall see later, in Chapter IX, there is only one First Cause, which is God.

as a finished thing, it does not depend upon the builder for its being. The builder therefore is not the cause of the being of the house except indirectly as the cause of its becoming.[7]

A second and rather easy distinction to make is based on the kind of similarity between the cause and effect.[8] Some causes and effects are exactly of the same nature. We can see this very clearly in the ordinary generation of living things: parent and offspring are of the same species. Similarly, the heat in the heater and in the thing heated are exactly the same kind of perfection. Any cause which has strictly the same kind of perfection as the effect is called a "univocal" cause. Sometimes, however, the perfection in the cause is not of the same kind as the perfection it brings about. At times, the cause is only a mediate cause. For examples, we can take the remote general causes of particular effects, such as atmospheric pressure, gravitation, sunlight in relation to growth, and so on. Here, the unlikeness between the (remote) cause and its effect is largely due to the proximate causes which are between the remote cause and the ultimate effect. Such causes, which are not univocal because they are not the immediate causes of their effects, we shall call "equivocal causes."[9] Similarly, when the efficient cause of a thing is actually a collection of partial causes, one of these partial causes, considered separately from the others, could well be an equivocal cause. But generally we are more interested in the efficient cause which is adequate in its own order to account for the effect, whether that cause be a collection of distinct things or a numerically single entity. Some causes, on the other hand, are somewhat unlike their effects because they act through knowledge: the bird is not identical in nature with its nest, the man is not of the same nature as the machine or the art work which he produces. A cause, which is somewhat unlike its effect because it causes through knowledge

[7] As a completed being, the house depends on other causes for its being: the substances out of which it is made, its structure, the earth, and so on.

[8] See Selected Passages, No. 20.

[9] Most authors use the terms, "equivocal," "analogical," and "analogous," as equivalent terms when they speak of causes. St. Thomas uses the various terms indifferently. We have chosen to make a distinction in order to handle the cases more clearly.

and not simply through nature, we shall call an analogous cause. The kind of analogy which is in question between an analogous cause and its effect shall be investigated below.

62. Types of agents: principal and instrumental causes

If I write *abc,* the fact that these are letters is due to me and not the pen. The power of the pen is to make ink marks when applied to paper, but the power to make letters is in me and not in the pen. Thus, we can distinguish two powers in the instrumental cause which are really distinct; the *natural* power which the instrument has of itself (a saw has power to cut, a typewriter to type, and so on), and the *instrumental* power which the instrument has from the principal agent.

There are two powers, but not two actions. In the working-together of principal and instrumental causes, for example, the writing of a letter, there is only one action and only one effect which is due to two causal factors. We can make a distinction of reason between the natural action of the instrument and the instrumental action; or, in the effect, we can make a distinction of reason between what is due to the instrument as a natural being and what is due to the instrument as instrument.

We can consider the relation of principal cause to the instrument from the part of each one of them. The instrument limits and particularizes the action of the principal cause; thus I get different effects with a pen, a pencil, a brush. On the other hand, the instrument as such is not active of itself; it is caused to be a cause, it is "moved" by the principal cause to produce an effect.

N.B. Distinguish between an instrument in the strict sense which is moved to cause by the principal cause and the instrumental use or application of a natural cause. Compare the instrumentality of an engraver in using a tool and in using an acid to engrave a name on a piece of metal. A chemist, in producing synthetics, uses some instruments and also makes instrumental applications of the proper natural effects of chemicals.

There can be wide variation in the principal-instrumental relation. Compare the relationship of a man with a pen to the work produced and that of a man to the electrical calculator he uses.

Many modern machines are extremely elaborate, and the nature of the effect is largely determined by the natural materials and the artificial structure of the machine: for example, the push-button machine which turns out automobile frames.

There is a similarity between the conception, "instrumental cause," and the conception, "secondary cause."[10] In both there is a dependence upon another cause (or causes). The instrument, to the extent that it is merely an instrument, is a cause only inasmuch as it receives and transmits the causality of the principal cause. The only evident example of such a purely passive instrument is in the area of local motion. For example, when a person uses a stick to push a stone, the causality of the stick is purely received; it moves the stone only to the extent that it itself is caused to move the stone. In the relationship of the principal to the instrumental cause we find this distinguishing trait: that the very causing of the instrument is received, not as a nature, not as a permanent possession (that is, by way of an inherent form), but as an essentially transient influence. The secondary cause, on the contrary, although it does depend on other causes so that without them it cannot cause, has a causality all its own and has a proper and positive influence. A secondary cause may need the co-operation of other causes; it may be moved to action by some other cause. But when it is moved to action, its causality is at least partly its own, an active expression of its own nature—although not exclusively so.

63. The exemplar cause

An intelligent agent engaged in the production of something has a more or less perfect knowledge of the thing he intends to make and directs his activity according to that knowledge. The object as known, according to which he directs activity, is called an "exemplar." (A man may use an external model, as when a painter has a bowl of fruit in front of him which he is copying, but the external model is not directly a cause; it has influence only in so far as it is known.) An exemplar is a true cause because it does have an influence upon the being of the effect—not immediately but through the agent.

[10] See Selected Passages, No. 21.

The type of causality of an exemplar is like that of *form;* that is, it specifies the effect. But instead of being the form of the effect directly and of itself, it is the form of the (intelligent) efficient cause. For this reason, the exemplar cause is sometimes called an "extrinsic formal cause."

64. The theorem of causality[11]

So far we have been considering the causality which we directly experience, that is, where we experience both the coming-to-be of the patient and the activity of the agent. In still other words, we understand that some things as a matter of fact come to be in dependence upon an agent. Or again, we understand that some things pass from potency to act under the influence of an agent which is in act.

Now the question arises: Is this necessarily so? In other words, can something come-to-be, pass from potency to act, without the influence of any agent in act? As far as our everyday knowledge is concerned, we know that every case of coming-to-be has an efficient cause somewhere or other—things don't just happen. So, too, the whole of science proceeds on the implicit understanding that events and things have causes which determine them to be and that with sufficient patience, skill, and instruments, these causes can be discovered. But our question is: Is this implicit knowledge correct?

DIGRESSION ON NECESSITY

In general, that is necessary which cannot not-be. What does it mean to say that something cannot not-be? It is relatively easy to understand this in the logical order, in the connections between concepts and between propositions. Examples of necessary con-

[11] Most authors call this the "principle of causality." Most of them then proceed to say that it is "self-evident" from the very analysis of the concepts or that it is deduced from the principle of sufficient reason, and so forth. These implications are historically attached to the term, "the principle of causality," and so this text avoids using it. What we are talking about is a proposition of a very general and inclusive character, whose truth can be established beyond doubt. Such a proposition is called a "principle," "law," or "theorem." On the nature and treatment of causality in its general formulations, see Joseph Owens, C.Ss.R., "The Causal Proposition," *The Modern Schoolman,* XXXII (1955), 159–171, 257–270, 323–339.

nection are: "If there is 'red,' there is 'color' "; "If Socrates is sitting, he is sitting." In the sense of these examples, that is necessary which must be granted if something else has been granted. Most logicians try to show that such relations are based on identity, and with this they are content. We can concede that anything which is called necessary can be expressed in a proposition or a set of propositions.

But we have noted earlier that the principles of knowledge, though by no means identical with being, are nevertheless based on being. So the question arises, Is there any necessity in being itself? We must be quite careful in handling this question, for logical relations based merely on identity are not real relations. Thus, the inclusion of the genus in the species ("red" includes "color") is not a case of the necessity of being, since the distinction between genus and species is a result of the mind's activity.

We can begin to consider this question by still understanding necessity as a connection between terms. Are there connections between things, such that if one thing is, another also is and cannot not-be? We know that there are causes which are not free but act by nature, and often they are adequate to produce their effect. If there is a natural adequate cause and a sufficiently disposed patient, then the effect necessarily follows, that is, the cause makes the effect to be, and its producing of the effect is the necessity itself. When the effect is being caused to be, it is not able not to be. We can truly call such a necessity a necessity of and in being.

What about the corresponding relation of the effect to the cause? We say that if something is being produced, there *must be* an adequate cause to produce it. But this is not properly a necessity in being; it is more accurately a necessity between two propositions: that is, if we grant that something is being produced, we must grant that a cause is producing it.

However, the notion of necessity is broader than that of a necessary connection between two terms. We began our consideration by saying that that is necessary which cannot not-be. We can therefore also legitimately consider necessity as the absence of potency. For example, a material thing has within its nature a real potency to become something else, and thus to cease to be itself; this potency is primary matter. But an angel is a pure form without an intrinsic potency to become something else. Therefore an angel is essentially speaking a necessary being. There is, indeed, a potency in an angel in the order of existence, namely, its essence. Now, essence is a potency to be, but it is not, properly speaking, a potency to nonbeing. Hence, we can even say that an angel is hypothetically necessary even in the order of existence. Why hypothetically? Because we must suppose that an angel is caused, and so on the hypothesis that its cause is operating, then the angel exists necessarily. As far as it is concerned, it cannot not-be; though it depends on its cause (see the next part of this section), it is possible that an existing angel not-exist only if that cause is a free cause. Only a being that is entirely without potency can be called a necessary being without qualification—a being that is entirely act ("pure act") cannot not-be simply.

From this broader and at the same time more profound metaphysical consideration, we can see the basis even for logical necessities. For all logical necessities are based on the principle of contradiction, and that principle is ultimately based on the correlative opposition between act and potency. Only in the difference between act and potency is it finally clear that whatever is, to the extent and in the sense that it *is*, cannot not-be—for esse is the correlative opposite of all potencies and all other perfections, as we have seen.

For convenience's sake, we will list some of the types of necessity, trying to point out the bases on which the various divisions are made. Necessities are:

(1) based on the source of the necessity, intrinsic (for example, acid necessarily reacts with certain metals) or extrinsic (a pencil moves necessarily as long as I, an efficient cause, am moving it).

(2) based on the scope of the necessity, absolute (under all conditions, a triangle must have three sides) or relative (exercise is necessary for a growing boy, but he can live without it).

(3) based on temporal or causal priority or posteriority in relation to the thing which is necessary, antecedent, or de jure (the actions of nonfree agents are antecedently necessary because they flow from the nature which is causally prior to action) or con-

sequent, or de facto (once Socrates is sitting, he sits necessarily [in virtue of the principle of contradiction]).

(4) based on the object of the necessity, logical (if the premises are true and correct, the conclusion must follow) or real (this event must come about if its necessary causes are actual).

(5) based on the objects of real necessity, essential (the essence of man necessarily makes him rational) or existential (God, Whose essence is identical with His act of existing, exists necessarily) or operational (any nonfree agent, like a dog or a chemical, necessarily performs its operations).

(6) based on the kind of causality, formal, telic (the necessity [or utility] of means in relation to goals), and efficient (sometimes called the necessity of coaction or violence).

The opposite of necessity is *contingence*, the possibility of undergoing change, of being and not-being, and so forth. Note that necessity and contingence are not so opposed that a thing is either completely necessary or completely contingent. No thing is so completely contingent that there are no necessities about it—the most contingent of beings and events has at least consequent necessity (now that it is, it cannot not-have-been) and some essential necessities (being what it is, while it is, it cannot not-be). On the other hand, though necessity as necessity is not contingent, there are some particular contingent necessities. For example, the necessity by which a nonfree agent acts is contingent upon its continued existence, the co-operation of other causes, and the like; something which is necessary with consequent necessity is contingent with regard to its antecedents. The essential (formal) necessities (e.g., if a man is to be, he *must* be rational, he *must* possess an intellect and will) of limited beings are existentially contingent (e.g., if man did not exist, there would be no one who must be rational, and man does not necessarily exist).[12] The concrete copresence of both necessity and contingence in the

---

[12] But one may say, "It is eternally true that man must be rational." Of course, but what does the verb "to be" mean in the dependent clause? Pure essences (which are not of real things) are negatively eternal and necessary: that is, if they are thought of, they can only be thought of in a certain way. Essences either are in things or are objects of thought, and this is the only being they have. See below, sec. 87, on the possibles.

same being is a point of great importance for this reason among others, that it shows how we can arrive at a knowledge of something which is necessary from beings which are contingent.

BECOMING, CONTINGENCE, AND LIMITATION IN RELATION TO CAUSALTY

Now, our question is: "Can something come-to-be without any agent?" Note that something which comes-to-be does not have before its becoming the perfection which it later acquires but is only in potency to it. Potency is ordered to act; but it is also and by its very nature distinct from act. It is not-act. To suppose that a being in potency can of itself acquire the act corresponding to that potency[13] is implicity to deny any significant difference between potency and act; it is to suppose that potency is a kind of *hidden* act. But this is not true and not even really intelligible; it is an implicit contradiction. If potency is not the same as act, then any transition from potency to act takes place under the influence of an agent in act. From these considerations we derive our first general statement about causality: Anything which comes-to-be—which passes *from* potency to act—does so under the influence of an agent. This statement of causal dependence is first discovered in immediate experience and is known to be true without exception by an analysis of the beings themselves and their intrinsic constitution. Such a proposition, which depends on no outside evidence except on the intrinsic intelligibility of the being about which it is said, can be called "self-evident," or "per se known."[14]

[13] Living things are said to "move themselves" (that is, from potency to act). This is by no means contrary to the causal dependence of things which change; for the living thing is not entirely in potency—it has its substantial act and its operative powers; moreover, many distinct causes (moisture, food, sunlight, and so forth) are necessary so that the living thing can continue to live and grow. See also, Selected Passages, No. 20, par. 1.

[14] Please note how the term, "self-evident," has been defined. Students sometimes think that "self-evident" means "evident to itself"; sometimes they think that a self-evident proposition is one that is explicitly known and admitted by all men—babies, barbarians, people who have never thought about it, and so on.

Philosophers have historically used the term "self-evident" in other senses; often, they have said that a self-evident proposition is known to be certain

Every thing which comes to be is existentially contingent; that is, of its nature or essence it is such that it can exist or not-exist. But contingent existence is more inclusive than the conception, "a thing which comes to be"; hence, at least as far as our knowledge of a thing is concerned, there may be some things whose temporal origin we know, but others about which we know first that they are contingent, and as yet know nothing about their origin. Hence, we can extend our question about causality to include those things about whose temporal origin we are ignorant. Let us suppose a being about which all we know is (a) that it does exist (for example, a pure spirit, or angel), and (b) that it is a limited being. A limited being is a limited actuality. We have seen that an act is not limited of itself as act but can only be limited by a potency distinct from it by which it is limited. Hence, that which is limited as a being is composed of two really distinct principles in the order of being itself, namely, essence and the act of existing.

We can make some definite statements about the relation between essence and the act of existing in a being in which these principles are really distinct. First of all, since the act of existing is not a quiddity or form, it can never be a *part* of an essence. Secondly, esse cannot be the property of any essence. A property is an accident which inheres in a substance, is necessarily connected with that substance, and is a natural and necessary consequence thereof, as risibility is a natural and necessary consequence of the essence of man. Now, that which is a consequence of an essence is caused by that essence and is posterior to it in nature. For to be a cause, a thing must first exist in itself. An essence which is really distinct from its act of existing exists only by the possession of that act of existing. And the act of existing, inasmuch as it is an act, is prior in nature to its correlative potency. To suppose that esse is the property of an essence really distinct from it therefore involves a contradiction. Such an essence would be both prior and posterior to its own esse and would have to exist before it existed—it would have to exist in order to

---

from an analysis of the concepts (and even of the terms!). There are some propositions which are known from an analysis of their concepts; the causal proposition is not one of them.

be a cause of esse; and this would be before it existed, since it is by its act of existing that a thing is. Therefore, in a limited being, esse cannot be a property of the essence. Esse is contingently had; it is never possessed by such an essence de jure.

Two statements can therefore be made about the esse of a limited thing. First, esse is not the essence or a part of the essence of a limited thing. Second, esse is not a property of the essence of a limited thing.[15] But esse is related to such an essence; this relation is one of non-necessary, or contingent, possession. Esse is possessed as an act and, therefore, as prior to its receptive subject. Yet it is prior in such a way as not to be a thing in itself, nor to have the essence as its property or possession. The essence, although it is posterior to the esse, is necessarily the subject of that act. Hence, the esse, even as prior and as act, cannot be independent. It depends on something other than itself. The "something other" cannot be the essence of the limited thing itself, as we have just seen. Hence, in order that a *limited being* can be, it must depend on a cause. Hence, every limited being is existentially contingent, and every existentially contingent being depends on a cause.

This statement of causal dependence is a very inclusive statement. It includes and goes beyond the first statement of causal dependence, and it is proved true by a reasoning process based on act and potency and the analysis of an essence really distinct from its act of existing. Hence, this proposition may appropriately be called a "theorem."

65. The analogy of causality

In considering the types of efficient causality, we noted that there are both univocal and nonunivocal causes. Univocal causes belong to the same species as their affects, whereas nonunivocal causes do not. Nonunivocal causes are in some way unlike their effects.

But we have also seen that an adequate cause of a thing must be

---

[15] Compare the statement of Bertrand Russell: "There does not even seem any logical necessity why there should be even one individual—why, in fact, there should be any world at all" (*Introduction to Mathematical Philosophy* [London, 1924], p. 203).

in some way like its effect. Since such a cause does not possess the caused perfection univocally, it must posses either a different but equivalent perfection[16] or a perfection which somehow includes the caused perfection though it is greater. In the former case, the analogy will be said to be "extrinsic"; in the latter, "intrinsic." For example, the food which conserves the health of an animal is truly called "healthy." But health, properly speaking, is a quality of a living thing; it can be the intrinsic modification only of a living thing. Therefore, the food—for example, a broiled steak—is not intrinsically healthy; yet it does have a relation to the health of a living man. For an example of intrinsic analogy, consider a bird building a nest. The bird does not have as its own intrinsic perfection the shape and structure which it gives to its effect, and so it must have some other perfection. We know that birds are beings capable of knowledge, and so we can see that the perfection, "having sensitive knowledge of a nest," is intrinsic to the bird. A man, inventing a marvelously complicated machine, and not being such a machine by nature, must possess a similar perfection through which he can bring about the perfection in the patient upon which he acts. This perfection is intellectual knowledge, which includes in some way the perfection of what is known. Hence, we can truly and intrinsically speak of a "powerful idea," a "mighty conception," and so on. Conversely, we can call the effect by the perfection of the cause, and this is usually an extrinsic analogy; for example, we speak of a "clever gadget."

The nonunivocal cause is either greater than or equivalent in perfection to the effect. Sometimes the relation is a definitely known proportion, and so we can correctly speak of an analogy of proportion between the nonunivocal cause and its effect. At

[16] Electrical energy is equivalent to local motion, and an electric motor is precisely a machine for converting one kind of energy into another. Again, photosynthesis in plants turns solar energy into the locked-up energy of chemical combination. For another example—good meat contains such a mixture of chemical compounds that the animal which feeds on it can maintain itself in good health. For still another example: the two parents of a plant hybrid together contain the equivalent of the perfection of the hybrid offspring; polyploidy in plants can be brought about by the normal processes of cell division interfered with by high energy rays; the rays together with the normal processes of the parent cell are equivalent to the peculiar structure of the new cell.

other times, we may find a nonunivocal cause whose nature we do not definitely know, at least so as to be able to state a definite proportion between it and its effect.[17] This causal analogy we will call "the analogy of eminence."

We have seen earlier[18] that there are two kinds of nonunivocal causes: analogous and equivocal. If we now recall that the analogy of causality can be either intrinsic or extrinsic, we can see a correspondence between the kinds of causes and the kinds of causality. An analogous cause acts through knowledge and so need not have a nature univocally the same as its effect; nevertheless the knowledge is intrinsic to the cause and shows a nature more perfect than the nature of the effect. An equivocal cause acts by nature; it is a remote or a partial cause, and so its effect need not be of the same nature, since the nature of the effect may be determined by a proximate cause or by one of the other partial causes (or by the concurrence of the causes, as in chance effects[19]). The equivocal cause truly causes and so can truly be denominated from the effect, but the denominated nature is extrinsic to the cause.

We can distinguish intrinsic analogies of causality from the extrinsic by seeing whether the perfection of the cause is different and equivalent or similar and inclusive and therefore greater and intrinsic. Note that this distinction rests on some kind of knowledge of the cause in itself and its intrinsic perfections. If we merely know that X is the cause of some perfection and is a nonunivocal cause, we are unable to tell whether it is an equivocal or an analogous cause, nor do we know that there is a definite proportion; consequently, we do not know whether the analogy is intrinsic or extrinsic, and the perfection must be predicated as indefinitely greater. This is the analogy of eminence, used indeterminately—a very useful analogy at the beginning of an investigation.

66. Definitions

Active condition is that which removes a hindrance that prevents another agent from acting. (For example, an agent who

---

[17] See Selected Passages, No. 22. On the analogy, see also below, sec. 124.
[18] See above, sec. 61.
[19] On chance, see below, sec. 71.

opens a shutter is a condition of the sun's illumination of the room.)

Passive condition, or disposition, is a state or modification of a patient influencing an activity after the manner of a material cause. (For example, the general run-down condition of a sick person can influence the way in which the action of a medicine is received.)

Occasion is that which provides an opportunity for an agent's action without acting itself. (For example, an anniversary celebration may be the occasion of a man's getting drunk.)

Cause is that which influences the act of existing of some thing.

Agent (or efficient cause) is that which by its activity influences the being of another. (For example, a sculptor)

Patient is that which is affected or being changed by another. (For example, marble)

Effect is that which is brought about by a cause. (For example, the statue)

Acting is the full intrinsic actuality of an operative power. (It is therefore a concrete, existential, and analogous act.)

Action (in the strict sense) is the change produced in a patient, considered as received from the agent. (For example, the taking-shape of the statue as brought about by the sculptor.)

Transient action is a more explicit term for action in the strict sense.

Passion is the change received from an agent, considered as taking place in the patient. (For example, the taking-shape of a statue under the influence of a sculptor, considered as a modification of the statue.)

Causality is the influence of the cause upon the effect.

Formal cause is the intrinsic principle of being which influences the being of the effect by communication of itself to the effect as the determining or specifying act. (For example, the soul of a living thing.)

Material cause is the intrinsic principle of being which influences the being of the effect by communication of itself to the effect as the subject and determinable, limiting factor. (For example, the body of a living thing.)

Efficient cause (or agent) is the extrinsic principle of being which influences the being of the effect by its activity. (This is a more formal definition.)

A *secondary cause* is one which depends upon one or more causes for its being and its activity.

First cause is one which does not depend on other causes for its being or its activity.

Principal cause is a cause which acts by its own power and is a source of causality. (N.B. This does not exclude the possibility that a principal cause may be previously caused by another.)

Instrumental cause or instrument is a cause which acts by the power of the principal cause and only to the extent that it is moved by the principal cause.

An *exemplar* is an object known by an intelligent cause, according to which that intelligent cause directs his activity.

Necessity is that condition or qualification of a being by which it is (or is what it is) and cannot not-be.

Existential necessity is the necessity by which a being which is cannot not-be.

Essential necessity is the necessity by which a being is *what* it is.

Absolute essential necessity is the necessity by which it is simply impossible that a being be otherwise than it is, and is based on the real identity of an essence with itself.

Relative essential necessity (physical or natural necessity) is the necessity by which distinct properties or activities are linked to the essence from which they flow and is based an formal causality.

Contingence is the condition or qualification of a being by which it can be otherwise than it is.

Univocal cause is one which belongs to the same species as its effect. (For example, a heater and the thing heated)

Analogous cause (in the strict sense) is one which does not belong to the same species as its effect but intrinsically possesses a perfection which includes and goes beyond the perfection of its effect. (For example, a man, possessing intellectual knowledge [the greater and more inclusive perfection] causes a structure in a collection of material things [a perfection of a different kind]). (In the wide sense, analogous cause and equivocal cause are used interchangeably.)

Equivocal cause (in the strict sense) is one which does not belong to the same species as its effect but possesses a different and equivalent perfection. (Healthy food, as cause of the health of an animal)

Analogy of eminence in causality is an analogy based on causal dependence of an effect on its nonunivocal cause, involving a true attribution of the perfection of the effect to the cause, in an indeterminately higher, greater, or "eminent" sense. The analogy is intrinsic if the cause is strictly analogous; extrinsic, if the cause is equivocal. (Conversely, the perfection of the cause can be truly attributed to the effect in an imperfect or lesser sense, and this perfection, too, can be either intrinsic or extrinsic.)

67. Proofs (to be developed)

A. Whatever comes to be has a cause.
B. Whatever exists contingently has a cause.
C. No effect can be greater than its total cause.

68. Readings

St. Thomas Aquinas, *Contra Gentiles*, Bk. II, chap. 21 (proportion between cause and effect); Bk. III, chap. 21 (tendency), chap. 69 (that creatures are truly causes of esse); *Summa Theologiae*, Pt. III, q. 19, art. 1, par. 2 (distinction between instrument and instrumental use of a natural cause), q. 62, art. 1, last par. (distinction between principal and instrumental causes); Pt. I, q. 46, art. 1 ad 6 (on the conditions under which a particular cause acts), q. 48, art. 1 ad 4 (on types of causing), q. 54, arts. 1–3 (a very important series of texts on being, substance, esse, acting, and power), q. 104, art. 1 (a difficult but very important text on the difference between the cause of coming-to-be and the cause of being); Pt. I–II, q. 72, art. 3 (the difference of causality of the four kinds of causes); *Commentary on the Metaphysics of Aristotle*, Bk. V, lesson 2, Nos. 736–776, pp. 305–308) (on the kinds of causes).

Aristotle, *Metaphysics*, Bk. IV, chaps. 1–2, 1013a–1014a24 (on principles and causes).

Etienne Gilson, *The Christian Philosophy of St. Thomas Aquinas* (New York, Random House, 1956), pp. 174–186; on causality.

Francis L. Harmon, *Principles of Psychology*, rev. ed. (Milwaukee, Bruce, 1951), pp. 202–204; a brief summary of the work of Michotte on the perception of causality.

Robert O. Johann, S.J., "A Comment on Secondary Causality," *The Modern Schoolman*, XXV (1947), 19–25.

Arthur A. Vogel, "Efficient Causation and the Categories," *The Modern Schoolman*, vol. XXXII (1955), 243–256; that causation is a reality that does not fit into the categories.

John Wild, "A Realistic Defense of Causal Efficacy," *Review of Metaphysics*, II (1949), 1–14.

SELECTED PASSAGES FROM ST. THOMAS AQUINAS

20. Kinds of Agents and Patients

Those artifacts which have such a nature [that is, one to be produced by art], as stones are the matter of a house, cannot be changed by themselves, for it is impossible that they be changed except by another. And this principle is true, not only in artifacts, but in natural things. For in this way the matter of fire cannot be changed to fire except by another. And hence it is that the form of fire is not generated except by another. . . .

Hence, it must be said that only living things are found to move themselves locally, but other things are moved by an exterior principle, either that which generates them, or that which removes a preventing condition, as is said in the eighth book of the *Physics;* so, too, only living things are found to change themselves according to the other kinds of change. This is because they are found to have different parts, one of which can be the agent, and the other the patient, and this is the situation which obtains in everything which moves itself, as is proved in the eighth book of the *Physics.* . . .

It is about such matter having in itself an active principle that the Philosopher is speaking here, and not about inanimate things. This is clear from the fact that he compares the matter of fire to the matter of a house in this regard, that both are moved to the form by an extrinsic agent. Yet it does not follow that the generation of inanimate things is not natural. For it is not necessary for natural change, that the principle of motion in that which is moved be an active and formal principle; sometimes it is passive and material. . . .

He had said above that everything which is generated is generated by something like it in species. But this is not the same in all cases, and so he intends here to show how this is found in different cases. . . . Everything which is generated from something, is generated from it per se, or per accidens. But what is generated from another per accidens, is not generated from it according as it is such as it is, and so it is not necessary that in the generator there is the likeness of that which is generated. Thus, the finding of a treasure has no likeness in him who, digging in order to plant, finds the treasure accidentally. But the per se generator, generates such as it itself is, as a generator. And so it is necessary that in a per se generator the likeness of the generated must be in some way.

But this comes about in three ways. In one way, the form of the generated pre-exists in the generator according to the same way of being, and in similar matter, as fire generates fire, or man generates a man. This is wholly univocal generation.

In another way, the form of the generated pre-exists in the generator, not according to the same way of being, nor in a substance of the same kind. Thus, the form of the house pre-exists in the builder, not according to its material mode of being, but according to an immaterial mode of being, which it has in the mind of the builder, but not in the stones and wood. This generation is partly univocal, as far as the form is concerned, partly equivocal, as far as the mode of being of the form in the subject is concerned.

In the third way, the whole form of the generated does not pre-exist in the generator, but some "part" of it, or some part of a part, as in hot medicine there pre-exists the warmth which is a part of health, or is something leading to a part of health. And this generation is in no way univocal.

> *Commentary on Aristotle's*
> Metaphysics, Bk. VII, lect. 8
> (ed. Cathala, Nos. 1440,
> 1442e, 1442z, 1444–1446).

21. Difference between Principal and Instrumental Causes

For a principal agent acts according to the requirements of its own form, and so the active power in it is some form or quality having complete reality according to its own nature. But an instrument acts inasmuch as it is moved by another. Hence, it has a power proportioned to this motion. But motion is not a complete being, but it is a way to being, as it were something between pure potency and pure act, as is said in the third book of the *Physics*. And so the power of an instrument inasmuch as it is an instrument, according as it acts to produce an effect beyond that which is proportioned to it according to its nature, is not a complete reality having a fixed being in its nature, but an incomplete reality (like the power of affecting sight which is in the air inasmuch as it is an instrument moved by an exterior visible thing).

> *Commentary on the Fourth*
> *Book of the* Sentences, dis. 1,
> q. 1, art. 4, qa. 1.

22. Analogy of Composition Compared to the Analogy of Eminence in Causality

The creator and the creature are reduced to one, with a community, not of univocation, but of analogy. This latter community can be of two kinds. It can consist in this, that several things share in one thing according to priority and posteriority, as potency and act share in being, and, similarly, substance and accident. Or this community can consist in this, that one receives its esse and its essence from the other, and this is the analogy of the creature to the creator. For the creature does not have an act of existing except inasmuch as it has come from the First Being; consequently, it is not called being except inasmuch as it imitates the First Being.

Commentary on the First Book of the Sentences, prologue, q. 1, art. 2, ad 2.

VIII

The Extrinsic Principles
of Being: II. The Goal of Action

69. The goal of action

So far, in our analysis of change and being, we have considered the material, formal, and efficient causes of becoming and being. Are these three causal factors sufficient? Or, at least in some cases, is it still possible and meaningful to ask, "Why?" For example, when we know who did this, what he did, and to whom he did it, are we satisfied that we fully understand the action? When we ask "Why?" do we not want to find out the *reason* or cause, which is, in the context, the purpose or motive of the action? In other words, when we have found material, formal, and efficient causes, we still have not discovered the full intelligibility of action and causality.

An inspection of various kinds of beings shows us that they have various kinds of activity; they are either conscious beings or beings without knowledge. We will consider each kind in turn.

A. ACTIONS WHOSE RESULTS ARE FORESEEN AND DESIRED

In the case of our own activities, we find that we often know, or at least think we know, the results of our transient actions. What is more important, we find ourselves wanting, desiring, choosing these results either for themselves or as a means to something else, and so we go on to perform those actions. For example, a man may want the money he can earn by his work, or he may want the product itself. In the former case, we speak of "the goal of the agent"; in the latter, of "the goal of the activity (or work)"—though the latter is also desired as a goal by the agent. In both cases, the goal is foreseen and desired by the agent.

We also often foresee and want our own vital activities for their own sake. For example, a student may want to know something, and the knowledge itself is the goal which he foresees and desires. Again, a man may travel in order to *see* and *experience* for himself the scenes or the customs of different countries. In these cases, the action itself is a goal which is foreseen and desired.

A goal which is foreseen and desired is called a "purpose." A purpose is a real cause of action, for it influences the coming-to-be of something, either a product or an immanent activity. A purpose is by no means an efficient cause. People sometimes think that an efficient cause pushes an object, and a purpose "attracts" or "pulls" it. Pulling is as much an efficiency as pushing, but we have to use some words to express the causality of a purpose, and these words are applied to purpose by an analogy with efficient causes. So, when we say that "A purpose moves an agent, or directs or influences him," we are understanding this of an influence which is not an efficiency. A purpose, then, causes by directing an agent to make actual that which is preconceived and desired. This direction to a goal we can call "goal orientation"; the goal as causing we can call "telic cause." An intellectually knowing agent is oriented by the knowledge it has of a goal to be made or gained.[1]

In the activities of brute animals, there is also indirect evidence of some foreknowledge and desire of goals. Certainly, we do not have the same evidence that we find in ourselves. But there is some; a hungry dog, for example, goes hunting for food. The dog does not know that it has a *purpose* as such; it only knows that it is hungry, that food will satisfy that hunger, and that food can

[1] A goal that is to be made is, for example, a picture to be painted, a house to be built. A goal that is to be gained is, for example, a house or a field or an automobile to be acquired. In the second case, the goal already exists, but not *as possessed by* the agent, and it is as a goal *to be possessed* that it moves the agent to act.

We use the words "goal" and "purpose" to translate the Latin *finis*, instead of the more common but misleading word "end." We use "telic cause" to translate *causa finalis*, rather than "final cause"; "teleology," rather than "finality"; "goal orientation" or "goal-directedness" rather than "finalization"; and "to orient," rather than "to finalize."

be found by looking for it. When we want to know why a particular dog is hunting, we are satisfied when we know that it is *looking for food*. (In saying this, we are intellectualizing the brute's activity; the brute doesn't think of a goal; it imagines and desires food, and we understand that this foreknowledge of food is as a matter of fact a knowledge of a goal.) The brute's activity of hunting is oriented by its knowledge of the sensible object. This sensible object is not known precisely *as a goal*, but it is known concretely and in the particular as something to be gained or avoided. Hence, we can speak also of the purposive activity of animals. A sensitively knowing agent is oriented by the knowledge it has of a sensible object (which is a goal) to be gained or avoided.

What exactly is the function of a purpose, that is, a consciously held goal? We want to know this, because from an analysis of our own purposive activity we can understand what is meant by the terms "goal," "telic cause." A purpose is obviously not one of the intrinsic causes or principles of our being, like matter and form or essence and the act of existing. First and foremost, a purpose is concerned with activity. How does purpose function in connection with activity? It is clearly not another efficient cause, for a known goal, as such, is not a real being and so has no activity in the strict sense of that word. We can see still more clearly the function of a purpose if we compare it with an exemplar. An exemplar causes by way of specifying some type of activity, but only conditionally; that is, if there is to be activity, it will be of such-and-such kind, as specified by the exemplar. But a purpose, as such, "moves" the agent to act; it is a determinant of *action* simply, and only secondarily of action of this or that *kind*. It functions as the correlative object of tendency (that is, of desiring, wanting and so forth). From this analysis, the conclusion emerges: a goal is that principle which influences the coming-to-be of an effect inasmuch as by being the object of tendency it influences the agent.

B. NATURAL ACTIVITY

There is not much difficulty in establishing the goal orientation of activity which flows from knowledge. But are other activities so oriented? There are many activities which do not flow from knowledge: the activities of nonliving things and of plants, and those actions in men and animals which are below the conscious level (such as digestion, growth, regeneration of tissue, reflex actions, sleep).² All such activities are called "natural activities." Clearly we cannot say that such actions are purposive in the sense that they proceed from the agent's own conscious knowledge. But can we in any sense speak of the goal orientation of these natural activities?

To help us see that this is a good question we can reflect that in some fields of natural activity we distinguish between a normal or natural result and a defective result. This is particularly the case in the generation of living things: plants, animals, and men are sometimes born defective in one way or another. The natural processes of generation tend to normal results; if we did not at least vaguely apprehend this tendency, we would never talk of monsters or of healthy, full-formed births. A somewhat similar indication can be found in some extremely complicated processes of nonliving things, for example, in the formation of crystals. Sometimes there are "defective" crystals which occur when the natural processes do not altogether succeed in reaching their goal.

This vague indication of goal-directedness needs to be carefully explored and analyzed. Suppose we begin with the activities of living things without knowledge (and with similar activities performed by agents which possess knowledge, but not as guides of these activities). For example, a tree's roots push through the ground to find water. A tree growing in wet ground will have a relatively shallow root system, whereas the same variety of tree growing in a dry spot will send its roots much deeper. The sprouting seed pushes through even hard ground to get to sunlight. The tendrils of a vine wind around supports to hold the vine upright. Certain plants turn their flowers or leaves with the apparent mo-

² Note that orientation is properly a characteristic of *action*. In the classic example of the archer and the arrow, the arrow in flight has a direction temporarily imposed on it—by the archer. Strictly, the arrow has no intrinsic orientation for the target, nor even for any local motion. Modern thinkers point out that local motion has no goal of itself—and that is true, for they are considering the thing which moves locally (that is, the thing which *is moved*). But orientation is to be looked for in the *agent*, not in the patient. This caution must be kept in mind throughout. Cf. *Summa Theologiae*, Pt. I, q. 103, art. 1 ad 3.

tion of the sun to get more sunlight. What do these various activities show us? First of all, we see that a distinct result *is reached:* some new being or some new effect is attained. Secondly, we see in living things a tendency, an impulse, a dynamism *toward these* results. Even before the results are reached, there is an orientation of the activity toward them. Vital activity is in fact goal-directed.

The analysis of the activity of nonliving things is more difficult than that of living things, and so our investigation will have to proceed more slowly. In the first place, nonvital activities do reach results. This fact is so obvious as not to need further explanation. Secondly, the results of nonvital activities are consistent results. Of course, there is not an absolute invariability of action and result. But there is a definite *constancy,* within limits, so much so that physicists and chemists can construct mathematical formulas for these activities, and so much so that in the past two generations entire industries have been built on the exact, universal knowledge acquired by scientists. Now, what does the constancy of nonvital activities show us? It shows us that nonliving things are, in a real sense, sources of activity. They are not independent sources, it is true; other surrounding things are necessary and frequently energy must be supplied. Nonliving things, therefore, are real, secondary causes. Furthermore, these nonliving things are intrinsically determined to their activities. If this were not so, they would be determined entirely by circumstances, and constancy would vanish. Therefore, nonliving things have some intrinsic principle of determination to their proper activities. Proximately, this principle is the power by which they act; ultimately, the determination is from the substantial form, by which each one of these things has its own given nature.

The result of this investigation can be summarized briefly: nonliving things, as agents, are intrinsically determined to some definite activities that have constant results. Now, we must ask a further question: "Are nonliving things determined to act, as well as to the kind of action? Or are they, on the contrary, pure instruments which cause only as long as they are being made-to-cause by another cause?" It must be admitted at once that there is much passivity in nonliving things. It was suggested above that local motion is a passion of the thing which moves rather than an action. It should also be admitted that in some cases we do not know very much about the activity of nonliving things. But there seem to be some clear cases of real activity. When energy is released through chemical action—for example, when phosphorus combines with oxygen—the material things themselves seem to be active, not merely to be moved like instruments. At some time in the past, energy was put in; but this merely means that such agents are caused causes, or, in other words, secondary causes. Again, there are activities like those of radium, which are quite clearly cases of activity that is not merely instrumental. By carrying this induction further, enough examples could be found to enable us to conclude that nonliving things are truly agents and of themselves tend to act, even if their agency or efficiency is a very limited one.[3]

If there were no agents, there would be no need for goals of action. For example, from the "point of view" of the lumber, the coming-to-be of a table is in no sense a goal. This is because the lumber is wholly passive in regard to the becoming of the table. But an agent is precisely in some sense or other *active*, and that means having a tendency and an impetus toward something. Since there cannot be an impetus which is not an impetus toward something, every action has a goal. Similarly, material things as such are purely passive in regard to their own local motion. As such, they are indifferent or "free" to move in any direction, and so there is no goal-orientation in local motion if we consider only that which moves. But from the point of view of that which moves it, that is, the agent (whether the agent moves by contact or gravitation), local motion does have a direction and, consequently, is oriented.

[3] Another way of discovering the goal-directedness of nonvital activity is by examining the activity itself. Many complex natural activities take time and occur in a series of distinguishable steps, which have an intrinsic relation to the results which they bring about. Modern chemistry finds it quite practical to determine, from a consideration of the product that is wanted (for example, a plastic of a certain hardness or resilience), the required materials and the various stages and order of production. The order of natural process is more strikingly evident when the activity of one agent is interfered with by that of another, although it can perhaps be found even in simpler activities.

We can now summarize the results of our investigation of the activity of nonliving things. Nonliving things, to the extent that they are agents, are intrinsically determined to some definite activities which have constant results and also intrinsically tend to perform these activities.

C. THE CAUSAL ANALYSIS OF ACTIVITY

In studying activity, we must try to see it as a whole and try to account for all its aspects. It is possible, and legitimate for certain purposes, to consider activity abstractly. But, in the philosophy of being, an abstract consideration is seen to be only a partial one. Just as being is considered concretely and as a whole, so, too, activity must be considered concretely and as a whole.

In Chapter V, we studied the intrinsic principles by which being is constituted and by which change is possible. The intrinsic principles of being are concerned with the being itself. As causal factors, they bring about the being in which they are. They determine, specify, or structure a being in relation to itself. For example, the form is that by which a being is what *it* is substantially, and the form brings with it certain properties (namely, accidents) which perfect that being *itself*. So, too, the act of existing is that by which a being *itself* exists. By understanding these principles, we can understand how change is possible. But, so far, we cannot say *that* change is actually taking place; nor can we exactly decide *what* the effect will be.

Hence, in Chapter VII, we discovered that change demands an extrinsic principle, the agent, by which the passive potencies of beings are actualized. Given that there is an agent with its tendencies (active powers), we can understand (1) that change actually occurs,[4] and (2) what the effect will concretely be;[5] and so we can have a full understanding of the coming-to-be of contingent things. "Given that there is an agent," we can understand activity. But why should any being be an agent? Why should any being be endowed with active and operative powers that are tendencies toward new actuality?

Here, the analysis of human purposive activity shows us a

[4] See above, Chap. VI, sec. 55.
[5] See above, Chap. VII, sec. 60.

fourth causal factor, the goal, on account of which an agent acts. We need to investigate this factor further, both in transient and in immanent activity.

In transient activity, the direction of efficient causality is toward the patient which, as such, is distinct from the agent. Transient activity is an impulse toward a new being which does not yet exist but is to come into being through that activity.[6] The fact that causality is directed toward the esse of another, namely, of the effect, requires a causal factor over and above the principles by which a being is constituted. And since the production of a distinct effect is found in all transient activity, we can truly say that every agent, as principle of transient activity, acts for a goal.

Living things have immanent activities, and immanent activity is, as such, the perfection of the agent which acts immanently. Plants bring themselves to their perfection by the immanent activities of growth and nourishment and the immanent aspect of generative activity. Animals and men perfect themselves by exercising their powers of knowledge and appetition. These activities are either desired for what they bring to the agent (and so are oriented to a further goal), or they are sought and valued for themselves, in other words, are themselves goals (for example, games, which are "for" nothing else, the contemplation of truth, the exercise of sympathy, love, and so forth).

Sometimes, it is true, we speak of "aimless activities"; what we mean is that where we expect a conscious purpose there is none. For example, semiautomatic actions, like scratching one's head or drumming one's fingers, are said to be aimless because they are activities which ordinarily flow from a conscious purpose. But here the purpose is not conscious, or perhaps the goal is not a humanly desirable one—but there is a goal nonetheless. In the explanation of immanent activity, therefore, the intrinsic principles explain what a thing is, and how it is possible for it to acquire further perfections. The thing in its substantial perfection itself is the agent which brings about the accidental perfection of immanent activity; but that the agent should act at

---

[6] Hence, the nature of a being which has only transient activity is profoundly different from one which has properly immanent action; see sec. 70.

all is precisely the function of the goal (telic cause).[7] Consequently, for both immanent and transient activity, the goal is the reason (cause) why the agent acts. In a word, every agent, no matter what its type of activity, acts for a goal.[8]

How is an agent oriented to its goal?[9] An agent which has knowledge (sensory or rational) is oriented by the object known, toward which it tends to by its conscious appetite. An agent which does not have knowledge is oriented by its nature (ultimately by its substantial form, proximately by the active powers which are the properties of that form; by these powers the agent is adapted to its goals). How can a substantial form be a formal cause and, at the same time, a principle of goal-directedness? This is an important question which cannot be answered at this point.[10]

70. Orientation in being

In the very intelligibility of the act-potency correlation we have a manifestation of goal orientation, for a being in potency is a being ordered to an act or perfection. For example, essence is ordered to the act of existing by its very nature, and so is intrinsically oriented. The same is true of the other instances of the act-potency correlation; matter is ordered to form, is "for" form; substance is "for" accidents. And all the beings which we directly know exist for their operations. In other words, not only is it true that all the agents we directly know act for goals, but also, because there are goals,[11] these agents act necessarily (with different kinds of necessity depending on their natures).

But as we have seen before, there are two basic types of operation, immanent and transient activity. Immanent activity, as we

[7] For a clear analysis of the causality of the goal and the mutual influence of the four causes on each other, see Selected Passages, No. 23.

[8] This proposition is often called "the principle of teleology" ("finality").

[9] Previously it has been mentioned that the passivity of a potency is not necessarily always passivity to the reception of an influence from an efficient cause (see sec. 48, n. 2, and sec. 60, n. 3). The fallacy of univocity in the explanation of the passivity of tendencies is as misleading as any other mistaken univocity. This remark concerns chiefly the theory of powers in the philosophy of human nature and the theory of premotion in natural theology.

[10] See below, sec. 83.

[11] Recall that as was explained in n. 1 of this chapter, some goals already exist and need only to be obtained; other goals must be produced.

have also seen, is the perfection of the agent, and so an agent with immanent activity has an internal goal: it acts for its own good, in some sense at least, and so, to that same extent, exists proximately for its own sake. This is least perfectly true of merely vegetative living things, for their highest operation, generation, is ultimately ordered to the production of a distinct living thing. It is more perfectly verified in animals, which have sensitive knowledge; but sensitive knowledge is very limited, as we shall see in the philosophy of human nature. It is most perfectly verified in intellectual beings, whose immediate goal is their own perfection, to be attained by the possession of the good which is the completion of their nature.[12]

On the contrary, beings which have only transient activities cannot be said to be for themselves. Their being is for the sake of their effects; in other words, their goals are wholly external. They share in activity only to the extent that they bring other things to perfection. That is why some philosophers have found only an extrinsic or instrumental teleology in nonliving things; for example, that they serve the goals and purposes of men, animals, and plants. But this is a confusion. Nonliving things have an intrinsic principle of goal-directedness, their nature, but their goals are always external.

71. Chance

The term "chance" is often used loosely to indicate that we do not know the efficient causes or agents of a particular event (coming-to-be). But if someone is ignorant of the causes of an event, or even if the event cannot be foreseen (foreknown), there is no philosophical problem about reality involved. For example, ignorance may keep a person from knowing what a gun is, but when such an ignorant person pulls the trigger and the gun fires, the firing of the bullet is not chance. Again, we may not be able to tell which way the dice will fall, but the *chance* we take is our ignorance, not the absence of causes for the event.

Some philosophers have taken the position that some events

---

[12] As we shall see in moral philosophy, the ultimate goal of man is the possession of the subsistent truth (for knowledge) and goodness (for appetite), which is God.

happen without efficient causes. Of course, they admit that within our immediate experience causes are always to be found and to be expected. But for various reasons (some of which shall be considered in the next chapter[13]), these philosophers maintain that some events remote in time or space occur without efficient causes, and they state this supposed situation by saying that these events happen "by chance." Note that this is no explanation. If, with these philosophers we would say, "Chance is the coming-to-be of some event without an efficient cause," then the statement, "An event has happened by chance," means, "An event has happened by the coming-to-be of that event without an efficient cause." This is the same as saying that something comes to be without a cause. And, as we have seen in the preceding chapter, every being which comes to be has a cause.

However, there is another meaning of the term "chance" which does offer a philosophical problem. We call that chance which happens without design or expectation. For example, a man in spading his garden comes upon a hidden treasure: we say he found it by chance. The miser who hid the treasure had the purpose of concealing or safeguarding it, not the purpose of having it found. The man who was spading his garden had no purpose of finding a treasure. Or another case: a man on his way to the store met a robber at an alley; the meeting of the two men was chance. What happens in such a case? There is a meeting of two lines of causality, each of which is purposive in itself, but the meeting of the two lines is not included in the purpose of either agent. In this sense of chance, all accidents are chance. In this sense also, we can correctly speak of chance even in the world below man. The stone on top of the mountain is pulled by gravity, which is a goal-directed activity, toward the bottom. A plant halfway up is engaged in the goal-directed activity of growing and nourishing itself. But the destruction of the plant by the descending stone is not due either to the causes which pull the stone down or to the activity of the plant; it is a chance result due to the interference of two lines of activity. For another example, we know that when molten iron cools without interference, it takes a crystalline structure which is relatively brittle.

[13] See below, sec. 76.

When it is violently pounded while cooling, it becomes tough and malleable. From the point of view of either the iron itself or the forge, the malleability of the iron is a chance result due to the interference of two unconnected lines of activity. Hence, we can define chance as "the concurrence or interference of several causal chains,[14] such that the concurrence is outside the goal of any of the causes taken singly."

Chance, considered from the viewpoint of the agents immediately involved, is certainly something real. Because this consideration is restricted to the immediate or proximate agents, we will call chance taken in this way "relative chance." But this is not the only way in which we can consider chance, as is clear from the example of the iron and the forge, for what is chance from the viewpoint of either of those causes is intended by the operator of the forge. If, then, we take into account all the causes involved in an event, both proximate and remote (or mediate) secondary[15] causes, we would have a complete consideration of all the causes in the universe, so that, if an event were a chance event with regard to all these causes, we could speak of "absolute chance."

Can there be an event which would be a chance occurrence with regard to absolutely all causes, even a cause outside the entire universe of limited beings—"total chance"? To answer this question we must first distinguish between a positive chance and a merely destructive one. Most chance events are less perfect (less actual, and so on) than the effects which the causes would have produced if they had not been interfered with. With such an event there is really no problem of causality and goal orientation.[16] But what about positive chance results? Let us suppose an effect arising from an interference of distinct causal lines,

[14] Recall that natural goal-directedness or deliberate purpose will be orienting each one of these lines of causality in itself.

[15] On the meaning of the term, "secondary cause," see above, sec. 61.

[16] Imperfection, or lack of act, does not need an efficient cause, since as such it *is* not. Supposing that God exists (which we have not yet considered philosophically): such a destructive result would indeed fall under His foreknowledge and providence and could not happen unless He permitted it; yet He would not be its cause.

which is more perfect than any single one of its proximate causes.[17] When we were considering efficient causality, we saw that an effect may possibly be more perfect, more actual, of a higher degree of being than any one of its proximate causes, but not more so than all of its causes taken together, else it would be really uncaused. The situation with regard to telic causes is not altogether the same. A positive effect may well escape the goal orientation of any of the proximate and particular causes and so be a relatively chance effect. Moreover, granted a real plurality of contingent beings, and granted especially the real internal freedom of some finite agents, a positive chance effect may escape the goal orientation of any and all secondary causes.[18] Is this a sufficient and complete analysis? If we were to say that an event or a being in its coming-to-be has escaped the goal orientation of every cause without any qualification at all, would we not, first, have separated two of the causal factors (agent and telic cause) and, second, have left the determinate nature of the effect without any cause, thus also separating the intrinsic principles of the effect from each other? And does this not violate both the nature of cause and of being as we have found them? This problem brings us to the topic of the next chapter.

72. Definitions

Goal, or telic cause, is that to which an activity is directed. It is that for the sake of which something exists or is done. It is the cause which influences the being of an effect by being the object of an agent's tendency.

---

[17] To the extent that more perfect living things were born of less perfect ones their origin would be ascribed to chance. How a nature can arise in this way will be considered in general below, sec. 83, and more specifically in the philosophy of nature; see G. P. Klubertanz, *Philosophy of Human Nature* (New York, Appleton-Century-Crofts, 1953), pp. 405–407; 422–425; "Chance and Equivocal Causality," *Proceedings of the XIth International Congress of Philosophy,* VI (1953), 203–208. This article also shows how the statistical character of some scientific laws is to be related to both efficiency and teleology.

[18] To suppose the opposite is to admit mechanical predetermination. Such a system of thought would hold that a sufficiently powerful intellect (for example, Laplace's demon), given an adequate knowledge of any moment of world history, could discover all the events which led up to it and predict all subsequent events.

Purpose is a *consciously held* goal.

Goal orientation is the being-directed toward a goal.

Teleology is the being-ordered or directed toward something which is a good or perfection in some sense.

The "principle of teleology" is the universal statement of the goal-directedness of every agent—"Every agent acts for a goal."

Chance is the concurrence or interference of several causal chains, such that the concurrence is outside the goal of any of the causes taken singly.

Relative chance is the concurrence of several causal chains which is outside the orientation of the proximate causes involved.

Absolute chance is the concurrence of several causal chains which is outside the orientation of all secondary causes.

Total chance would be a concurrence of several causal chains which would be totally uncaused.

73. Proof

Action is either immanent or transient.

But: immanent action is itself a perfection of the agent and so a goal; transient action flows either from a conscious purpose or from a nature so structured as to act toward constant and determined results.

Therefore: every agent acts for a goal.

74. Readings

St. Thomas Aquinas, *Contra Gentiles*, Bk. III, chaps. 2 and 3 (every agents acts for a goal which is a good), chap. 16 (every limited being has a goal); *Summa Theologiae*, Pt. I, q. 5, art. 4 (how the causes are related), q. 44, art. 4 (God is the goal of all beings); Pt. I-II. q. 1, arts. 1 and 2 (teleology in human activity), q. 26, art. 1 (love and the good).

Etienne Gilson, *The Spirit of Mediaeval Philosophy*, trans. A. H. C. Downes (New York, Scribner, 1936), pp. 102–107.

A. D. Sertillanges, *Foundations of Thomistic Philosophy*, trans. Godfrey Anstruther (St. Louis, Herder, 1931), pp. 148–158.

George P. Klubertanz, S.J., "St. Thomas's Treatment of the Axiom, 'Omne Agens Agit Propter Finem,'" in *An Etienne Gilson Tribute* (Milwaukee, Marquette Univ. Press, 1960), 101–117.

Leo R. Ward, C.S.C., *God and the World Order* (St. Louis, B. Herder, 1961).

SELECTED PASSAGES FROM ST. THOMAS AQUINAS

23. That the Goal Is a Cause

The fourth kind of cause is the goal (end). This is that for the sake of which something happens, as health is the cause of walking. Because it is less evident that the end is a cause, since it is the last to come to be, therefore also was it omitted from consideration by earlier philosophers, as is noted in the first book. Hence [Aristotle] proves in a special manner that the end is a cause. For the question, "Why?" or "On what account?" is a question about a cause. For when someone asks us, "Why, or for what reason, is someone walking?" we give a suitable answer when we say, "For his health." And in answering this way, we think we are giving the cause. Hence it is clear that the end is a cause. Not only the ultimate end for which the agent acts is a cause with regard to those things which precede it, but all the intermediate steps between the first agent and the ultimate end are called ends with regard to what precedes them. In the same way, the intermediaries are called the agent cause and source of motion with regard to what follows them. . . .

Since the term *cause* has many meanings, it happens that there are many causes of one thing, not accidentally, but properly. . . . For the cause of the statue, in itself and not accidentally, is the sculptor and the brass, but not in the same way. . . .

He says that it also happens that two things are causes with regard to each other—but this is impossible in the same kind of causality. This indeed becomes clear if we consider that causes are of many kinds. For example, the pain from a wound is a cause of health, as efficient cause or the principle of change; but health is a cause of that pain, as end. For according to one and the same kind of causality it is impossible that one thing be both cause and caused. . . .

We ought to understand that, of the four kinds of causes previously mentioned, two of them correspond to each other, and the other two also. For the efficient cause and the end correspond to each other, in that the efficient cause is the principle of change, and the end is its term. Similarly, matter and form correspond to each other, for the form gives esse, but the matter receives it. Therefore, the efficient cause is the cause of the end, and the end is the cause of the efficient cause. The efficient cause is the cause of the end, inasmuch as it makes it to be, because by bringing about change, the efficient cause makes the end exist. But the end is a cause of the efficient cause, not indeed of its being, but with regard to its causality. For the efficient cause is a cause inasmuch as it acts, and it does not act except for the sake of an end. Therefore, the efficient cause has its causality from the end.

Form and matter are causes of being with regard to each other.

Form is the cause of matter, inasmuch as it makes the latter to be in act; but matter is the cause of form, inasmuch as it sustains it. But I say that both of these are causes of being for each other, either simply or in some regard. For the substantial form gives being to matter simply. But the accidental form does so in a qualified manner, inasmuch as it too is a form. Furthermore, the matter does not always sustain the form in being simply, but inasmuch as the form is the form of this matter, having its being in it, as the human body is related to the human soul.

Commentary on Aristotle's Metaphysics, Bk. V, lect. 2 (ed. Cathala, Nos. 771, 773, 774–775).

IX

God, the Cause of Limited Being

75. The problem[1]

In studying the being and action of things around us, we have found certain structures and characteristics that are analogously common to all of them. We have seen that every being of our experience is something that has an act of existing, ·that it is consequently a limited being, and that it is therefore existentially contingent.[2] In studying the action and causality of these beings which are limited, we have seen that every one of them is a secondary cause. In other words, the very action and causality of these beings is dependent in one way or another on other distinct beings, and that in the two dimensions of efficiency and goal-directedness.[3] The question now arises: "Is all reality of this same nature and structure?" "Or, as most men hold, is there a being or beings of quite a different sort, commonly called by them God?"

This question is complicated by a difficulty raised by some recent philosophers. They want to know how anyone could claim to know a reality which was allegedly outside experience. Of course, we can think of many things which we have never

---

[1] It was explained above (sec. 5) that metaphysics and natural theology are not two distinct philosophical disciplines, that a complete metaphysics includes natural theology. On the other hand, not even a preliminary study of limited and particular being is complete without a consideration of its adequate cause. The student should note, however, that much more can be naturally known about God than can be taken up at this point. Even the points taken up in this single chapter could be treated adequately only in a series of books.

[2] Above, secs. 15, 25, 43, 55(3), 64.

[3] Above, secs. 60, 61, 64, 71.

experienced, but it is maintained that all such "things" are either possible material things (like the spaceship not yet built) or simply unreal objects (like the chimera or the objects of mathematics). The question then is: "How do we come to know real things of which we have no immediate experience?"

Furthermore, some people assert that there is evidence to show that there is no God. They allege, and rightly, that almost all who accept the existence of God agree that He is good. How, they ask, can a good God be the source of imperfection, suffering, evil, and sin? Are not evil and disorder evidences that the world did not proceed from an all-good source?

76. Solutions

In general, all who accept the existence of God in any way, are called "theists." Conversely, those who do not, are called "atheists."[4] More accurately, an atheist is one who denies that there is a distinct intelligent cause of the material universe. Usually, an atheist also has some positive doctrine about the ultimate nature of reality. Most atheists are materialists of one sort or another.

Materialism is the doctrine that only mass and motion are ultimately real, or that matter is the only substance. Mechanism, which is now almost entirely obsolete, held that all activity in the universe could be reduced to mass and motion.[5] Modern materialism admits that conscious activities cannot be reduced to local motion but maintains that nevertheless all being is material.

[4] On atheism, see the very illuminating study by Jacques Maritain, "The Meaning of Contemporary Atheism," *The Range of Reason* (New York, Scribner's, 1952), pp. 103-120. For a more extended and literary treatment, see Henri de Lubac, S.J., *The Drama of Atheistic Humanism* (New York, Sheed and Ward, 1949).

[5] The term, "reduce," has a special meaning in the area of knowledge. We say that A can be reduced to B when B is shown to give us the essential intelligibility of A. Thus, by means of the parallelogram of forces, two forces acting at an angle to each other can be shown to be equivalent to a single force, and the direction and speed of the motion deduced. Similarly, complex motions can be reduced to a series of simple motions. In this way, too, materialists would like to be able to show that vital activity is only an enormously complicated series of physicochemical activity, and conscious activity is only a very, very complicated vital activity. Sometimes, such attempted reduction is called "the fallacy of nothing but."

If materialism includes an explanation of human history as determined by evolving material conditions, it is usually called dialectical materialism (or theoretical Marxism). Dogmatic materialism maintains that matter is an adequate and satisfying explanation; at the present time this philosophy is more commonly called "scientific naturalism" or "scientific humanism."[6] Critical or positivistic materialism holds that the search for any ultimate explanation is impossible, meaningless, or futile; the modern form of this doctrine used to be called "logical positivism" or "logical empiricism"; in its contemporary stage of development it is often called "philosophical analysis" or "analytic philosophy"; in an extreme form it is called "general semantics."

Pantheism is the doctrine that the world is God or God is the world. It has taken and takes many forms: nature-pantheism, idealistic pantheism (which holds that sensible things either have no reality at all or only the partial reality of illusion), atheistic idealism (which denies the existence both of matter and of a God distinct from the spirit, mind, or idea), and so on.

Theists we have defined above as all who in any way accept the existence of God. For our purposes, we need to make a distinction among theists, for some of them hold that we can *certainly know* the existence of God, and others do not. Agnosticism is the doctrine that we cannot know or at least cannot know with certitude that there is a being outside the material universe. Agnostics who are theists usually accept God for some noncognitive reason. Sentimentalists maintain that although we cannot know there is a God we can feel his reality. Fideists claim that we cannot know or at least cannot prove the existence of God, but we accept it on faith or tradition. Pragmatists who are theists hold that God's existence is a meaningful postulate and "true" in the sense that it is important in a man's life. Neo-Kantians hold that the postulate of God's existence is not only important but necessary for freedom and moral action; they maintain, how-

---

[6] "Humanism" in this sense is obviously something quite different from the humanism which is the aim of the liberal arts program; the latter is called humanism because it aims to educate the "whole man"; the former, because it denies that there is any reality superior to man.

ever, that it cannot be proved in the sense of a rational demonstration.

77. The question of knowledge

In asking the question, Does God exist? we must clearly understand its import. We are not asking whether we can know God in Himself without relation to the world.[7] Some thinkers have tried to assert that we can have an immediate experience of God by means of a natural mysticism.[8] There is no question but that there can be a mystical experience of God in some way; but we can safely assume that this is not the common experience of men. Moreover, it can be proved that as long as we are in our present condition of knowing, it is impossible to have an immediate knowledge of God as He is in Himself.[9]

Our knowledge of the existence of God is therefore some kind of mediate knowledge of God inasmuch as He has some relation to the universe. At the level of unreflective, spontaneous knowledge[10] most people know with certitude that God exists. We are not going to question this knowledge; in other words, we are not going to doubt God's existence. Our question is, Can there be a demonstrative (scientific) knowledge of the existence of God as the cause of the beings of our experience?

When we ask a question about the cause of the material universe, what kind of cause are we concerned with? We have seen that there are two kinds of causes, univocal and nonunivocal.[11] A univocal cause is one that has the same nature in its effect. Now, the material universe contains things which belong to different species, even to different degrees of being. From this point of view, we could not be asking about a univocal cause of all the

[7] On the kind of knowledge we can have of God and of other spiritual things, see Selected Passages, No. 24.

[8] "Mysticism" means (a) a kind of internal experience of some remarkable working of God in the soul; (b) the theoretical explanation of such experience.

[9] See, for example, St. Thomas Aquinas, *Summa Theologiae*, Pt. 1, q. 12, arts. 2, 3, and 4; also see below, secs. 81 and 82, for a brief statement of the kind of knowledge we do have of God.

[10] See above, sec. 1.

[11] On the distinction between univocal, analogous, and equivocal causes, see above, sec. 61.

things in the world. Furthermore, since a univocal cause is of the same species as its effect, when we find the univocal cause of this individual effect, we have, it is true, found out why this individual effect is, but a new question can arise about its cause, which in turn needs its cause, and so on. A univocal cause always is what we called above a "secondary" cause, that is, it presupposes other causes and a pre-existing patient upon which to act. Hence, a univocal cause is never the total cause of the whole being of the effect.

We could also ask about a nonunivocal cause. However, at the start of our investigation, we do not know whether there is such a cause, much less what kind of nonunivocal cause it is. Therefore, we do not know whether it has a definite relation to its effect; we must begin with a cause which has an "indefinitely greater" relation, and which might be an equivocal or a strictly analogous cause. We will therefore be using the analogy of eminence in causality.[12]

What sort of cause can we come to know? The answer to this question depends upon what the limitations of our knowledge are. If, for example, we knew only beings as material (the primitive conception of being), we could not possibly go beyond a cause which was also a material being. We would be even more limited if we could know only the things which we immediately experience. That is another reason why we must have first arrived at the metaphysical conception of being as being, for without it we could never hope to arrive at a scientific proof of the cause of the material universe.

78. The question of proof

To answer the question, Are there men? we need but point and then show that what we point to verifies or realizes what we mean by *man*. Strictly speaking, this is not a proof; at most it is a pointing out of the evidence which is immediately available. To answer the question, "is there a city called Montreal?" we might have to have recourse to the testimony of some one who had been in contact with immediately available evidence. Strictly speaking, this also is not a demonstration; testimony never makes us

[12] See above, sec. 65.

see the truth of what we believe on testimony. And it should be noted that testimony can never be use precisely to testify to the existence of the testifier (it may testify to his name ["Are you John Smith?"] or his nature, substantial or accidental ["Are you English by descent?"]).

Anyone who asks, "Is there a God?" is asking because he has not had any immediate experience of that being. We do not mean to imply that such experience is possible or not possible; we are concerned only with the fact. As students of metaphysics, we are dealing with being and the causes (principles) of being accord- ing to the proper intelligibility of being and not with what authoritative witnesses or documents may have had to say about it. As far as investigating testimony is concerned, that is not the job of philosophy (but of history or at least of an historical sci- ence). Hence, neither the way of immediate evidence nor that of testimony is available to us. And so we must use some kind of proof.

KINDS OF PROOF

Proofs can be classified in many ways; what concerns us now is the point of departure which is used in a proof. From this point of view proofs are divided into those which proceed from cause to effect and those which proceed from effect to cause. The former we will call "causal proof" (sometimes called a *propter quid* demonstration, for it tells us that a thing is and also why it is); the latter is called a "fact proof" (or *quia* proof, for it tells us only *that* something is).

Strictly speaking, it is impossible to use a causal proof to prove the existence of a First Cause, for precisely what we mean by a "First Cause" is one that itself has no cause. But it may be possible to use something which for us (considering our way of knowing) is in the place of a cause; such a proof can be called "proof from a prior reason" (*a simultaneo*, because it proceeds from something which is really identical with the existence of the First Cause but with regard to our way of knowing is prior). The "proof from a prior reason" can be formulated in several ways. St. Anselm expressed it thus: (1) God exists in the mind— we can think of Him. (2) God is that than which a greater cannot be thought of. (3) To exist both in reality and in the mind is greater than to exist in the mind alone. (4) God exists in reality. Leibniz puts his proof this way: (1) God is a necessary being. (2) If a necessary being is possible, it exists. (3) The necessary being is possible. (4) Therefore He exists. Both of these proofs depend for their validity on the implied premise that God is real. St. Anselm, of course, was working within faith—he already believed that God exists; but independently of faith, all that St. Anselm's proof proves is that unless we think of an existing God we are not thinking of God at all.[13] Leibniz's proof hinges on this: that the necessary being is not merely possible-to-be-thought-of but is really possible. But how anyone is to arrive at such a knowledge prior to his knowledge that there is a God is inexplicable. Since these two formulations of the "proof from a prior reason" are considered by all who try to use such a proof to be the very best ways to put this proof, we can conclude that such a proof is either impossible or presupposes what it claims to prove. Therefore, the only way we can prove the existence of God is by a fact proof.[14]

What precisely does a fact proof do? In general, it proves that something is or is such and such by means of a point of departure which in the course of proof becomes known to be dependent upon what is to be proved. The structure of that proof, still in general, is something like this: "Given X as a fact, we see by inspection and analysis of X that it depends upon Y; therefore Y." The fact proof has two major forms: one in which we proceed from an effect to its univocal cause. The effect-to-cause relationship can be either formal (when we argue from a property to an essence) or efficient (when we argue to a cause of exactly the same kind as its effect). These two proofs can be put into an Aristotelian syllogism, and because the difference here is so very important, an example of each kind of proof will be given.

(Formal): Twinkling stars are close to the earth; this star twinkles; therefore it is close to the earth.

[13] We are not investigating what St. Anselm himself meant by his argument or what his contemporaries understood but rather what our contemporaries would make of it.

[14] On the sources of our knowledge of God, see Selected Passages, No. 27.

(Efficient): A man has died of wounds which were not self-inflicted; such wounds are inflicted only by a killer; therefore there is a killer.

The second type of fact-proof seeks to answer the question, Is there a nonunivocal cause of this existent fact? Actually we find ourselves required to answer a double question, and by one and the same process of reasoning: first, we need to find evidence that a cause is required and at the same time we must see the reason why the cause is nonunivocal.

THE FIRST ASPECT OF THE PROOF:
INITIAL EVIDENCE AND CLARIFICATION

When we began our study of causality, we noted that we first discover causes in the act of causing some given effect, and in such cases we do not argue *to* the existence of a cause, though we may argue about the kind of relation that is present, and so on. As our experience of things increases, we come to know that certain events are effects and that they pertain to particular kinds of causes. So we say, "There were men living in this cave so many thousand years ago," "This man died of uremic poisoning," and so on. Could we in a similar fashion say, "Here is an effect that only God can produce, therefore God exists"? *Prior* to the proof, such an attempted argument is circular, for we suppose that there is an effect proper to God. We must therefore start with some event which we know already to be an effect. In our study of the beings of our experience, we have noted that whenever something begins to be, that beginning is an effect and so a cause is operating.

This fact needs closer attention. In some cases, at least, we observe that there are not only two beings involved—the experienced cause and its effect—but that "the cause" is really a series, one of which causes another to cause. For example, when a man pushes something with a stick, the stick moves the object only inasmuch as it is itself moved. We will call the intermediate cause a "caused-cause" and we will use the hyphen to mean that it is a cause which is caused to cause. We then have the following series: a cause, a caused-cause, an effect. What sort of series is this?

A series or sequence of causes and effects can be simply a

temporal or historical series. An example of such a series is a series
of "fathers and sons" in human generation. Suppose we were to
ask whether a given man had a father and whether this father in
turn had a father. We would find a series within which there is
an order. The intermediate links (a father who was also a son) are
both caused and causes, but they are not caused to be causes by
their being born in such a sequence. Hence, this order is accidental
(contingent),[15] not necessary. Moreover, it is a series of univocal
causes, and so cannot help us in our search.

The series—cause, caused-cause, effect—is a necessary series;
the links must be precisely where they are because of the causal
relation itself. The order of the series is therefore intrinsic to the
series as well as necessary, so we will call it "a per se ordered series
of causes." Can nonunivocal causes then, stand in such a series?
We have seen earlier that the relationship between an effect and
its nonunivocal cause involves both a dependence of the effect on
the cause and an inequality of perfection in effect and cause. In
this relationship there is no reason why nonunivocal causes cannot
stand in a per se ordered series.

We have already noted that the order of a per se series is necessary and intrinsic. We must also note that it is not a time sequence. The influence and dependence are simultaneous and
nonmutual: the order cannot be reversed.

THE SECOND ASPECT OF THE PROOF:
ANALYSIS AND EXCLUSION

There are, then, causal series in the material universe. Some
people think that an argument can be built up on the accidental
(historical) series of causes. They hold that no series can be
infinite. Hence they conclude that the entire world had a be-
gining in time, and that therefore there must be a cause which is

[15] This order is accidental, because "to cause this individual effect," and
"to be caused by this particular agent" belong neither to the constitutive
essence (substantial or accidental) nor to the properties of the things concerned.

On the other hand, the order of instrument to principal cause is essential
or necessary, for the instrument as instrument actually exists as such only
when it is moved by the principal cause.

outside the world, distinct from it, and originally made the entire universe.[16] This argument is not nearly so simple as it looks at first sight, and we will make no use of it.[17]

What about the per se ordered series? In our first look at this series, we were mainly interested in the "middle" link, the caused-cause. Now, we need to look for a moment at the "cause," which we did not examine. In our example, a man was the principal cause. Is he also a caused-cause? We know from experience that men are moved to act by various causes—ideas, feelings, commands, changes in their body or their environment, and so on. True, man is free, but nevertheless all his actions have causes, and these causes account for his beginning an action. The case is similar with animals, except that animals are necessitated by the causes which influence their actions. Plants, too, are caused to cause. Finally, the whole subliving world is constantly in change, constantly receiving causal influence and acting under that influence. Hence, it seems that all the things of our experience are really caused-causes. Where, then, does the "causality get its start"?

Some philosophers have thought that the question is wrongly put. They think that the series of causes would indeed have to get a start if the series were finite, but not if the series is infinite. We need then to consider the question, "Can a series of caused-causes be infinite in such a way that it does not depend on a cause outside the series?" An infinite series does not have a "first"; its members are simply unnumberable. So, these philosophers hold, the causality of every member of the series is derived from a prior cause, but since there is always a prior cause the causality

---

[16] Distinguish between the statement, "An historical series cannot be infinite," and the statement, "Scientific evidence indicates that our universe (in its present form) in fact began its evolution at a specified point in time." Modern cosmogonies almost all demand a temporal origin—billions of years ago—for the present stars and nebulae. But they do not unequivocally prove that this point is an absolute beginning.

[17] St. Thomas wrote a special treatise, *On the Eternity of the World*, in which he concludes that it cannot be proved that an historical (or accidental) series *cannot* be infinite. Of course we know, by an infallible revelation, that the universe in fact began in time, but this is not our question—knowledge by faith is not the point of our present investigation. An argument which is not rationally certain should not be used in philosophy, especially since we do have really sound arguments at our disposal.

is accounted for; the series itself is neither cause nor uncaused, but simply infinite; hence, there need be only caused-causes in existence; as an ultimate consequence, there is no reason to assert the existence of God. To clarify their statement that the series itself does not require the existence of a cause, they appeal to a general rule: A set does not have the qualities of its members. What they mean can be illustrated from an example that is often used: In a set of three brothers, each one is a male and has a brother; the set itself is neither male nor does it have a brother.

Now, this position needs careful consideration. We do not know how many causes are operative in a per se ordered series culminating in a particular event. Even if every being in our sensible universe were involved in the causality of every event, it is by no means clear that the multitude of beings in that universe is infinite. Let us suppose that there literally is an infinite series in the sense in which mathematicians talk about the "infinite." The point to note is that, infinitely many or not, each member of the series is a caused-cause. Our question now is, if they are all caused-causes, is there any causality to be communicated? To see what this means, let us in our turn, make up an example. Suppose there is a set of beings, none of which is good in itself, but each of which is good in relation to another (is a pure means); let us suppose further that these beings stand in a per se series, such that *A* is good by relation to *B*, which is good by relation to *C*, and so on; and finally, let us suppose that there is no being which is good in itself. In this supposition, what happens to the "good" which we started out with? By the conditions of the supposition, there is no good by relation to which other beings could possibly be good. It does not help the case any to say "But the series is infinite!" For the mathematician is dealing with a static relation of order (having a unit prior to itself) which is *intrinsic* to each unit. But the *derived* goodness of the means is neither static nor intrinsic to it; it must by the nature of the case *be* and be *intrinsic* to something before it can be derived.

In the light of this example, we can now examine the question of efficient causality. We find as a fact that there are caused-causes. The supposition that there are only caused-causes— whether there be a finite number of them or an infinite series

—provides no being in reality for the causality to be inherent in, and therefore is tantamount to denying that causality happens. What about the argument that, "Though all the individuals of the world are caused, it does not follow that the world is caused, and so there need be no 'cause of the world'?" From our preceding analysis, we can say: if all the individuals of the world are caused, and if this is a per se ordered series, then there is a cause, not a member of the world, which is a cause of all the individuals of the world. What one further says about the "world" as a logical set makes no difference.

This very extended discussion can now be summarized. We will do it in two stages. In the first, we will stress particularly the causality, since this is the most easily grasped of all the arguments. But causality is closely connected with being, so that by shifting our point of view slightly, we can construct a parallel argument. The advantage of doing this is that it enables us to consider God, not merely as the cause of the causality of things, but explicitly as the cause of their being. This point of view has particular importance in the philosophy of being.

79. Summary of evidence and argumentation (I)

(1) It is given in immediate experience that change is going on (in the general sense that there are transitions from potency to act, as for example, some local motion is beginning, growth is going on, someone is beginning to know), and that this change is brought about by caused-causes.

(2) [a] Something passes from potency to act only through the agency of a being in act.[18]

[b] It is impossible that there be caused-causes in an ordered series and no uncaused-cause as the source of that causality.

[c] Therefore there *is* a First Cause of the actual existential causality of per se ordered causes. This cause is, and is a cause, by the analogy of eminence in causality. Because it is a *First* Cause, it is in no way caused by another and so cannot have any real potency; it is pure act.

(3) Therefore, a First Cause exists, which as First is unique and supreme, and this is the Cause which we call God.

[18] See above, Chap. VII, secs. 60 and 64.

80. Evidence and argumentation (II)

(1) It is given in immediate experience that contingent beings exist (for anything which changes is existentially contingent, such that what-it-is is really distinct from its act of existing).

(2) [a] But that which is existentially contingent depends on a cause for its existence.[19]

[b] It is impossible that there be an infinite series of existentially contingent beings such that each of them depends on another for its act of existing.

N.B. An existentially contingent being *is* because of another which here and now is the cause of its being (as every effect, formally speaking, depends on its cause, here and now, for its being as effect). To say A exists because of B, and so on, implying thereby that none of the existential causes exists of itself, is to say that things both exist and do not exist.

[c] Therefore, there exists an existentially necessary being on which all contingent beings depend precisely for their existing, and in this being essence is necessarily identical with its act of existing. Hence, this being is pure act in the order of existence and so is absolutely unlimited, fully actual of its nature, completely perfect.[20]

(3) Therefore, there exists a First Cause in the order of existence, which is pure act in that order, whose essence is identical with its act of existing, which is therefore properly named "Who *is*" (without any limitation), and this is God.

81. The analogy of participation

The basis for our argument has been the existential dependence of secondary causes and of contingent beings upon an efficient cause. Previously[21] we have seen that nonunivocal causes are similar to their effects according to the analogy of eminence in causality. But this relationship, taken by itself and in the abstract, does not enable us to decide whether the nonunivocal cause is analogous or equivocal—in other words, whether the cause is intrinsically and properly in itself analogous to the effect or

[19] See above, sec. 64.
[20] See above, sec. 51.
[21] See above, sec. 65.

is only truly denominated such (as a healthy climate is not properly "healthy" but is truly denominated healthy because of its influence upon the health of living things).

Let us look at the analogy between God and sensible things, no longer vaguely as an instance of eminence in causality but concretely, in regard to what is truly said of God in our conclusion. We say *that* God *is*. And we mean that He is, in the sense that He is actually exerting a causal influence upon the causality and existence of real things in the proper sense of the term *real*. We have seen above[22] that "is" in the metaphysician's sense means "exercising or having an act of existing." We have seen[23] that the causality of an efficient cause is an expression of the intrinsic dynamism of the act of existing;[24] and that conversely that which does not exist cannot be an agent. Therefore, the "is" which we predicate of God means a real and intrinsic act of existing, and so is predicated according to the intrinsic analogy of eminence in causality.[25]

Furthermore, God is the *First* Cause. Therefore, no other being can be related to Him as cause to effect. Since potency is unintelligible and impossible unless there is an act of which this potency precisely is the potency,[26] there can be no intrinsic or receptive potency in God. He is therefore pure act—not the act which is the act of a potency and is received into the potency as a principle of being but an act which is the subsistent thing itself. And this act is the act of existing. Hence, God is a subsistent act of existing. We have seen above[27] that an act is limited and

[22] Secs. 15 and 17.
[23] Above, sec. 60.
[24] This statement need not imply that an agent acts necessarily. Only when an existing agent is a nonfree agent does it act necessarily; a free agent acts freely. But whether an agent acts freely or necessarily, its activity and its causality both are a kind of "superabundance" of act, a kind of overflowing of the actuality of esse. Less metaphorically, esse is the source within a being of all its other acts.
[25] Because the form of argument we use to arrive at a knowledge of the existence directly does not enable us to decide whether the eminent cause is analogous or equivocal (see above, sec. 65), and because no abstractly common perfection is involved, no direct knowledge of subsistent esse is implied; see St. Thomas, *Summa Theologiae*, Pt. I, q. 3, art. 4, ad 2.
[26] See above, sec. 53; see also below, sec. 87.
[27] Sec. 52.

multiplied only by a potency in which it is received. If an act is subsistent and not received, it is necessarily perfect, unlimited, and unique, and thereby distinguished from all received acts.[28] Hence, God, as a pure act of existing, is the perfection of all existence, infinite and unique and distinct from all the beings which *have* an act of existing. His nature, inasmuch as we can use the term "nature" of God, is to be—simply, without any limitation.

If God, by His nature or essence, is His act of existing, it follows that we can say that His essence is to exist; God is by His very essence. All beings other than God are because they share or participate in a "common" act of existing; they are by participation (namely, by participating in the act of existing). Here then we have a new analogy, which we may well call "the analogy of participation."[29] When we say, "God is," we designate an act of existing which *is a nature;* when we say, "A limited (contingent, caused) thing is," we designate an act of existing

---

[28] On this distinction between God and creatures, see Selected Passages, No. 26, at the end of this chapter.

[29] The relation in *being* between God and any finite thing is the only instance of the analogy of participation in being. In the next chapter, we will see that the analogy of participation in the transcendentals (good, true, and so on) also is found between God and any finite being. See also, Selected Passages, No. 25.

In addition to these basic, essential instances of the analogy of participation, where efficient causality is intrinsically involved in the analogy, it may be helpful to mention that there are other instances of the analogy of participation in which efficient causality is not directly involved. We can correctly speak of the analogy of participation whenever one being is by nature what another is by nonessential (that is, which is not a part of the essence) received act. Thus, human beings are not, in the strict sense of the word, *intelligent* by nature but rather *rational*, which implies a connection with sensory life. Nevertheless, men do occasionally perform acts of simple intelligence through their power of intellect, which, as operative power, is an accidental act in relation to substance. Angels, on the other hand, are simply intellectual by nature (though not by being), for the only operations they have are on the intellectual level. Hence, man, in his acts of simple intelligence, can be said to participate in angelic intelligence. We can find another instance of participation within man himself. Thus, man's higher sensory powers, through the reception of an influence from his intellect, sometimes act in a way which is imperfectly similar to the way in which intellect acts by its nature. In this meaning of the term, a man's emotional life can be said to be *reasonable*, not by nature but by participation.

possessed by, received in, and limited to, a potential subject-essence.

Being and the properties of being (the transcendentals) are properly predicated of God according to the analogy of participation.[30] What about some perfections which in man are strictly accidental, such as the perfection of wisdom? Such perfections or attributes, if they are really and unqualifiedly perfections, can be predicated of God positively and properly, by the same analogy of participation, but also by an analogy of proper proportionality. For example, once the existence of God is known, and also His complete perfection, we can truly predicate the perfection of wisdom of God, for, as a wise man orders all his actions according to their real value, so God's effects are ordered according to their intrinsic values.[31] But let it be noted that no analogy of proper proportionality between God and any finite things can be used until we first know the existence of God.

Now that we have seen, at least in outline, the whole scope of analogy, it will be useful to organize and interrelate all the kinds of analogy. The analogy of participation is the last to be discovered, but it is the primary and basic one. God is by His essence, and when He, as an analogous cause, makes things to be, He communicates to them the perfection of being in a partial and limited way, so that these things are by participation. Through the analogy of eminence in causality there arise many participants in being. Each thing which is by participation is something-having-esse and thus, according to its intrinsic perfections, being related to God in an analogy of proportionality. As having esse, each created being is related to every other created being by an analogy of individual communication. Created beings which belong to different grades of essential perfection are analogous according to the analogy of proper proportionality.

Because any thing which has esse is intrinsically composite, and because such a nature is a substance which acquires perfections which are accidents, within a being there is an analogy of composition, so that all the internal principles of a being can themselves

[30] How we can name God is discussed more fully in Selected Passages, No. 30.
[31] See, in addition, Selected Passages, No. 27.

be called beings. Because these internal principles stand in a series of similar relations to each other, we discover the act-potency correlation and find that act and potency are analogously verified in the case of the constitutive principles of being according to an analogy of proper proportionality.[32] Because things which exist by participation are capable of being modified—in all cases accidentally, in some also substantially—they can stand in multiple causal relations with each other. Among these are causal situations wherein the effect receives the communicated perfection in an essentially imperfect way. Hence, even among secondary causes there is to be found the analogy of eminence in causality.[33]

The dependence of all beings on God is a total dependence. Hence, our universe of experience, and all contingent beings, exist by creation, that is, their whole being is from God. By creation we understand the complete and total dependence of one being with regard to its entire being upon another as upon its total cause. An equivalent definition is the more common statement that creation is the production of a thing, no subject and no other cause being presupposed.

When did creation happen? The arguments we have used, as well as the other arguments of St. Thomas, conclude that the entire universe exists by creation. These arguments simply do not enable us to decide whether created things have been in existence for a limited time or from all eternity.

82. Answers to objections

Against the second argument (which is the "third way" of St. Thomas), some writers object: "A conclusion cannot be stronger than the premises; but we begin with contingent things; therefore we can only reach a contingent being in our conclusion." The answer to this is: the beings with which we begin are contingent;

---

[32] In addition, "act" is said of esse and of form analogously, according to the analogy of proportion; this is an extrinsic analogy, as explained above, sec. 55. n. 16.

Furthermore, there is an analogy of proportion, according to which the intrinsic principles of composite substance are called substance; form is called substance more properly, matter, less properly, inasmuch as it is related to and perfected by form. See above, sec. 41.

[33] For an outline summary of analogy, see Chap. XIV, sec. 124.

but *that they are contingent* is true with absolute, even though only consequent necessity. Furthermore, the link from effect to cause (no matter what the nature of the effect, provided only that it *is*), is absolutely necessary. Hence, the argument to a necessary being is completely valid.

The objections of agnostics and positivistic empiricists are based on a consideration of purely conceptual (therefore univocal) knowledge and on essences. They maintain, either explicitly or implicitly, that we must know *what* a thing is before we can know that it is, or, at the very least, that we must be able to state its essence. But we maintain that there is knowledge in addition to the conceptual knowledge of essences, namely, judgmental knowledge, and that there is a principle of reality beyond essence, namely, the acts of existing and activity. It is true that the knowledge we ultimately arrive at is analogical and strictly limited. We do not know with any proper knowledge *what* God is. We know, first of all, that the statement, "God is," is true. But further reflection on the implications of the fact proof by which we know that God is gives us the conclusion that in God there is no receptive potency, so that He is a pure act (subsistent act) of existing. We know, further, that this perfection of existing, which we cannot comprehend, englobes in a unity the perfections of creatures in an eminent way. Hence, we can summarize our knowledge about God thus: it is positive inasmuch as we assert truly that God is the cause of the various perfections which we experience and that therefore He is, simply and unqualifiedly; it is negative inasmuch as all univocal perfections, and even more all imperfections, must be denied of Him; it is knowledge by eminence, inasmuch as the act of existing—which even in creatures is the act of all other acts—when it is a subsistent act, is, in a simple way which we cannot grasp in a concept or any number of concepts, all the perfections of creatures and infinitely more.

The objections against the existence of God which are based on the reality of evil cannot be answered in such a way that evil will cease to trouble us. But the following things can be said. (*a*) No creature can be absolutely perfect; it is necessarily a limited being. Moreover, as limited in being, it is contingent, and so in one way or another is able to fail. (*b*) No one creature can be as good an effect as a universe composed of many differing kinds of beings. But this very plurality, which is good, entails necessarily the possibility of conflict, contrariety, and the like, between those creatures. (*c*) Rational and free beings are the greatest, most perfect kinds of creatures (as we will see in the philosophy of man). But if God really means to create a large number of free beings, who are good inasmuch as they freely fulfill the law of their nature and destiny, then, being really free and limited (contingent), it is absolutely necessary that they be able (and hence be allowed by God) to fall into moral evil. (*d*) Finally, if God who is good is to be the author of a created universe in which there is to be evil, this can happen only if God can and does draw forth good from that evil. In some cases we can see this: from physical evil, God brings forth moral good that otherwise would not have come about; from moral evil itself we sometimes see the greater good of penance, greater love of God, and so forth arise; in other cases, we see that some evil men are the occasion for good in others. However, there are also many instances where we cannot see this: we only know that in ways unknown to us God is able to draw forth good from evil. This is enough to break down the force of the objection.

83. The creative intellect and the goal-directedness of natural causes

We have seen, in the first argument for the existence of a First Cause, that God is the First Cause of the activity of all created beings. As *First* Cause, God cannot be caused by anything else in any way, and so there can be no potency of any kind in Him.[34] In other words, He is pure act. Consequently, God cannot be material, for to be material involves the presence of a real potency, namely, primary matter. Hence, God is a nonmaterial being, or, in other words, a spiritual being. Consequently, God cannot be the source of activity after the manner of a material being; He cannot cause activity by contact or gravitation or any other material activity. Now, we have in ourselves the experience of a principle of activity which is not itself moved by any type of

[34] See below, sec. 87, the discussion of possibility.

material motion, namely, our acts of willing.[35] Hence, God is the source of activity in created things by an act of will. But will presupposes intellectual knowledge. Hence, God is an intellectual being.

We have also seen that an effect cannot be more perfect than its cause.[36] But God is the cause of all contingent beings, and so is the cause of men, who are intellectual beings. Hence, God must be an intellectual being.

God, therefore, is the total cause of contingent beings, on Whom the whole reality of these beings depends. And He is a cause through intellect and will.

With these conclusions as a background, we can now complete the analysis of goal orientation, which we left incomplete in Chapter VIII.[37] We saw there that every agent acts for a goal. We saw also that there are two types of agents, those with knowledge and those without it. Knowing agents foreknow the results of their activities; and these results, inasmuch as they are foreknown and desired, are in the full sense goals, or telic causes. But how is the goal present, and how does it cause, in agents which do not have knowledge?

We can derive some understanding of this from human activity. The products of human activity are artifacts and are made for purposes. This is perhaps most clearly evident in machines. A machine is made for a purpose; when it acts, it acts for that purpose, and its activity is determined by its purpose. Of course, a machine is only an accidental structure; the various substances in it are not produced by man (even synthetics are products of nature-guided-by-man; they are not simply artifacts). God, on the other hand, is the creative cause of the whole being, and so there is only a feeble analogy between an inventor and the Creator. But it helps us to see the causality of the goal. The goal is a true cause of mechanical activity, inasmuch as it was foreseen by the inventor and desired by him, and, by being a determinant of the mechanical structure, is a determinant of the consequent

[35] This is discussed at great length in the philosophy of human nature.
[36] See above, sec. 64.
[37] See above, sec. 71.

mechanical activity. So, too, the goal is a real cause of the activity
of noncognoscitive agents, inasmuch as it was foreseen and desired by the First, creative Cause of those agents, and, by being a
determinant of the intrinsic constitution of that nature, is a determinant of natural activity.

When we studied telic causality in the preceding chapter,[38]
we saw that it is possible for two causes to interfere with each
other's activity. Most often, such interference is negative in character—the effect is an accident, something less perfect, of a lower
order of being than either cause. And we saw that such interference, since as such it does not produce new being, in the strict
sense of the word also does not require a cause. But we also saw
that occasionally the interference of two secondary causes may
bring about a positive effect which is different in kind from
either of the causes directly concerned. Such an effect—a chance
effect—is a real and positive reality. What is uncaused, at the
level of the causes immediately concerned, is the interference
itself. If another secondary cause brings about the interference
(for example, a man), we have called it an instance of "relative
chance," for it is chance in relation to the immediate causes but is
goal-directed by the cause of the interference. We have also seen
that some interferences are not brought about by any secondary
cause at all—there is not only relative chance but real, irreducible
chance and contingency, absolute chance.

At this point of our investigation (in the same chapter) we
asked ourselves whether this analysis was sufficient, and we concluded that it was not. Why? Because the causality of the cross-
interfering causes, *as received in the patient*, is such as to lead to
the production of a new being. Where is the orientation by which
such a change leads to such a kind of being? Not in the process
itself, for the process is precisely that which *is oriented*. Not in
the new being, for it does not yet exist. Nor in either or any of
the interfering causes, for the orientation of their natural activity
is directed to a univocal and not to a chance (or equivocal) result.
Now that we know that there is a God, Who is an intelligent

[38] See above, sec. 71.

being, and a cause by creation of natures, we have found an intellect where the order of process to term is known and intended. Hence, the unity and finality of positive chance results lies in the order of beings as understood in the Divine Intellect.

Therefore, though on the one hand, as against determinists we find and admit real, absolute chance and contingency in the material universe, we cannot admit chance as a total and ultimate explanation. In other words, there is chance, not merely in relation to *some* created agents but absolutely, even when all created agents are considered. But chance is not total, for the finality of the interference of causes and the order of process to term which escapes the orientation of any and all secondary causes is contained within the orientation known by the Divine Intellect, which is the creative cause of the whole universe.[89]

84. Definitions

A per se ordered series is a group of objects which by their very nature have determinate relations of priority and posteriority. (For example, the series of natural numbers; the parts of a real definition; the biological stages of a plant: seed, plant, flower, seed.)

A *per se ordered series of causes* is a group of several causes which by their very nature as causes depend on the next higher in the group for their very character of being causes. (For example, principal and instrumental causes; knowledge and desire; nerve impulse and muscle movement.)

Proof (demonstration) is a kind of mediate knowledge (reasoning) which because of the clear truth of its premises and the explicit and full form of procedure leads to a certainly true conclusion.

Causal proof is one which not only establishes a conclusion as true but shows why it must be so.

Fact proof is a proof which establishes that a conclusion is true without any reference to the ontological cause of the conclusion. (For example, any proof of a cause from its effect.)

Analogy of participation is a nonunivocal similarity of two

[89] For a summary statement of God's causal relation to the world, see Selected Passages, No. 29.

analogates, one of which is by nature or essence (and therefore wholly) what the other is partially by received act.

Pure act is an act which is not the act of a potency, not a principle, but subsistent and complete in its own order.

Total chance is a happening or being which is alleged to have come to be without any determination from a telic cause, including the First Cause as well as all secondary causes.

85. Readings

St. Thomas Aquinas, *Summa Theologiae*, Pt. I, q. 2, arts. 1-3 (the proof for the existence of God); q. 1, art. 2 ad 3 and q. 12, arts. 4 and 12 (the limits of our knowledge of the Divine Essence); q. 13, arts. 1, 3, 4, 5, 11 and 12 (how we can name God); *Commentary on the Metaphysics of Aristotle*, Bk. II, lessons 8 and 9, Nos. 301–330, pp. 125–133; Bk. XII, lesson 5, Nos. 2488–2499, pp. 876–879 (on the existence of God).

E. F. Caldin, *Science and Christian Apologetic*, Aquinas Papers, No. 17 (London, Blackfriars, 1951), pp. 18–21, on the proof for the existence of God.

Hilary Carpenter, O.P., "The Philosophical Approach to God in Thomism," *The Thomist*, vol. I (1939), 45–61.

Jean Daniélou, S.J., *God and the Ways of Knowing*, trans. Walter Roberts (New York, Meridian Books, 1957), chap. 2; limits of our natural knowledge.

Etienne Gilson, *The Christian Philosophy of St. Thomas Aquinas* (New York, Random House, 1956), pp. 59–83, 103–109, 443 n.50, 458, n.51.

———*Being and Some Philosophers*, 2d ed. (Toronto, Pontifical Institute of Mediaeval Studies, 1952), pp. 160–167, 172–179, on the meaning of being and on existential contingency.

——— "Can the Existence of God Still be Demonstrated?" *McAuley Lectures, 1960* (Hartford, Conn., St. Joseph's College, 1961).

G. P. Klubertanz, S.J., "Being and God According to Contemporary Scholastics," *The Modern Schoolman*, Vol. XXXII (1954), pp. 1–17.

Jacques Maritain, *The Range of Reason* (New York, Scribner's, 1952), "A New Approach to God," pp. 86–102; "The Meaning of Contemporary Atheism," pp. 103–120.

——— *Approaches to God* (New York, Harper, 1954).

Piux XII, "Modern Science and the Existence of God," *The Catholic Mind*, L, No. 1071 (March, 1952), 182–193. In this address, the Pope makes two points: first, that the modern science shows the mutability (and therefore the contingence) of all material being, and secondly, that the researches of modern science on the formation of the solar system and the stars indicate (though they do not prove), that the universe as we know it had an origin in time. These indications, however, are not yet of the nature of an established hypothesis, and, if established, they would prove an absolute origin of the universe *as we know it*; they cannot prove whether this absolute origin was preceded by another mode of material reality or whether this absolute origin was an absolute origin of material being.

A. D. Sertillanges, *Foundations of Thomistic Philosophy*, trans. Godfrey Anstruther (St. Louis, Herder, 1931), pp. 45–90; this author stresses the "difference" in analogical predication so much that sometimes he seems to be an agnostic; he should be read according to his intention, which is to follow and expound St. Thomas's doctrine of analogy.

SELECTED PASSAGES FROM ST. THOMAS AQUINAS

24. How We Can Know God at All

For we cannot know the essences of the separated substances by demonstrative knowledge, for these essences are per se intelligible—by an intellect proportioned to this. But it is not possible to gather a knowledge of them from principles prior to them. But by speculative knowledge we can know of them whether they are, and what they are not, and something according to a likeness found in lower things.

> *Commentary on the* Posterior Analytics *of Aristotle*, Bk. I, lect. 41.

Human reason is deficient in the knowledge of separated substances, which nonetheless are most knowable in their nature. With regard to the knowledge of them, our intellect is like the eye of the owl to the light of the sun, as is said in *Metaphysics*, II, and therefore it is said in *De Animalibus*, XI, that about them we can know extremely little by reason, although that little which we do know about them is pleasing and dear to us.

> *Commentary on the Second Book of the* Sentences, dis. 3, q. 1, art. 3.

25. The Analogy of Participation

Only God is his own esse, existing, as it were essentially, that is, inasmuch as his esse is his substance. This can be said of no other being. For subsisting esse can be only one, as also subsisting whiteness could be only one. Therefore, it is necessary that any other thing is a being by participation, so that there is a distinction in it between the substance partaking of esse, and the esse which is participated. But everything which participates is like potency to act; consequently, the substance of every created being is related to its esse as potency to act.

Quodlibet III, art. 20.

There are two ways of predicating one thing of another: essentially, and by participation. For light is predicated of an illuminated body by participation; but if there were a separated light, it would be predicated of that essentially. According to this, it must be said that being is predicated essentially of God alone, because the divine esse is a subsisting and absolute esse. But of any creature it is predicated by participation, for no creature is its esse, but is something having esse. Thus also God is called good essentially, because He is goodness itself; but creatures are good by participation, because they have goodness; for everything, inasmuch as it is, is good. . . . Whenever something is predicated of another by participation, it is necessary that there be something there besides that which is participated, and therefore in every creature the creature itself which has esse is not the same as its esse, and this is what Boethius says in his book, *De Hebdomadibus,* "In everything which is, besides the First, esse is other than that which is."

But it is to be noted, that there are two ways of participating. One way is, as being of the substance of that which participates, as the genus is participated by the species. This is not the way that esse is participated by the creature, for that is of the substance of a thing which falls into its definition. But "being" is not of the definition of any creature, for it is neither genus nor difference. But it is participated as not being of the essence of the thing. Hence, the question, "Is it?" is a different one from, "What is it?" Consequently, since everything which is outside the essence of the things, is called an accident, and so the Commentator says, on *Metaphysics,* V, that this proposition, "Socrates is," has an accidental predicate, inasmuch as it signifies the being of the thing, or the truth of the proposition. Now, it is true that this term *being,* inasmuch as it implies the thing to which such an esse belongs, in this sense signifies the essence of the thing, and is divided into the ten genera, but not univocally, because esse does not belong to all things in the same way, but it belongs to substance of itself, but to other things in another way. If, therefore, there is in the angel a composition of essence and esse, this is not a composition of parts of substance, but as of substance and that which adheres to substance. . . .

In reply to the second argument, it is to be said that esse is an accident, not as if it were accidental to the thing, but as the actuality of every substance. Consequently God, who is His own actuality, is His own esse.

Quodlibet II, art. 3.

Although the esse of a thing is other than its essence, we are not to think that esse is something superadded after the manner of an accident, but it is as it were constituted by the principles of the essence.

> Commentary on Aristotle's
> Metaphysics, Bk. IV, lect.
> 1 (ed. Cathala, No. 558).

26. How God Is Distinguished from Creatures

A thing is said to be determinate in two senses: the first, by reason of limitation; the second, by reason of distinction. But the divine essence is not something determinate in the first way; only in the second way. For a form is not limited except by this, that it is received in another, to which the matter is proportioned. But in the divine essence, there is not anything which is received in another, because His esse is the subsisting divine nature itself. But such a situation is not to be found in any other thing. For every other thing has an esse which has been received, and thus limited, and hence it is that the divine essence is distinguished from all others by this not-being-received-in-another. Thus, if there were a whiteness not in a subject, by this very fact it would be distinguished from every whiteness existing in a subject, although as whiteness it would not be received and so not limited. Therefore, it is clear that the divine essence is not something general in being, since it is distinguished from all other things, but it is general only in causing, because that which is by itself is the cause of all those things which are not by themselves. Consequently, the per se subsisting esse is the cause of every other esse received in another.

> Quodlibet VII, art. 1, ad
> 1.

27. The Sources and Nature of Our Knowledge of God

First he shows what they knew about God, secondly, he shows from whom they received this knowledge . . . thirdly, he shows how. . . . For there was in them a true knowledge of God with regard to some points, for "that of God which is known," that is, which is knowable about God by man's reason, "is manifest in them," that is, is manifest to them by something which is in them, that is, by an intrinsic light. We must therefore know that something concerning God is entirely unknown to man in this life, namely, what God is. Hence, St. Paul found at Athens an altar inscribed, "To the unknown God." This is because the knowledge of man begins with those things which are connatural to him, that is, with sensible creatures, which are not proportioned to represent the divine essence.

But man can know God from such creatures in a threefold way, as

Dionysius says. The first way is that of causality, for since such creatures are able to cease to be and are changeable, it is necessary that
we argue back to some unchangeable and perfect principle, and in
this way we know that God is. The second way is that of eminence;
for we do not go from all creatures to the first principle, as to a proper
and univocal cause, as for example, a man generated a man, but as to a
common and greater cause, and in this way we know that God is
above all. The third way is that of negation, because, if God is a
greater cause, none of the perfections which are in creatures can
pertain to God. . . . And in this way we say that God is unchangeable and infinite, and anything else which is expressed in this way. And
this knowledge they had by the inborn light of reason. . . . Then
. . . he shows from whom such knowledge was manifested to them,
and he says that God manifested it to them. . . . Here we must consider, that one man manifests to another, explaining his conception
by some external signs, for example, by word or by writing. But God
manifests something to men in two ways. First, by giving him an
internal light, by which man knows. . . . Secondly, by placing before
him exterior signs of his wisdom, that is, sensible creatures. . . . Thus,
therefore, God manifested to them, both by giving an internal light,
and by exteriorly showing sensible creatures, in which, as in a book,
the knowledge of God can be found.

*Commentary on the Epistle
to the Romans,* chap. 1,
lect. 6.

28. Meaning of "Substance" as Applied to God

God, absolutely speaking, is not an accident, but neither can He
with entire propriety be called a substance, both because the term
substance is derived from "standing-under [accidents]," and because
substance names the quiddity which is distinct from its esse. Consequently, this [distinction of substance and accident] is a distinction
of created being. But if one does not insist on this, in an extended
sense of the term God can be called a substance (which is understood
to be above all created substance), in so far as substance has perfection, such as not to be in another and so on, and then it is identical
in the subject and predicate, as is the case with everything that is
predicated of God. . . . Consequently, because of the different mode
of predicating, substance is not used of God and creatures univocally,
but analogously.

*Commentary on the First
Book of the* Sentences, dis.
8, q. 4, art. 2, ad 1.

29. Relation Between Creatures and God

For God is He by Whom all things are, as by their efficient cause, and for Whose sake all things are, as by their final cause. For all things are for Him, because they are for the sake of His goodness which is to be communicated to them. And this was the reason which moved God to produce things, and so ultimately, all things are for God. . . . They are also effectively by Him. . . . Therefore He is the principle and the end of all.

Commentary on the Epistle
to the Hebrews, chap. 2,
lect. 3.

30. How Different Names and Attributes Can Be Predicated of God

Because God according to one simple act of existing is perfect in all the ways which are indicated by the names we give Him . . . therefore these names positively belong to Him. . . . The intelligibilities of the attributes are truly in God. . . . The plurality of names comes from the fact that God is greater than our intellect. And the fact that God is greater than our intellect, on God's part, is because of the fullness of His perfection, and on our part, our intellect deficiently understands Him. So it is clear that the plurality of those intelligibilities arises not only from the side of our intellect, but also from the side of God, inasmuch as his perfection is greater than every conception of our intellect. Thus, to the plurality of intelligibilities there corresponds something from the side of God's reality—not indeed a real plurality, but a full perfection because of 'which all these conceptions are suited to him. . . . On the side of our intellect, and also of the effects [from which we come to now God] [something corresponds] because our intellect cannot conceive the divine perfection with one conception only, but needs many. . . . Therefore there is something in God which corresponds to all these conceptions, namely, his full and every-sided perfection, according to which any name signifying any of these conceptions is truly and properly predicated of God.

Commentary on the First
Book of the Sentences, dis.
2, q. 1, art. 3.

X

The Transcendentals

86. Being is a transcendental

Some predicates[1] can be said only of particular classes or kinds of things, and these predicates are usually univocal ones; for example, "white" (which can only be said of things that are extended); "square" (which can only be said of things that have a surface). These predicates will be considered in Chapters XI, XII, and XIII. But the predicates to be treated here are common to many kinds of things, and so their community must be one of analogy, as we have already seen with regard to *being* and *substance*. A predicate which is not restricted to any category, type, or class of reality, but goes beyond, or "transcends," all limited areas of reality and all distinctions within reality is called a "transcendental." The transcendentals are predicates.

We have seen that *is* can be said or predicated of *all* real things. From our study of being, which we know is common by way of analogical inclusion, we can see that being is not a genus, not even the widest possible genus. For genus is always abstract; and the wider and more universal the genus, the more abstract and potential it is. For example, *material substance* is a predicate that can be applied to every thing in our material universe; it is also a very abstract concept and is in potency to all the specific

---

[1] The term "predicate" is here taken in a very wide sense to include verb-predicates (such as "runs," "is") as well as nouns and adjectives. For a discussion of those "metaphysicians" and logicians who wish to reduce all two-element propositions (*de secundo adjacente*) to three-element ones (*de tertio adjacente*), see Etienne Gilson, *Being and Some Philosophers*, 2d ed. (Toronto, Pontifical Institute of Mediaeval Studies, 1952), pp. 190–205.

determinations—merely material, living, sensitive, rational. But *being* as it is understood in its first and proper metaphysical sense is named from that which is most actual and concrete, namely, the act of existing. Being is *not* the "widest in extension and the least in comprehension," because the logical rule of the inverse variation of extension and comprehension holds only for universals. Being is at once the widest in extension—for *is* can be said of all things—and the fullest in (implicit) comprehension—for any real act or perfection *is*. Being includes all reality; indeed, all the reality of any and all individuals. Therefore, *being* (understood as "the being of metaphysics") is a transcendental.

This conclusion is simple and obvious. A series of problems, however, remains. We have seen that *is* has many meanings and that in addition to its strictly metaphysical meaning, it is also used of things which are real only in the wide sense, and even of purely mental objects. We must therefore also consider how these meanings are related to the metaphysical sense. Moreover, there are some terms which are used more or less in the same sense as *being,* and so we should give a brief consideration to these terms. Finally, some philosophers have raised a question about the sense in which being is *a* transcendental. We will take up these topics in inverse order.

The question, "In what sense is being *a* transcendental?" is a question about the unity of being.[2] The question, "Is being one?" has many meanings. It may mean, "Is there only one being?" and immediate experience shows us many distinct individuals. The question may mean, "Is being univocal?" The reflection which we have made in Chapter III (and the following chapters) shows us that being is analogous. The question may mean, "Is there only one 'kind' of being, for example, material being or limited being?" and a study of the being of metaphysics and of the proof for the existence of God leads us to the conclusion that there are many kinds of beings, which are analogous with several kinds of analogy (analogy of eminince in causality, analogy of proportion, analogy of participation). The question may mean, "Granted

---

[2] See above, Chap. II, sec. 17, nn. 17 and 21, and Chap. III, sec. 24, n. 3. St. Thomas explicitly says, "There is no single intelligibility in the things which are said analogously" (*Summa Theologiae,* Pt. I, q. 13, art. 5).

that beings as they are are many and analogous, can they be correctly understood as beings by one concept?" An attentive reflection on our knowledge of being has shown us that it is impossible to have a *concept* of being in its first and proper sense, and so the unity of being is not even of one concept.[3] The community of the act of existing is only an analogical one, and so being is *one* transcendental only by the unity of analogy (according to all the kinds of analogy which we found in being).

Finally, the question about the unity of being may mean, "Is there at least an indirect way in which some, if not all, the analogates can be understood in one act of understanding?" Now, concepts are formed by abstraction, and in the first instance directly from the things which we wish to grasp. Conceptions, however, are formed from judgments; they can be formed either by abstraction (from an attributive judgment, from which we derive a composite essence, e.g., gold mountain) or by a negative judgment. Can we form a conception of being? We can if it is possible to make a series of judgments from which the same conception can be derived. Now, we have noticed that among the analogies of being there are some in which one analogate is prior and the other is posterior, and that in such analogies, the secondary analogate (as far as our *knowledge* of the two is concerned) is defined through the first, whereas the first does not include the secondary analogates. Thus, substance is prior to accident and to the other intrinsic principles of being, and sensible creatures are prior in our knowledge to God. Thus, we can form a common conception of being, so that, when we say, without any further qualification, "Something is," or name an object, "something which is," we are understood to mean, "A sensible subsistent exists," "an individual sensible subsistent which is." In this derivative and limited sense we can truly speak of a single conception of being.

We can now take up the consideration of the terms which have somewhat the same meaning as *being*. One of these terms which we have already used is "reality," or "the real." As we have seen, this is a term which belongs to the level of everyday, spontaneous knowledge; hence, it is often used in a loose or less precise sense

---

[3] For a more elaborate discussion of our knowledge of being, see below, Chap. XIV, sec. 123.

than the term "being." "Thing" as a term from the level of everyday knowledge is like "reality." As used on the level of demonstrative knowledge, "thing" stresses the essence or quiddity and connotes the act of existing (whereas "being" includes the act of existing more directly). "Something," as a technical term on the level of demonstrative knowledge, means the same as "thing," but connotes, in addition, the division of that which is named "something" from other things. In other words, "something" is a term which implies that there are other things in addition to the one we call "something." Hence, it implies the unity of the thing (it is *a* thing) as well as the diversity or multiplicity of things.

87. Possibles

As we have already noted, the properly real is being, that which has an act of existing. Nevertheless, we understand that some things *can* be in the real order which here and now actually are not. We understand this from the contingent real things which we experience. For these beings manifest themselves as contingently existing. They are composed in the order of being itself—namely, of an essence and an act of existing—and consequently we can consider things in relation to existence even though they are not.

When we consider a thing inasmuch as it is able *to be*, we call it a possible.[4] A thing which is not, whether it be possible or a mere fiction, is simply nothing in the real order. Such a thing, under the aspect that it simply is not, is not the subject of any form of knowledge at all. If we consider a thing as simply an object of the mind, we are not thinking of a possible; we may be thinking of a logical entity; we may be studying the content of dreams as a psychologist might do. If we investigate an essence down to the last detail, but only from the point of view of *what* it is, we are not dealing with a possible as possible and so are not dealing with it from the point of view of the philosophy of being

---

[4] By a "pure possible," we mean something which does not exist, but is an object of knowledge with a reference to what could be extramental. We can also, however, consider the possibility of a being which exists; in this case we are not thinking about a possible in the strict sense of the word (sometimes called a "mixed possible").

—we may be engaged in mathematics or one of the sciences. But when we consider an essence (a thing) inasmuch as some properly real thing can or could correspond to it, then we are considering the possible as possible, that is, in relation to being. A possible considered in this way belongs to the subject of metaphysics.

The intelligibility of a possible, therefore, lies in its relation to being. As a possible thing, an essence has the possibility of having an act of existing; in other words, it is known as that to which in the real order there could correspond a contingently existing thing.

Now, to understand an essence with a relation to an act of existing there must be a foundation. This foundation is twofold: (*a*) in essence, and this consists in the noncontradictoriness of the constituent elements of that essence; (*b*) in an act of existing —not its own, of course, because a possible has no act of existing —the act of existing of some actual cause, past, present, or future. Hence, the intelligibility of a possible depends on its essence (understood with reference to an act of existing which a corresponding real being might have); its possibility of *being* depends on the act of existing of some cause (or causes) adequate to produce an actually existing (real) being corresponding to the knowledge we have.

Possibility, therefore, can readily be divided into two parts: essential possibility (the noncontradictoriness or consistency of its constituent intelligible notes, understood with reference to a being which might exist), and existential possibility, for only that can truly exist which exists necessarily of itself or is produced by an existing cause.

Because the possibility of being depends on a cause, and causes can be proximate or remote and variously disposed to act, possibility itself can have degrees. Moreover, because that which is possible depends for its possibility on an actual being, a possible can be said to be by an analogy of proportion—although the relationship of a possible to an act of existing is mediate and indirect—namely, through the esse of a distinct real being which is its cause.

88. Beings of reason and pure intelligibilities

Whenever we think of something, that "something" can be either a being in the proper sense of that term or some principle of being or something pertaining to a being or sometimes not a being in itself at all (for example, a fiction).[5] All of these "things," however, can be considered *as known*, and as such they can be called intelligible objects or intelligibilities[6] (in the wide sense). These intelligibilities, from the viewpoint of being, can be classed into three groups: real beings, beings of reason, and pure intelligibilities (*rationes*), that is, intelligibilities in the strict sense. So far in this book we have been considering mainly real beings, although there have been occasional references to the other two groups.

A being of reason is an object which can be thought of but which does not and *cannot* exist in itself. Consequently, in the proper sense of being, such objects are simply not beings. Nevertheless, they are understood *after the manner of beings*. They are objects conceived or mentally constructed with reference to the real order; yet they have no direct correspondent in that order.[7]

Beings of reason are of three kinds. (1) Negations and privations (for example, "nobody," "a hole"; "blindness," "ignorance") obviously do not correspond to any real existent or to any real principle of being. A negative or privative proposition may be true or false, yet the truth of a negative proposition does not imply the existence of a negation. (2) Relations of reason are beings of reason, either because they join together objects which exist only in a mind (for example, the relations of genus, property, subject and predicate) or because they are mentally applied to real beings without a direct and a real foundation in the real, for example, the "right" side of a table (transferred to tables from the distinction between the sides of an animal body), the "top" of a box whose top and bottom are constructed the same, and so forth. (3) There are also mental constructs which are beings of reason, because as such they cannot exist, and are only indirectly

[5] See Selected Passages, No. 32.
[6] See Selected Passages, No. 33, especially par. 1, where intelligible objects are divided into three classes.
[7] See Selected Passages, No. 31.

related to the real, that is, through some other real being from which the construct is derived. Among such constructs there are to be found some second-level abstractions (for example, "humanity," which, although it is understood after the manner of the substantial form of a being, is rather the abstracted formal intelligibility of "man," which is the product of a total abstraction) and some transferred intelligibilities.[8]

Beings of reason are beings *because* that is the way we think of them. They are understood as having the nature of being. Because beings of reason are correlative with the real on which they are modeled, the predication is by proportion; because beings of reason are not intrinsic constitutive principles of being but are understood after the manner of beings, the analogy is not intrinsic but extrinsic. Hence, we may say that beings of reason are by an extrinsic analogy of proportion.

Why do men produce or invent beings of reason? For the purpose of a better understanding of, and a more efficient dealing with, real beings. For example, consider how awkward it would be to think and talk of "digging a hole," "curing an illness," "being in debt," without making use of any beings of reason. Again, consider the poverty of our literature if all metaphors were removed from it. Thirdly, our direct (or ontological) understanding of beings is frequently very limited. There are many things which we cannot directly understand in themselves, particularly as soon as we get beyond immediate experience into science. (To say that science makes use of constructs is by no means derogatory to the dignity of science; in a way it is a glorification of the human mind, for although the human intellect is limited by being the intellect of a rational animal, it can at least to some extent transcend its limitations by means of the products of its own activity.)[9]

[8] For example, many metaphors like "John Doe is a pig," where we understand John Doe's greediness in terms of the understood nature of a pig. In such metaphors, we attribute an alien nature to the subject. The "pig" we are speaking of is not an existent individual (for such a predication would be false); nor is it a being of reason (for beings of reason cannot be directly predicated of existents like John). See above, Chap. III, n. 8, and the article there cited.

[9] For a fuller discussion of the nature of constructural knowledge and its difference from ontological knowledge, see below, sec. 115.

Besides real beings and beings of reason, there is a third class of intelligibilities, the pure intelligibilities.[10] Universals, for example, are pure intelligibilities: they are neither merely constructed mental objects nor real beings. With regard to universals, we must distinguish between that which is known and the manner in which the known is in the mind. "Man," for example, can be truly said to be the knowledge of a real being, because that which we know when we know "man" is wholly and entirely real. But the manner in which we know "man"—namely, as abstract and universal—is unlike the manner in which a man exists—namely, as concrete and singular. Similarly, many of the objects which we speak of in metaphysics are pure intelligibilities. To see the difference between a pure intelligibility and a being of reason it may help to compare two conceptions. As an example of a pure intelligibility we will take the act of existing of a being with respect to what is known when we know it. This act is real (for it is that principle in a being by which it *is*); but with respect to the manner in which it is known, it is not immediately real (since it is known as if it were a subject). As an example of a being of reason, we will take the concept of existence,[11] namely, "the form by which a real being is." Existence is a positive formalization, to which no being or principle in the real order directly corresponds. In the real order, there is the esse of some being. This esse is referred to indirectly by the concept "existence." The mind constructs and conceives, after the manner of a form, a substitute representation of a real intelligible which in itself is not essential or formal. In other words, the mind essentializes and formalizes by way of a construct (derived from a real principle) what it recognizes in the real as belonging to the existential order.

89. The transcendental "one"

The term "one" is used in two quite different senses. The numerical "one" is used in counting and, at the level of demonstra-

[10] See also, Selected Passages, No. 33, for a very full explanation of what an intelligibility is.

[11] For the difference between the "concept of existence," which is a constructural concept, and the "conception of the act of existing," which is a direct intelligibility, see above, sec. 17 (n. 17, 21), sec. 24 (n. 3), and below, sec. 123; see also, G. P. Klubertanz, *The Philosophy of Human Nature* (New York, Appleton-Century-Crofts, Inc., 1953), pp. 179–180.

tive knowledge, in arithmetic. At present we are not going to deal with the numerical "one" at all. The transcendental "one" means "actually undivided"—for example, in the expression, "in one piece." The transcendental "one" is an absolute adjective; it does not in any sense imply that there are other things. In form, it is a positive term; but as far as its meaning is concerned, it is negative, for it means "not actually divided." Terms related to "one" are "unique," which means "one and only one"; "whole," which implies that the thing which is actually undivided is capable of division into parts; and "simple," which means "not only undivided but indivisible, having no parts."[12]

"One" is the first "property"[13] or attribute of being. It is the *first* property, because it refers to being absolutely, considered in itself (and so is prior by nature to the other transcendentals which belong to being relatively, as we shall see). "One" does not add anything positive to being; it is the being in itself which is undivided. However, we understand this absence of division after the manner of an added qualification.

Every being is one. For a being is either simple, that is, indivisible and so, of course, actually undivided, or it is composed. But parts do not make up a being unless they are *united* in some way or other. And there are a number of kinds of unity.

ONE

per se	{ according to one act of existing[14] according to one essence (nature)
per accidens	{ by composition of substance and accident (or two accidents, according to their inherence in the same substance)
accidental	{ of many substances according to some accident: dynamic: joined in operation (activity) static: joined in place, structure, and so forth

[12] See also, Selected Passages, No. 34.

[13] From the Latin, *proprietas* or *passio entis*.

[14] Ordinarily, both these types of per se unity are found together, for the undividedness of essence and of the act of existing are naturally proportioned to each other. Hence, for many purposes, that can be said to be "per se one" which has one essence or nature. But it is still the undividedness of the act of existing which is the most basic reason for denominating a being *one* being.

"One" and "being" are clearly not synonyms. On the other hand, they clearly do not refer to really distinct principles. Hence, there is a distinction of reason between "one" and "being." Moreover, since "that which is actually undivided" is a being, and *a* being is actually undivided, the distinction between "one" and "being" must be a minor distinction of reason.[15]

The opposite of "one" is "many" or "the divided" or "the distinct" or "the different" or "the diverse." Which one will be precisely the opposite of "one" in any given case depends upon the precise connotations in the particular usage of "one."

90. Being-in-itself and being-for-another

In most of metaphysics—up to this point in our present study— the being that we consider is the being which a thing has in itself. However, in most of our prior experience and probably much of the experience we will have in the future, the being which a thing has *for us* is more significant.[16] In the practical order, our world for us is a biocultural world. The biological world is the world of immediate vital utility. The cultural world, which in the last century has become very profoundly a technological world, is the world in which we spend most of our time. Thus, our ordinary world is a world in which things have a meaning as food, shelter, tools, artifacts, and symbols. But, when we are looking at our surroundings in terms of food, shelter, tables, roads, traffic signals, pianos, books, and on the persons surrounding us as parents, friends, enemies, strangers, we are not considering them according to the reality which they have in themselves, but rather according to the being which they have for us. A thing has being-for-us to the extent that it is known, is the object of some tendency (love, hatred, and so on), or is the object of our transient activity.

As far as noncognitive things are concerned, their being-for-us is not part of their intrinsic reality, except that things must have in themselves the possibility of entering into relations with us.

[15] See above, sec. 33.
[16] It is not metaphysics alone that considers being-in-itself; it is a mark of all purely intellectual knowledge and especially of all the kinds of speculative (theoretical) scientific knowledge to be directed to the object as it is in itself. See secs. 116, 119.

The being-for-man for such a thing is therefore principally a fact about man. The anthropologist is the one who is interested in knowing that an oddly shaped piece of stone is an arrowhead, not the geologist.

Persons, however, not only have being-for-another, but in turn are aware of this being. As a result, their being-for-another intrinsically affects them. A child, for example, first sees his own value as a reflection of the value which he thinks others put on him. Similarly, he reacts to his surroundings primarily in terms of their being-for-him, and habitual reactions structure his personality. However important such relations are for our practical life as well as for psychologists, artists, educators, and the like, the contingent forms which they take have little meaning for speculative science of any kind.[17]

Nevertheless, the basic fact that persons and things have being-for-us, and that we have being-for-other persons needs to be investigated further.

91. The transcendental "true"

The first kind of being-for-another is being-known. We can begin our investigation by considering the relationships between knowledge and the things which are known.

In logic and theory of knowledge there are many references to "truth." There, "truth" means the "conformity of the mind to things" and, when we are speaking accurately, should always be called *logical* truth. So, too, when we ask whether something is true, we are ordinarily speaking of logical truth. And we use "falsehood" or "falsity" in the same kind of way. However, even in our ordinary speech, we occasionally use the term "true" and especially "false" in a related but quite different sense, as in the expressions "false teeth," "true love," "a true albino." In this sense, we are talking about the conformity of the thing to its definition, essence, and so forth, or, more generally, to knowledge or a mind. (Compare the meaning of the verb "to true.") This is the sense in which we speak of the true in metaphysics, namely, the conformity or conformability of a thing to a mind.

---

[17] This is another reason why a universally valid metaphysics can hardly be begun starting with "subjective," personal experience of "our world."

The true is not a negation or a negative attribute, for it expresses something positive, namely, conformability with intellect. But "true" does not add anything really distinct to "being," for "true" is simply "being" expressed in its relation to intellect. Hence, the distinction between "being" and "the true" is a minor distinction of reason.

When we say, "The true is being in relation to intellect," we must determine explicitly which intellect we are referring to. Since the beings of our experience, by their very participation in being, are related to the First Being, it is to the Divine Intellect that the true has an essential relation. Because the beings of our experience exist by creation and God creates through intellect and will, all created beings are actually conformed in their being to the Divine Intellect. The predicate *true*, therefore, when applied to creatures, means "made so as to conform to the Divine Intellect." When applied to God Himself, however, the predicate *true* means essentially that God, Who is a subsistent intellect and act of understanding, knows Himself so perfectly that what He is and what He knows of Himself are entirely and completely identical.

But in addition to the Divine Intellect there are also other, contingently existing intelligent beings; and, of these, we are especially concerned with man. Note that only those beings are necessarily conformed to the human intellect which come into being in dependence upon a human agent. In the case of artifacts, *true* means "made so as to conform to the artist's mind." In the case of all other finite things, however, there is no necessary relation of actual conformity to the human intellect. Some things are in fact known by man. With regard to the nature and existence of these things, it is extrinsic and accidental to them that they be in fact known by some man. Therefore, *true* in the sense of "actually conformed to a human mind," when applied to artifacts, is an essential predicate; when applied to natural beings, it is an accidental and extrinsic predicate.

The relation between being and the human intellect can be considered in terms of conformability rather than conformity. By this we mean that whether such things are known or not, they can be known, they are knowable. The relationship of conformability to some created intellect is a necessary one, given the existence of these things and of an intellect, but it is secondary (the primary essential relation is to the Divine Intellect). The relationship of conformability to any given individual created intellect or to any kind of created intellect—for example, that of man—is contingent or accidental, for it is not necessary that men exist. Applied to creatures, therefore, the term "true" in the sense of conformability means that they are such as can be known by man. Some things, of course, are here and now not actually knowable by man—things hidden from man's experience within the earth or at the far reaches of the stellar universe or among the multitude of angels. But the reason these things cannot be known at present is some hindrance external to the nature of the things—their lack of contact with us, for example. Hence, we can state what is sometimes called the "principle of intelligibility"— "All things are intelligible."

We can also ask whether the predicate *true* in the sense of conformability to the human intellect can be applied to God. Prior to our knowledge that God exists we cannot, of course, say that He is true. But now that we know that He exists, it is evident that He can be known by man.

True, in the sense of conformability to some created intellect, is a necessary but secondary predicate of all things. In the sense of conformability to some particular created intellect or to some kind of created intellect, *true* is an accidental and extrinsic predicate.

Being-true is, then, being-knowable and (sometimes) being-known by another. When the being which is knowable and known is a person, then this being-for-another which is (ontological) truth is the foundation for truthfulness in communication, which in turn is one of the foundations of society. Being-true is also the foundation for particular relationships, such as that of fidelity to promises, or of the knowledge aspect of friendship.

According to the various meanings of *true* which we have been considering, it is a relative attribute: it describes a thing as related to something else (namely, an intellect). In other words, it denominates a thing from something distinct from it (an intellect), to which it has a relation.[18] Does *true* have any absolute signification? In other words, does it say anything about the being in itself? Yes, because a being to be conformed and conformable to intellect must be of a certain kind. Intelligibility supposes that being has a certain structure. We have previously seen that potency, as such, is not knowable in itself but through act and in relation to act.[19] We have also seen that the first and primary of all acts is the act of existing. Hence, the primary one among the absolute meanings of *true* is the one which designates the act of existing of a thing:[20] "The *true* is the esse of things." On this basis we can see why every being is true. For being is "that-which-is," "something having an act of existing." The act of existing is intelligible, even if we cannot have a simple apprehension or direct abstractive concept of it. At the very least, we can know in a judgment that a being is. This does not imply that every being is perfectly or completely intelligible to man; it only means that no being is completely unintelligible to man. Therefore, *true*, in its first absolute meaning, designates the basic internal actuality of a being, its act of existing.

 Moreover, act is also form, especially substantial form. Hence, a second absolute meaning of transcendental truth is the actual possession of a form and, consequently, of a nature. Again, inasmuch as act is intelligible, the being which possesses an act— that is, a form—is thereby intelligible. Here, however, not all beings are equally true, that is, equally conformable to the human intellect. Sensible things can be directly known by us. But pure forms—the angels and God—cannot be directly known in themselves to the human mind, because it is impossible for us to have an abstractive concept of such forms. Therefore, *true*, in the secondary, absolute sense of the possession of a form or nature, can be predicated of all beings, but in different ways of sensible things, separate substances, and God.

[18] Recall what was said above, that the relation in question is not something added to being; it is only rationally distinct.

[19] See above, sec. 53.

[20] St. Thomas most often gives among the "absolute" meanings of the *true* the esse of things; but there are also other meanings; cf. for example, *"veritas humanae naturae,"* in *Summa Theologiae*, Pt. III, q. 5, arts. 1 and 2.

The transcendental true is related to knowledge as that which can be grasped and that which is to be grasped. As goal of knowledge, it is a telic cause of knowledge. Two consequences follow from this. One is that we meet again a reason for rejecting materialism, since even the sensible, as being, is intrinsically ordered to knowledge. Thus, the very material being, as true, implies the existence of a knower. Secondly, we mentioned in the beginning of this course that metaphysics can start from the fact of knowledge. The transcendental true is the reason why such a procedure is possible; for, if being as being is true, then from the fact of true knowledge we can work back to the necessary conditions of being and of knowledge.[21] For one example of this in metaphysics, we could work from the experienced fact of universal concepts to the composition of matter and form in things. For another example, we could work from the coexistence of a being which is both knower and known and another being which is only known but not a knower, to the role of act (esse and form) as source of intelligibility, and the contrary role of (primary) matter as that principle in a being which impedes full intelligibility.

Hence, we can sum up the entire discussion of transcendental truth in this way. The transcendental true is analogous. First, there is the subsistent truth of God Who is pure act, perfectly known to Himself. Then there are the participated truths, which are primarily true inasmuch as beings by participation are conformed to the creative intellect, and secondarily true, as such beings are conformable to some created intellect. In a derived sense, *true* designates the absolute (that is, nonrelative) perfection of a being, and here, too, there are degrees of truth. That is most true which is pure, subsistent act. That is more or less true which has more or less of act—primarily the act of existing, secondarily other acts, especially substantial form and essence.

The opposite of the true is the false. Being is not, absolutely speaking, false, for that which has, absolutely speaking, no act of existing in any sense is not a being. However, a being may be called false from some limited point of view. For example, when

[21] This method is quite popular; it is sometimes called the "method of transcendental deduction." sometimes, of "reduction."

we speak of "false teeth," we mean "some things which are not really teeth, but have something of the appearance of teeth and perform some of their functions."

92. The transcendental "good"

The second kind of being-for-another is being-loved or being the object of some activity. We have already seen, in our discussion of telic causality, that the correlative of tendency and action is "the good."

THE PROPER GOOD

The predicate "good" is used in many ways. In its unqualified sense (for example, "John is a good man"), it means "that which is perfect according to its kind." In this sense of the term "good," the goodness of a thing is proper to it; and the goodness of one kind of thing is different from the goodness of another kind. For example, a pen is good when it writes well; a race horse is good when it runs fast; a man is good when he has the virtues and other qualities which human nature ought to have. The unqualified "good" is therefore also called the "proper good." The proper good is clearly not possessed by every thing, for there are bad men, bad bargains, bad food. Moreover, in the beings of our experience, their proper good is a perfection distinct from their substance and so is an accidental perfection. (The proper good of man is studied in ethics or moral philosophy.)

The opposite of the proper good is the evil. Taken concretely, "evil" or "bad" designates some thing which is without (deprived of) some particular good which it should have according to its kind. Taken abstractly, "evil" or "badness" is the privation[22] itself; and privation itself is not a real being (just as blindness is not a being) but a being of reason. An evil thing, of course—"evil" taken concretely—is a real being, real with the reality of the thing that lacks a good which is due to it according to its nature.

But goodness and evil are not simply absolute predicates, like perfect and imperfect. In the full sense of the term "good," a

[22] Distinguish between privation and the simple absence of something. Privation means "the absence of something which is due, or suitable, or necessary." On evil as a privation, see Selected Passages, No. 36.

thing is good when it is not only perfect in its kind but is at the same time an object of appetite, or tendency. Good food, for example, is not merely a material substance with all the accidents suitable to its nature but also one which corresponds to a particular appetite, namely, the biological tendency of a living thing toward that which nourishes it. Similarly, a good race horse is not merely one which exercises the particular activity of running rapidly; that activity is also desired by someone. Again, a good man is not merely one who has certain virtues; he has the virtues he *ought* to have—and *ought* expresses the basic natural tendency of man to be in the condition of possessing such virtues. These examples—similar ones can easily be found—show us that *good* is a perfection for which there is an appetite (tendency) either in the thing itself which possesses or is capable of possessing the perfection or in something else.

Thus, the proper good is always a goal for that whose good it is. Conversely, all goals are objects of striving or tending, and are (or are thought to be) proportioned to the needs or capacities of the agent and its powers. Hence, every goal is also good. So we can say not only that every agent acts for a goal, but also that every agent acts for a good.

But men commit sins, that is, seek things that are evil; and the effects of natural causes are often evil. Quite so, and the understanding of how these facts are related to the statement that every agent acts for a good will be an advantage. First then as to sin. Sin involves a double aspect: that man does not will the good which he should be willing and that he wills something which is not, properly speaking, good for him. But the fact that a man does not accept as the actual goal of his activity that good to which he should be tending does not change the fact that that good is his proper good and that he should be striving for it, and this aversion from his proper good is not the primary object of his will, but rather something else which he wants which is incompatible with that good. On the other hand, what the sinner does actually take is considered by him at that point to be the good which he wants, and it is viewed as a good for him under some limited aspect or for a particular power (for example, sense pleasure, even against reasonable use, is a good for the senses considered in themselves; being responsible to no one could be considered good if a man forgets that he is a limited and dependent being; and so on). That is why we said above that every goal is a good or is thought to be a good. Second, as to evil effects from the operation of natural causes. Here we must remember two things that we have seen. First, that every physical change necessarily involves the passing-away of something, else the new thing could not come to be; so some evil (loss) is necessarily included in every change. But change is for the sake of what comes to be. Second, we must also remember that causal changes can interfere with each other; this chance result is not intended by either of the causes, but rather is accidental. But since the physical evil that results from the action of natural causes is accidental, it remains true that every agent acts for a good.

The proper good is not always able to be obtained immediately; sometimes we must make use of other things, or engage in a series of actions, which are necessary in order that finally we may obtain the good that is desired. Objects or actions that are necessary or useful to obtain a proper good are called "means." By a *pure* means, we mean one that is not desirable for its own sake, but only for the good which it leads to; thus, an unpleasant medicine is sometimes good for a sick man—not that it is desired for itself, but because it is a means to recovering good health. Other things and actions not only are means to something else which is good, but are desirable also in themselves, such as a well-prepared meal. Means which are also good in themselves are often called "intermediate goals."

Since proper goods are proportioned to natures, and so differ as the natures differ, *good* in its unqualified sense will be predicated relationally and proportionally. Is it univocal or analogous? Natures not only differ, but what it means for one to have the perfection which is suited to it is quite different from what it means for another kind of nature. For example, a nature which has knowledge derives from the possession of its proper good pleasure or joy, whereas a nature without knowledge cannot be said to enjoy its goods; again, for man, the perfecting of his sensory nature is quite different from that of his rational nature.

Hence, *good* is analogous, and so it will be analogous with the analogy of proper proportionality. Means are proportioned to the goals; hence, they are analogously good by the analogy of proportion.

THE TRANSCENDENTAL GOOD

The purpose of this analysis of the proper, or unqualified, good, has been to help to clarify the question, Is being good? Obviously, this question cannot be asked about the proper good, since it is a fact of immediate experience that there are evils. We must therefore mean something different by *good*, and yet not simply and entirely different, or there would be no point in using the same term. What then have we found in analyzing the unqualified good? There are three parts to the description of this good: (1) There is some real, intrinsic perfection which is (2) suited, or proportioned to, (3) a tendency. In order that we can call something a proper good we must know something of the proper nature of the perfection and of the tendency. What happens to this understanding of *good* if we substitute "being" for "nature"? We recall that a thing is properly a *being* if it has the act of existing: being is that which is. Now, the act of existing, as an act, is a perfection. Hence, every being, as being, possesses at least this perfection: the act of existing. Moreover, we have also seen that the act of existing is the act of its own proper potency, namely, essence, and that every potency is ordered to, and proportioned to, its act. From this we can conclude that the act of existing is a good and that every being, as being, *has* a good.

Is this enough to enable us to say that every being, as being, is good?[23] Here we must recall what we saw earlier about the nature of agency and goal-directedness. Some beings have only transient activity; that is, their goals are all outside themselves; in other words, they do not act *for themselves*. But action follows being, as we also saw. Such beings, then, do not have any self-directed tendencies, and thus are not good as beings if they are considered by themselves in isolation from all other beings. Other kinds of being, living and cognitive beings, do have themselves

---

[23] On the transcendental good, see Selected Passages, No. 35.

and their own perfection among the goals which they act for; hence, they act for themselves, and thus can also be said to *be for themselves*. Living beings, even considered in an isolated way, are truly goods for themselves as beings. Cognitive beings, and especially intellectual beings, are for themselves—not for themselves as absolute goals, as we shall see, but still truly for themselves.

One of the ways in which this truth is made clearer is in the tendency of living things to continue in being. Plants and animals resist death in ways proportioned to their nature and will work very hard to keep themselves alive for their normal life span (whether this be a few hours or hundreds of years). Men resist death and try to avoid it; one's own death is feared and disliked; even those who commit suicide voluntarily do so under the impression that life for them is so joined with evils that they seem greater than the evil of death.

We have already seen that the material things we know form an interconnected dynamic whole; they act for the good of the universe as an on-going process. In this limited sense, these material beings are good, not in themselves as isolated, but in relation to the other material things. They are the objects of tendency with respect to each other. Moreover, in a general way, merely material things serve the needs and tendencies of the living and the cognitive beings, and this is another sense in which we can say that these beings are good.

But can we from this analysis say that *every* being is good? Could there not be somewhere a material thing, not a part of our universe nor a part of any other universe, which would not be the object of any tendency, have no transient action, and not be the object of any transient action? This is very difficult to show from the argument as we have so far seen it, and the easiest way to approach it is indirectly.

We have seen that God is by His essence; He is the pure and subsistent actuality of being. So it follows that He is absolutely perfect as being. Because He is an intelligent being, He also has an intellectual tendency, a will. It is only natural that His own infinite perfection should be an object of this intellectual tendency, since He is a living being, and, therefore, the infinite perfection of God is also infinite goodness.[24] "Infinite" goodness means goodness without limit, without flaw.

We have seen that God is the cause of the world by creation, through intellect and will. Because the things He makes are willed by Him, it follows that creatures can be named good through the analogy of eminence (and deficiency). Is the goodness of creatures as such merely an extrinsic denomination?[25] or is it also an intrinsic perfection? Recall that the relation in being between God and creatures is proved to be an *intrinsic* analogy of eminence in causality and, therefore, also the analogy of participation. Since God is good inasmuch as He is by His nature, whatever participates in being also and to that same degree participates in goodness. And since every being is either being by essence or being by participation, every being is good.

This answer to the question, "Is every being good?" has been a priori.[26] But it enables us to come back to the question we left unanswered: Could there be a being, purely material in its own nature and not part of any universe? We now see that this supposition is impossible, since creatures must be willed as *good* by their Creator; a material thing cannot be good unless it enters into activity, as we have seen;[27] and merely material things have only transient activity. Conversely, every being which is part of the universe, as part, is good.

Since all beings are good, persons also are (ontologically) good as beings. Being-lovable, being-loved, and being-perfective-of-

[24] Since the nature of God is identically the act of existing, the transcendental goodness of God is identically His proper goodness. And since God is an intelligent being, His proper goodness is also moral goodness. This identity of perfection is not found in any other being.

[25] "Extrinsic denominations" will be treated more fully later on, in secs. 109, and 110. Here, it will suffice to define *extrinsic denomination* as "a name and a conception truly applied to one being because of another." Hence, it is evident that an extrinsic denomination is not a real being: it does not designate an intrinsic or inherent perfection or act. It is an intelligibility.

[26] The a priori approach to transcendental goodness is not in conflict with the truth previously stated that we have no direct, immediate knowledge of God, that we know Him only through creatures. For in the a priori approach as it is used here, we do begin with an immediate experience; namely, the experience of proper goodness. From this, by way of analogy and negation, we proceed to find transcendental goodness in the fullness of being, which is also an object of tendency.

[27] See above, sec. 44.

others is the foundation for that mutual love which is friendship. It is likewise the basis for justice, especially for those parts of justice which are often overlooked, such as respect, allowing the other person freedom and equality of opportunity, and the like. Thus it is also the remote basis for society, as well as for the duty of giving good example.

What is the relation of the transcendental good to being? The transcendental good is being inasmuch as it is in act. Consequently, good is not something really distinct from being and added to being, but in the real order is identical with being itself. But the conception, *good*, is not identical with the conception, *being*, for the very intelligibility of *good* adds to being the relation to some tendency or appetite. Therefore, the transcendental good adds to being the relation to appetite and so is distinct from being by a minor distinction of reason.

The beautiful is similar to the good.[28] Among the many definitions of beauty that have been offered, the most useful preliminary one is the one which declares beauty to be the capacity of some being to satisfy (please) in being known. Because man has different powers of knowledge and different tendencies, there will be, descriptively, different kinds of beauty: sensible beauty (especially visual and auditory[29]), intellectual beauty, moral beauty. In all cases, it is the very knowing of the being which causes the pleasure, and thus it can be said that beauty includes both truth and goodness.

Just as the first good we come to know is the proper good, so the first beauty we recognize is proper beauty. And, as the proper good has an opposite, the evil, so proper beauty has an opposite, the ugly. Yet beauty is not a univocal quality: the beauty of a

[28] In an introductory book, the study of the beautiful must necessarily be brief. But as proper truth is studied in a special discipline, logic, and proper good, in ethics, so beauty is studied in aesthetics. For those students who wish to do further reading in the philosophical analysis of beauty, two books can be recommended: Jacques Maritain, *Creative Intuition in Art and Poetry* (New York, Meridian Books, 1960) and Etienne Gilson, *Painting and Reality* (New York, Pantheon Books, 1957).

[29] Sight and hearing are the two senses that can be used for the sake of knowing alone. The other senses tend to be subordinated to biological utility, and thus to prevent the perception of beauty.

sunset is not that of a tree; the beauty of a sun-drenched land-scape is not that of a statue; the beauty of a poem is not that of a symphony. It appears, therefore, that the beautiful is analogous with the analogy of proper proportionality. Since it is analogous, we cannot give a definition that is both adequate and fully determinate; we must be content with a vague and general one. If we look at the various objects which we call beautiful, we find these elements: an ordered multiplicity and a certain excellence of form and cognoscibility.

Is there also transcendental beauty? Is every being beautiful inasmuch as it is? Every being, inasmuch as it is a being, possesses actuality; all finite beings are made up of an ordered multiplicity of "parts" or principles—whereas God, Who is the simple actuality of existing, with regard to our knowledge of Him is a virtual ordered multiplicity of unified perfections; every being has at least some splendor of actuality, be it only the act of existing; and every being can be related to both knowledge and appetite, and in some way we can take pleasure in the knowledge of it. This is the a posteriori approach to transcendental beauty.

The a priori approach to transcendental beauty is richer and fuller. We find beauty in created things, and in them beauty is a perfection without any intrinsic limitation or imperfection. Hence, God, the creative cause of all being, must also be beautiful. And any perfection predicated of God must be predicated infinitely, without any limitation, and as identical with His essence and act of existing. Hence, God is subsistent beauty, beauty by essence, infinite beauty inasmuch as He is. Therefore, all His creatures, which are beings by participation, also possess transcendental beauty by participation. Therefore, every being is beautiful inasmuch as it is, either essentially or by participation.[30]

[30] There are also some analogous perfections (like life, knowledge, understanding, willing), which are similar to the transcendentals. These perfections are not strictly transcendental, for they are not found in all beings, and are not "properties" of being as being. Their similarity lies in their analogy. In its analogous sense, "life" is a special way of existing; knowledge, understanding, and willing are special ways of acting immanently. Note, however, that life, understanding, and willing are also used in univocal senses. These differences are explained in the philosophy of human nature.

93. Definitions

A transcendental is a "predicate" and a perfection which transcends all genera and differences.

Thing (as a scientific term in metaphysics) is that which has an essence or quiddity, and, only by implication, an act of existing.

Something is a thing which is distinct from other things.

A possible is something which could be or could have been.

A being of reason is an object (an essence or form) whose actuality is the act of being-understood, which, as such, cannot have an act of existing (in the proper sense of that term) but which is understood after the manner of a being.

An *intelligibility* (in Latin, *ratio*) is that which the intellect understands of the meaning of some term. (This is a purely descriptive definition.) In the strict sense, an intelligibility is neither a being of reason (for *what* is understood exists), nor a real being (for it does not exist in the way in which it is known).

The transcendental *one* is that which is actually undivided.

Simple is that which is undivided and undivisible, that which has no parts.

Whole or composite is that which is actually undivided but can be divided, that which has real parts.

Per se one is that which is one of itself, not by an external principle.

Per accidens one is that which is one by inherence.

Accidental one is that which is substantially many and is one by some distinct accident.

Logical truth is the conformity of the mind to the object.

Transcendental truth (ontological truth) is the conformity or the conformability of being to knowledge.

The *good* is that which is desirable. (This is the preliminary, descriptive definition.)

The proper good is some actuality or perfection in relation to the appetite of a certain *kind* of being.

Transcendental goodness is the actuality or perfection of a thing inasmuch as it is the object of some tendency.

Evil, taken concretely, is a being deprived of some particular good.

Evil, taken abstractly, is the privation of a particular good in a subject apt to have that good.

94. Proofs (to be completed)

A. Every being is one.
B. Every being is true.
C. Every being is good.

95. Readings

St. Thomas Aquinas, *Summa Theologiae*, Pt. I, q. 11, arts. 1 and 2 (on the meaning of transcendental unity and its relation to multiplicity), q. 76, art. 3 (on per se unity), q. 16, arts. 1–6 (on the various meanings of truth, its relation to being and to God), q. 17, arts. 1 and 4 (on falsity and its relation to truth), q. 5, arts. 1–5, q. 6, arts. 1-4 (on goodness, its relation to being; the goodness of God and of creatures), q. 37, art. 2 (on "quasi-forms"); Pt. I–II, q. 94, art. 2 (on the relationship of the various transcendentals, and the analytical [logical] priority of being); *On the Power of God*, q. 7, art. 11, ad 2 (on the order of the transcendentals to each other); *Truth*, q. 1, art. 1 (the meaning of truth), q. 21, arts. 1 and 2 (the meaning of good and its relation to being); *Contra Gentiles*, Bk. III, chaps. 18, 19, 20, and 24 (good and the will; relation between good and final cause); *Commentary on the Metaphysics of Aristotle*, Bk. X, lesson 1, Nos. 1920–1936, pp. 708–711 (on unity).

St. Augustine, *Confessions*, Bk. 10, chaps. 27, 33–34 (some passages on beauty).

Etienne Gilson, *Elements of Christian Philosophy* (New York, Doubleday, 1960), pp. 145–163.

Clifford G. Kossell, S.J., "Principles of St. Thomas's Distinction between the *Esse* and *Ratio* of Relation," *The Modern Schoolman*, XXIV (1946), 28–36; an excellent exposition of what is meant by an "intelligibility."

Jacques Maritain, *Art and Scholasticism*, trans. J. F. Scanlan (New York, Scribner's, 1930), pp. 23–38, 167–172, 161–166; the first two selections deal with beauty and its characteristics; the third with the perception of the beautiful.

Anton C. Pegis, "The Dilemma of Being and Unity," *Essays in Thomism* (New York, Sheed and Ward, 1942), 151–183; 379–382.

Gerald B. Phelan, "Verum Sequitur Esse Rerum," *Mediaeval Studies*, vol. I (1939), 11–22.

SELECTED PASSAGES FROM ST. THOMAS AQUINAS

31. Substance and Accident Contrasted with Beings of Reason

. . . the quasi-definition of "being" is "something having esse." But substance alone is that which subsists. Accidents, however, are called beings, not because they are, but rather because by them something is; as "whiteness" is said to be, because its subject is white. Hence, [Aristotle] says that accidents are not simply called beings, but beings of being, such as quality and motion.

Nor is it to be wondered at, that accidents are called beings though they are not beings simply, because even privations and negations are said to be somehow beings, as "not-white is," not because not-white has an act of existing, but because a subject is deprived of whiteness. This, therefore, is common to accidents and privations, that being is applied to them by reason of their subject. But they differ in this, that the subject has esse to some extent according to accidents, but according to privations it does not have esse in any sense, but rather is deficient in esse.

> *Commentary on Aristotle's* Metaphysics, Bk. XII, lect. 1 (ed. Cathala, Nos. 2419– 2420).

32. The Difference Between Being and Being-known

It is clear to anyone who carefully considers the arguments of Plato, that he arrived at his erroneous positions, because he believed that the manner of being of the thing understood is like the manner of understanding the thing . . . But this is not necessary. For even if the intellect understands things by this, that it is like to them as far as the intelligible species (by which it is put into act) is concerned; yet it is not necessary that this species be in the intellect according to the way in which it is in the thing understood. For everything which is in a subject, is, according to the manner of the subject in which it is. Therefore, on account of the very nature of the intellect, which is different from the nature of the thing understood, it is necessary that the mode of understanding by which the intellect understands be different from the mode of being by which the thing exists. For, though that which the intellect understands must be in the thing, it need not be there in the same way.

> *Commentary on Aristotle's* Metaphysics, Bk. I, lect. 10 (ed. Cathala, No. 158).

33. The Meaning of "Intelligibility"

There are three ways in which things are signified by words. For there are some things which according to their entire and complete being are outside the mind, and these are complete beings, like "man" and "stone." There are other things which in no way are outside the mind, like dream-objects and the image of a chimera. There are still other things which have a foundation in reality outside the mind, but the completion of their intelligibility, with regard to what is formal in them, is by the operation of the mind, as is clear in the universals. For "humanity" is something in reality, but does not have the nature of a universal, since there is no humanity common to many outside the mind. But in the way "humanity" is present in the intellect, there is joined to it an intention ["intention" here means "a note or characteristic added to the understood form 'humanity' because of the latter's relation to many things"], according to which it is called a species. Similarly, "time" has a foundation in motion—namely, what is before and after in the motion itself—but with regard to what is formal in time—namely, the measuring [of duration or motion]—it is completed by the operation of the intellect which measures. I make the same distinction with regard to truth. Truth has a foundation in the thing, but its intelligibility is completed by the action of the intellect—when, that is, the thing is apprehended in the way it is. Therefore, the Philosopher says [*Metaphysics*, Bk. VI, 1027b26] that the true and the false are in the mind, but good and evil are in things. Now, in the thing there are its essence and its esse; truth is founded rather on the esse of the thing than on the essence. As the name "being" is given to something from the act of existing, so in the operation of the intellect which takes the esse of the thing as it is (by becoming like to it), the relation of equality is completed, and the intelligibility of truth consists in this relation. Therefore, I assert that the very esse of the thing (as it is in the knowledge of the intellect) is the cause of truth.

> Commentary on the First
> Book of the Sentences, dis.
> 19, q. 5, art. 1.

An intelligibility (*ratio*), as it is taken here, is nothing other than that which the intellect understands of the meaning of some name. In those things which have a definition, the intelligibility is the definition itself, as the Philosopher says, "The intelligibility signified by the name is the definition" (*Metaphysics*, Bk. IV, 1012a25). But some things have an intelligibility in the present meaning of the term, which have no definition, as (for example) quantity and quality and similar things, which are not defined, because they are the most general genera. Yet, the intelligibility of quality is that which is signified by the name "quality," and this is that by which quality is quality. Hence, it makes no difference whether the things which are said to have an intelligibility have or do not have a definition. Thus, it is clear that the intelligibility of wisdom which is predicated of God, is that which is conceived as the meaning of this noun, although the Divine wisdom itself cannot be defined. Yet the noun *intelligibility* does not mean the conception itself, for this latter is signified by the noun "wisdom," or by some other name of a thing, but it signifies the intention of this conception, just as the noun *definition* signifies an intention, and so also other nouns of second imposition.

From this it is clear . . . how an intelligibility is said to be in reality. For this does not mean that the intention which we signify by the noun *intelligibility*, is in reality, nor even that the conception to which this intention applies is in reality outside the mind—since it is in the mind as in its subject—but it is said to be in the thing, inasmuch as in the thing outside the mind, there is something which corresponds to the conception of the mind, in the way in which that which is signified corresponds to its sign.

> *Commentary on the First Book of the* Sentences, dis. 2, q. 1, art. 3.
> Cf. *Responsio ad F. Joann. Vercellens. de art. 108,* a. 1.

34. The Transcendental "One"

"One" . . . is used in two senses. In one way, inasmuch as it is convertible with being, and thus, every thing is one by its essence . . . and "one" does not add anything to being except only the intelligibility of "being undivided." In the second way, "one" is used, inasmuch as it signifies the intelligibility of the first measure, either simply, or in some genus.

> *Commentary on Aristotle's* Metaphysics, Bk. III, lect. 12 (ed. Cathala, No. 501).

For "one" which is convertible with being designates being itself, adding the intelligibility of indivision, which, since it is a negation or a privation, does not posit any nature added to being. And thus "one" in no way differs from being in reality, but only in intelligibility. For negation and privation are not beings in the real order, but beings of reason.

> *Commentary on Aristotle's* Metaphysics, Bk. IV, lect. 2 (ed. Cathala, No. 560).

He says, therefore, that "one" is said to be per se and per accidens. And he shows that we must consider the per accidens one primarily in singular terms, and this in two ways. In one way, there is a per accidens one, according as an accident is compared with a subject; in the other way, according as one accident is compared with another. In both cases, there are three things to consider: one composite, and two simple principles. For if we take the one per accidens according to the comparison of an accident to a subject, we have, for example: first, Coriscus, second, "musically-inclined," third, "the musically-inclined Coriscus." And these three are one per accidens, for "Coriscus" and "musically-inclined" are one in subject. Similarly, when we compare an accident to an accident, there are three things: of which the first is "musically-inclined," the second "just," the third, the "musically-inclined, just Coriscus." And these examples are said to be one per accidens, but in different ways.

For "just" and "musically-inclined," which are the two simple principles in the second way, are called "one per accidens," because they happen to one subject. But "musically-inclined" and "Coriscus," which are the two simple principles in the first way, are called one per accidens, because "one of them," that is, "musically-inclined," happens to the other, that is, Coriscus.

Commentary on Aristotle's
Metaphysics, Bk. V, lect. 7
(ed. Cathala, Nos. 843–844).

35. The Transcendental "Good"

The good according to its proper intelligibility is a cause, in the way in which a goal is a cause. This is clear, because the good is that which all seek after. But that, to which an appetite [tendency] tends, is the end. Therefore, good, according to its proper intelligibility, is a cause after the manner of causing of an end.

Commentary on Aristotle's
Metaphysics, Bk. I, lect. 11
(ed. Cathala, No. 179).

36. Evil Is a Privation

"Evil," like "white," can be said in two ways. For, in one way, when we say "white," we can understand "that which is the subject of whiteness"; in a second way, "white" is "that which is white inasmuch as it is white," that is, the accident itself. In like manner, "evil" can be understood in one way as "that which is the subject of evil," and this is something. In another way, we can understand "evil itself"; this is not anything, but is the privation of something good.

To see this, we must realize that good, properly speaking, is "something inasmuch as it is appetible"; for, according to the Philosopher (Ethics, Book I), those philosophers gave an excellent definition of good who said, "Good is that which all seek"; evil, however, is said to be "that which is opposed to good." Therefore, it is necessary that evil is that which is opposed to the appetible as such. That which is opposed to the appetible as such cannot be something, for three reasons: First, because the appetible is an end, and the order of ends is like the order of agents. For, if an agent is higher and more universal, the end for which it acts is a more universal good, for every agent acts for an end and for a good. . . . Since in efficient causes there is no infinite regress—for we must arrive at one first agent which is the universal cause of being—it is necessary that there is some universal good to which all other goods are ordered. The reason is that, since the appetible moves the appetite, and the first mover must be unmoved, the first and universal appetible must necessarily be the first and universal good, which does all things because of its love of itself. Consequently, as whatever there is in the real order must derive from the first and universal cause of being, so, whatever there is in the real order must derive from the first and universal good. But that which comes from the first and universal good can only be a particular good, just as what comes from the first and universal cause of being is some particular being. Therefore, whatever is something in the real order must necessarily be some particular good. But that which is good cannot, inasmuch as it is, be opposed to good. Hence, finally, evil, inasmuch as it is evil, cannot be something in the real order, but is the privation of some particular good, inhering in some particular good.

The second reason demonstrates the same truth. Whatever is in the real order has some inclination and tendency toward that which is suited to it. But that which is appetible is thereby good. Therefore, whatever is in the real order is proportioned to some good. Evil, however, as such is not proportioned to good but rather is opposed to it. Therefore, evil is not something in the real order. But even if evil were some thing, it would have no tendency, nor be the object of any tendency; hence, it would have no action or change, because nothing acts or is moved except on account of the appetite for some good.

The third reason leads to the same truth. Being itself most especially is that which is desired. That is why we find that every thing naturally tends to conserve its being, and avoids what destroys it, and resists destruction as it is able. Therefore, being itself, inasmuch as it is appetible, is good. Therefore, it is necessary that evil which is entirely opposed to good is also opposed to the very act of being. But that which is opposed to the act of being cannot be something. Hence, I conclude that that which is evil itself is not something; that to which evil happens is something, inasmuch as evil deprives its subject only of some particular good (just as blindness itself is not something, but that to which blindness happens is something).

De Malo, q. 1, art. 1.

XI

The Predicaments: Substance and Supposit

96. The predicaments in general

To locate the present discussion, it will be helpful to consider in summary form the matter to be investigated in this and the following two chapters. The predicaments are *intelligibilities*[1] derived from being in its first and proper sense (or, "metaphysical being," "that-which-is"). Substance is derived by total abstraction, accidents by total and formal abstraction. With the exception of quantity and quality, the predicamental accidents also involve formalization. Each of these predicamental intelligibilities is considered as an entity, that is, as analogous to an individual real being. Thus, we can speak *predicamentally* of substance and its esse and accidents and their esse's, although in the real order there is but one esse of the substance together with its accidents. Hence, in relation to extramental beings, the predicaments are secondary analogates by the analogy of proportion. Among the predicaments—because in the real order accidents have esse only through substance, and predicamental accidents are by their nature modifications of substance—these accidents are secondary analogates of predicamental being; substance is the primary analogate of predicamental being.

The predicaments, or categories, are the highest (that is, the

[1] It may be advantageous to review sec. 88 on intelligibilities or to re-read Selected Passages, No. 33.

most general) classes of things known. From the point of view of
Aristotelian logic, all predicates are attributes. From the point of
view of grammar, predicates could be classified as substantive or
adjectival. But when we are studying the predicaments, we are
not studying the operation of our mind by which we join one
concept to another, much less the structure of verbal propositions.
Of course, both logic and grammar will be to some extent useful
tools. But we are going to investigate the various ways of determining the mode (or way) of being of things in relation to our
knowledge.[2] This consideration we shall call "predicamental
being."[3]

To facilitate our understanding of the predicaments (predicamental being) and to establish their place in metaphysics, it is
necessary to recall briefly some of the discoveries we have already
made about being. Being, in its first and proper sense, is that
which is, or any thing having an act of existing (esse). As evi-
denced by the existents of our experience, being in this primary
sense comprises two principles: the "that-which (-is)," or "thing-
principle" and the principle by which the thing exists, the "esse-
principle." This pair of principles—though not the first to be discovered—is the most basic potency-act correlationship of being.
In this correlationship, the thing-principle is, of course, potential,
and the esse-principle is its correlated act. Primarily, then, the
thing-principle is a whole principle which exists by its proper
esse. It is an entire individual of a definite kind with all its components and modifications and all its capacities.

As the existents of our experience show, the thing-principle is
itself a composite of various other principles, namely, matter and
substantial form and substance and accidents. These, as we have
seen, constitute other potency-act correlations within a being.
They are rightly called principles of being, precisely because they
are components of the entire thing-principle whose proper act is
esse. For this reason, too, they are rightly called beings according
to an analogy of composition. But, let us note, they are so called

[2] See also, Selected Passages, No. 38; this is an extremely important group
of texts.
[3] See Selected Passages, No. 37.

only by reference to being in its first and proper sense; that is to say, because they, as intrinsic principles, in some way contribute to the structure of being (in that sense).

Thus, we see that being, metaphysically taken, has many meanings. By analogy of composition the whole thing-principle and its intrinsic components are called beings. This whole thing-principle presents its complex make-up to us as follows: (1) The experienced thing presents itself as directly ordered to esse; and according to this presentation, it is called substance. As designating this presentation "substance" means "that to which esse belongs in itself." (2) The same thing-principle also presents itself as a principle of a certain kind, or essence (nature). Our understanding of this presentation involves both natural (total) abstraction and judgment (for example, "This is a man").[4] (3) The same thing-principle presents itself as basically composed of primary matter and substantial form. What this presentation involves has already been analyzed.[5] (4) The same thing-principle presents itself to us as intrinsically modified in various ways. These modifications are called accidents, and the thing-principle, inasmuch as it is a potency for these accidents, is called their substantial subject or, simply, their substance. A substance according to this presentation means "a subject of accidents." All these presentations of being are *metaphysical,* as has been indicated, and directly experiential.

Bearing these distinctions in mind, we are now in a position to consider the nature of predicamental being and its relation to metaphysical being, which we have just summarily considered. First of all, we should note that it is being in the sense of *thing-principle* (and so being by an analogy of composition) which furnishes the foundation of predicamental being. It is precisely the thing-principle *as a principle of being in its first and proper sense* that gives rise to the predicaments. This is the basic fact

---

[4] Men do not commonly perform acts of simple apprehension. Usually simple apprehensions are (virtual) parts or functions of judgments. Only a relatively sophisticated person makes simple apprehensions. On this point, see G. P. Klubertanz, *The Philosophy of Human Nature* (New York, Appleton-Century-Crofts, Inc., 1953), pp. 173–177.

[5] See above, secs. 41 and 42.

which gives the predicaments their rightful place in metaphysics.

From the thing-principle, as we have observed, we can by means of total abstraction obtain an intelligibility which we call an "absolute nature" (for example, man, horse, tree).[6] This absolute nature can be predicated of various individual existents. It expresses their substantial nature. Substance as obtained in this way and used as a predicate is called "predicamental substance" or "second substance." Predicamental substance, thus, is nothing else than any absolute substantial nature predicable of real individual existents.

Again, the thing-principle presents itself as modified in various ways. Some of these modifications pertain to it precisely as this individual, while others pertain to it by reason of its nature, or the *kind* of thing it is. These modifications are called accidents. By means of formal abstraction, we can consider these modifications (accidents) in themselves apart from any substance. Indeed, we can consider them *as if* they were substances (*per modum substantiae*); and it is precisely as considered in this way that they are placed in the predicaments. We will take up the consideration of accidents in some detail in the two following chapters.

Why is the analysis of the principles of being (as we made it, for example, in Chapter V) not sufficient? This analysis is sufficient to understand real things in the real order, but not sufficient to enable us to deal with them intellectually. In examining the structure of real things in the real order, we have found that the essence (the thing-principle, *that-which-is*), is composed of two principles, a principle by which the being is something having esse in itself (substance), and other principles (accidents) by which that something is variously modified. When we consider substance and accident as principles *by* which something has esse in itself and *by* which something is modified, we are trying to understand them according to the manner in which things exist. Such an understanding is difficult and roundabout—a fact which is manifested by the awkward circumlocutions necessary to express it. On the other hand, it is very easy to understand and deal

[6] See above, secs. 2, 23, and 42.

with these principles when they are conceived as things; in other words, it is easy to deal with the principles of things by means of intelligibilities. When we classify these intelligibilities according to what they represent, we have the predicaments. The predicaments, therefore, are conceived in the manner proper to the human understanding. Since what the predicaments intelligibly contain directly relates to the real order, they are "first intention" predicates.[7] But we must be careful not to confuse the manner in which they are conceived with the ontological mode of being which they ultimately signify.

One further general consideration is necessary. Because predicamental being is so called by an intrinsic analogy of composition to metaphysical being, it is traditional to ask about the principles of predicamental being. As we have seen, the analysis of metaphysical being can be partially represented in a diagram like the following:

$$\text{(metaphysical)} \quad \text{being} \begin{cases} \text{essence}^8 \begin{cases} \text{substance} \\ \text{accident} \end{cases} \\ \text{esse} \end{cases}$$

By an analogy of proportion—this time an extrinsic analogy, inasmuch as our mind *considers* predicamental being according to the model provided by extramental being—predicamental being is *considered* as composed in the following way:

---

[7] A "first intention" is a knowledge (concept, judgment, reasoning) about some object, either a real thing or something conceived after the manner of a real thing, and referring to the kind of existence proper to such an object. It is contrasted with "second intentions." A second intention is a knowledge about some object according as it is understood and referring to the kind of being that an object has in a mind, that is, to its intelligible nature as understood. A second intention is called "second," because we must first know an object before we can think about our knowledge of that object.

Among the second intentions there are the "predicables" spoken of in logic. The predicables are classes of predicates according to the intelligible relations they have to subjects. The predicables are genus, difference, species, property, accident. Because they are second intentions, the predicables are beings of reason.

[8] This is not the strict sense of *essence* but a wide one; see above, sec. 43.

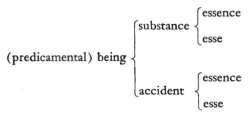

The similarity-in-difference between these two analyses has caused much confusion, and it will be necessary that we take great care in the discussion of both substance and accident. We will take up the point of the "esse" of predicamental being in detail in the next chapter. For the moment, however, let us carefully note that the understanding of substance as composed of essence and esse does turn out to be quite similar to the nature of metaphysical substance which has been made in this section. However, there are differences. Esse, as considered to be a principle of predicamental substance, is called "substantial esse," or "esse without qualification." Taken this way, substantial esse is an intelligibility, not an immediate principle of metaphysical being.

97. The division of the predicaments

A "thing" can share in being in ten basically different ways,[9] inasmuch as

it has being simply or substantially .... Substance
it has being in a qualified manner or accidentally ....
  on account of something intrinsic to the thing
    which is absolute
      and follows upon matter .... Quantity
      or follows upon form .... Quality
    or relative, that is, ordering one to another .... Relation
  or on account of something extrinsic to the thing
    partially
      of which the thing is principle .... Action
    or of which it is the term
      (that is, term of another's activity) .... Passion
    wholly extrinsic
      as measure of the thing
        according to time .... When
        according to place

[9] For a fuller presentation of the derivation of the predicaments, see Selected Passages, No. 39.

simply .... Where
considering also the order of
  the parts among themselves .... Situs
as joined to a thing according to
  some human purpose .... Habitus

To understand the predicaments in particular, it may help to look at some sample sentences employing the predicaments. The order of these examples will follow the order of the predicaments as given above. (1) "John Smith is a *man*"; "John Smith is *rational.*" (2) "My dog, Rover, is *large.*" (3) "The house is *white* and *square.*" (4) "John Doe is the *son* of Richard Doe." (5) "John Doe is *building* a house." (6) "This house is *being built* by John Doe." (7) "That manuscript is *ancient.*" (8) "Yesterday's storm was *local.*" (9) "The broken step is the *bottom* one." (10) "That man is warmly *clothed*"; "The work horses are *shod.*"

All the accidental predicaments are *denominations*,[10] that is to say, they are understood as expressing the subject (that which is) under some formal determination. They do not express a part or principle of the subject, for, if they did, they could not be predicated of the subject directly. But, though all the predicaments are understood after the manner of forms, in the thing itself they do not all have the same mode of being. Substance, as the principle by which the thing has subsistence, is a composite of matter and form. Quantity and quality, as principles by which a thing is quantified and qualified, are forms or at least quasi forms, which are inherent perfections of the thing itself. But the other predicaments, though also understood as forms, are not forms in themselves, though some of them are acts of, and inherent in, the subject, while others are more or less extrinsic to the thing which is.

98. Substance

Real being manifests itself to us in our experience as something which exists in itself and is variously modified, for example, "this brown horse." That principle of being, which we find in real being, by which that real being is (exists) *in itself* and not in another and which therefore can properly be said to be, is sub-

[10] On this point, see Selected Passages, No. 40.

stance. In all our experience of real beings, even if we understand no more about them than can be expressed in the words, "This is," we have already implicitly reached substance. For that which we designate by the word "this" exists in itself. We may be ignorant of, or mistaken about, what the substance is, but at least we know it as substance, implicitly. If someone were to imagine that he could directly experience an accident without experiencing substance, he would involve himself in a contradiction. For an accident is that principle of being to whose nature it belongs to be in another. Hence, to say, "We can experience that which is in another without experiencing the other in which it is," is a contradiction.[11]

Note that the word substance and its primitive meaning refer directly to "a permanent subject of accidental changes." But by reflection and analysis we see that this is a superficial description; we see that the ultimate subject of accidental change has to have an act of existing in itself, whereas not everything which is in itself necessarily has to be a subject of change. Hence, we define substance as that to whose nature it belongs to be in itself (not in another subject).

If we ask about the divisions or kinds of substance, substance can be divided in various ways. The substances we know are composite substances, made up of principles related to each other as act and potency (that is, matter and form); the contrary of composite substance would be simple substance, one not divisible into substantial principles or parts. The substances which are found in our immediate experience are material substances; the contrary of this would be spiritual substance which contains no matter. It would therefore be a simple, or incomposite, substance (for example, an angel).[12]

Sometimes writers on philosophy speak of complete and incom-

---

[11] If, by a miracle, in a particular case sensible qualities exist in quantity which has an act of existing after the manner of a substance, our experience is not thereby faulty, though we may make the mistake of *judging* that in this case quantity itself is in a subject (as is the nature of accidents). See below, sec. 105.

[12] Note however, that spiritual substance is not in the predicament of substance. When we say, "An angel is a substance," the term and conception substance is used analogously not univocally. See Selected Passages, Nos. 24 and 28.

plete substance; by complete substance they mean substance as we have been speaking of it; by incomplete substance they mean the substantial principles, matter and form. Finally, there is the distinction into "first" and "second" substance. "First" substance is the singular substance which exists as such in the real order (George Washington, the Charter oak). First substance is never a predicate; it is not in a subject but is the subject itself. (Grammatically, the subject of a sentence may be placed in a predicate *position;* but we are not talking about word order, we are dealing with the thing which is known and its intelligible function in a proposition.) "Second" substance is the substance which is a predicate (man, oak); it does not exist as such in the real order, for it is an absolute nature which is abstracted from individuality. It is called "second" substance, because it presupposes the existence of first substances in the real order of which it can be predicated.[13]

99. Supposit and person

First substance is not a predicament at all, because it is never a predicate. The first substance is the singular substance which exists. When we want to designate the being precisely as an existing, substantial, complete individual, we call it a "supposit." To stress the fact that the supposit is a complete individual, not something common to many (like second substance) or just a part (not an integral part, like a hand, or an essential part, like the body of a living thing), we say that the property of a supposit is "incommunicability."

N.B. Distinguish the supposit as spoken of in metaphysics (the incommunicable first substance) from the supposit spoken of in logic (the ultimate subject of predication). The supposit of logic is a second intention; it is considered as receiving predicates. The supposit in logic may be a thing (Peter, a tree); it may be a collection (three men, a flock); it may be an abstraction (humanity) or a being of reason (nothing).

The traditional definition of a supposit is "a distinct subsistent individual in a particular nature." The terms "distinct" and "individual" are used to exclude the communication of a nature to an

[13] See Selected Passages, No. 41.

individual or another supposit. The term "subsistent" is used to mean "something which exists with its own proper and proportionate act of existing." What then is the difference between an individual thing and a supposit? Ordinarily and naturally, an individual being has its own proper act of existing, even though there is a real distinction between the nature or essence and the act of existing. But the term "individual thing" only connotes an act of existing, while the term "supposit" explicitly means "having its own proper act of existing." A technical term sometimes used for "supposit" is the word "hypostasis."

The supposit in a rational nature has a special term, namely, "person." A person, therefore, from the point of view of metaphysics, is a "rational supposit," that is, "a distinct subsistent individual in a rational nature." Personality, therefore, namely, that (quasi form) by which a person is precisely a person, is the proper act of existing proportioned to a rational nature. In other words, a human being is a person by having his own act of existing.

N.B. Distinguish this metaphysical meaning of person and personality from the everyday and psychological meanings of those terms. The everyday meanings can easily be found in a dictionary. The meaning of "personality" in the science of psychology can be expressed thus: "the sum total of knowledge, attitudes, habits, ways of acting, and so forth, formed into a single pattern."[14]

100. Digression on the backgrounds of the problem of personality

Why distinguish between a person and an individual rational nature, since as was said above the individual nature of a being ordinarily and naturally has its own proper act of existing? Historically, the problem arises from a theological consideration. According to Christian theology, Jesus Christ is a Divine Person (namely, the Second Person of the Blessed Trinity), who became man without ceasing to be God; in other words, he assumed a human nature. Obviously, Christ did not assume universal human nature but a singular human nature, as singular and sensible as

[14] Cf. Francis L. Harmon, *Principles of Psychology* (Milwaukee, Bruce, 1951), pp. 595–597.

that of any mere man. But in becoming a man, Christ remained a Divine Person; hence, it cannot be said that Christ was a *human* person, for then he would be two persons, one of which was God, the other an ordinary man. Hence, there is one case of a singular, individual human nature, with an act of existing, and this nature is not a human person. Our theological explanation of this is that the Divine Person supplies the esse to the human nature; hence, Christ's human nature exists, but not with the esse proper to such a nature. This theological explanation is in harmony with the analysis of nature and personality that has been given above. (However, other theological explanations are current; from this fact alone we can see that faith [and theology] does not determine the solution given to the problem, though it has historically provided the impetus for its investigation.)

101. Definitions

Predicamental being is the thing-principle of extramental (metaphysical) being considered as a whole in relation to our knowledge. It is divided into the ten predicaments. (The thing-principle is "that-which [-is]"; it is "being" by an analogy of proportion to metaphysical being.)

Metaphysical being is being in its first and proper sense: "that-which-is."

A *predicament* (category) is one of the highest classes or genera of things known. For example, substance, quantity, quality.

A predicable is a predicate considered precisely as predicated, according to its relationship to the subject. It is a second intention. For example, "man as a species."

A substance is that by which a being has esse in itself. (This is a definition of substance as a principle of metaphysical being.)

A substance is that which properly and in the first place is said to be. (This is a definition of predicamental substance.) For example, "John is a *man*."

An accident is that by which a being exists in some modified way. (This is a definition of accident as a principle of metaphysical being.)

An accident is that whose being is inherence (in a subject). (This is a definition of predicamental accident.)

First substance is the singular existing substance.

Second substance is the absolute nature which is predicated as substance.

A supposit is a distinct, subsistent individual in a particular nature, whose property it is to be incommunicable.

A person is a rational supposit.

Personality, that by which a human individual is a person, is the proper act of existing proportioned to a human nature.

Hypostasis is another name for supposit or person.

102. Readings

St. Thomas Aquinas, *Summa Theologiae*, Pt. I, q. 3, art. 6 (substance and accident in creatures and in God), q. 29, arts. 1 and 2 (the meaning of "person"), q. 50, art. 1 (the nature of a pure form), q. 30, art. 4 (how the term "person" is said of the Persons in God); Pt. III, q. 2, art. 2 (the Hypostatic Union), q. 17, art. 2 (Christ as one being according to esse); *On Being and Essence*, chap. 2, par. 1–3 (meaning of "essence" in sensible things); *On the Power of God*, q. 2, art. 2, ad 2 (relation of one predicament to another), q. 7, art. 3 (on substance and genus); *Commentary on the Metaphysics of Aristotle*, Bk. IV, lesson 1, Nos. 546–547, pp. 219–220; Bk. VI, lesson 1, Nos. 1245–1269, pp. 488–494 (on substance and accident).

Ralph B. Gehring, S.J., "The Knowledge of Material Essence According To St. Thomas Aquinas," *The Modern Schoolman*, vol. XXXIII (1956), 153–181.

Etienne Gilson, *Spirit of Mediaeval Philosophy*, trans. A. H. C. Downes (New York, Scribner's, 1936), pp. 191–206.

Andrew J. Reck, "Substance, Language and Symbolic Logic," *The Modern Schoolman*, vol. XXXV (1958), 155–171.

William A. Van Roo, S.J., "A Study of Genus," *The Modern Schoolman*, vol. XX (1943), 89–104, 165–181, 230–244.

SELECTED PASSAGES FROM ST. THOMAS AQUINAS

37. The Meaning of "Predicamental Being"

The term "being," inasmuch as it signifies the thing to which esse belongs, thus signifies essence, and is divided into the ten kinds. But it is not divided univocally, since esse does not belong to all these kinds in the same way, but it belongs to substance per se, to the other, in other ways.

Quodlibet II, art. 3.

"Being" which is divided by the ten predicaments signifies the natures of the ten kinds according as they are in act or in potency.

Commentary on Aristotle's
Metaphysics, Bk. X, lect. 3
(ed. Cathala, No. 1982).

38. Predicamental Being Compared with Being-known

Being is used in two ways [St. Thomas does not say *only* two]. . . . In one way it signifies the essence of a thing, and is divided into the ten predicaments. . . . In another way, it signifies the truth of a composition.

Contra Gentiles, Bk. III,
chap. 9.

Being is used in two ways. In one way it signifies the nature of the ten predicaments, and in this sense neither evil nor any other privation is "being" or "something." In another way [it signifies] the answer to the question, "Is it?" and in this sense evil is, as also blindness is.

De Malo, q. 1, art. 1, ad 19.

Being is used in two ways. In one way, it signifies the entity [*entitas*] of a thing, as it is divided into the ten predicaments, and in this sense it is coextensive with "thing." In this sense, no privation is a being, and consequently neither is evil. In another way, being signifies the truth of a proposition which consists in a composition, whose characteristic note is the verb *is*, and this is the being with which we answer the question, "Is it?" Thus, we say that blindness is in the eye . . .

Summa Theologiae, Pt. I,
q. 48, art. 2, ad 2.

39. The Derivation of the Ten Predicaments

Being is divided into the ten predicaments, not univocally, as a genus is divided into species, but according to a different way of being. But the ways of being are proportional to the ways of predicating. For when we predicate one thing of something else, we say, "This is that," and so the ten kinds of being are called ten predicaments.

Predication is done in three ways. The first way is, when something pertaining to the essence of a thing is predicated of a subject, as when I say, "Socrates is a man," or, "Man is an animal," and in this way there is the predicament of substance. The second way is that by which something, which is not of something's essence, but inheres in it, is predicated of that thing. That which inheres either pertains to the matter of the subject, and thus there is the predicament of quantity, for quantity properly follows upon matter. . . . Or, that which inheres follows the form, and thus there is the predicament of quality. Therefore, the qualities are founded upon quantity, as color on surface, and figure on lines or surfaces. Or, that which inheres is with regard to another, and thus there is the predicament of relation. For when I say, "Man is a father," nothing absolute is predicated of man but a regard [respect], which is in man to something outside him. The third way of predicating is, when something extrinsic to that thing is predicated of it after the manner of a denomination. For it is as denominations that the intrinsic accidents are predicated of substance; we do not say, "Man is whiteness," but, "Man is white."

But to be denominated from something extrinsic is found to some extent commonly in all things, and to some extent especially in those which pertain only to man. Now, something is commonly denominated from something extrinsic, either according to the intelligibility of cause, or according to that of measure (for something is denominated "caused" and "measured" from something extrinsic). Since there are four kinds of causes, two of them, that is, matter and form, are parts of the essence. Consequently, the predication which takes place according to these two principles, pertains to the predicament of substance; for example, if we say, "Man is rational," and "Man is corporeal." But the final cause does not cause anything separately from the agent. For the end is a cause, inasmuch as it moves the agent. Therefore, there remains only the efficient cause from which something can be denominated as from something extrinsic. Thus, therefore, inasmuch as something is denominated from the agent, there is the predicament of passion, for "to undergo" [*pati*] is nothing other than to receive something from an agent. But, conversely, according as something is denominated an agent from an effect, there is the predicament of action. For action is the act from the agent in something else, as was said above.

A measure may be extrinsic or intrinsic. An intrinsic [measure], for example, is the proper length of something, or its width, or depth; from these, therefore, something is denominated as from an intrinsic inherent, and so they pertain to the predicament of quantity. But the extrinsic measures are time and place. Inasmuch as something is denominated from time, there is the predicament "when"; and inasmuch as something is denominated from place, there are the predicaments "where" and "situs" (which adds to "where" the order of parts in place). (But such a distinction was not necessary with regard to time, since the order of parts in time is involved in the very intelligibility of time, for time is the numbering of motion according to the prior and the posterior.) Thus, therefore, something is said to be *when* or *where* by denomination from time or place.

Finally, there is a special denomination with reference to men. For in other animals, nature has sufficiently supplied the things which

pertain to the preservation of life, such as horns for defence, a thick
and hairy hide for covering, claws for cutting without being hurt, and
so on. And so, when such animals are said to be armed or clothed or
shod, in a way they are not denominated from something extrinsic,
but from some of their parts. Consequently, these predicates are referred in them to the predicament of substance, as if we were to say
that "Man is handed," or "footed." But such parts could not be given
to man by nature, both because they are not suited to the delicacy of
his bodily constitution, and because of the many kinds of activities
which are suitable to man inasmuch as he possesses reason, to which
determined instruments could not be adapted by nature. But in
place of all such instruments, man has reason, by which he prepared
exterior things for himself, in place of the parts which animals have
intrinsically. Hence, when man is said to be armed, or clothed, or
shod, he is denominated from something extrinsic, which does not
have the intelligibility of a cause nor of a measure. Hence, this is a
special predicament, and is called "habitus." But it is to be noted, that
this predicament is attributed to other animals, not as they are considered in their nature, but as they come into human use, as if we say
that "A horse is trapped, or saddled, or armed."

Commentary on Aristotle's
Physics, Bk. III, lect 5.

40. The Predicaments as Denominations

[Aristotle] says that there must be something of which all forms are
predicated, on the condition that we understand this subject . . . to be
a different quiddity and essence.

We must note that what has just been said is not to be understood
of univocal predication according to which genera are predicated of
the species which are defined by the genera. For "animal" and "man"
[as predicated of each other] are not essentially distinct. But we must
understand this of denominative predication, as when "white" is
predicated of "man." For "white" and "man" are essentially distinct.

. . . denominative predication, in the way in which accidents are
predicated of substance. For this proposition, "Man is white," is true,
but not, "Man is whiteness," nor "Humanity is whiteness." In the same
way, the proposition, "This material thing is a man," is true, but not,
"Matter is man," nor, "Matter is humanity." The very fact of concrete
or denominative predication shows, that, as substance is essentially
distinct from accidents, so matter is essentially distinct from substantial forms.

*Commentary on the Seventh
Book of the* Metaphysics, lect.
2 (ed. Cathala, Nos. 1287–
1289).

41. The Meaning of "Substance"

And first he posits that there are said to be substances existing in the real order, some of which are admitted by all, namely, the sensible substances, such as the earth and the water and other elements, and likewise, according to the order of nobility and perfection, plants and animals and their parts, and finally the heavens, and their parts. . . .

He posits the ways of taking "substance" according to the acceptance of reason. . . . one of which is that "substance" is called the quiddity of some natural substance and this is nothing other than the whatness of a natural thing.

> Commentary on Aristotle's Metaphysics, Bk. VIII, lect. 1 (ed. Cathala, Nos. 1683–1684).

"Substance" is used in two senses. In one way, it means the supposit in the genus of substance, which is called "first substance" and "hypostasis," to which it properly belongs to subsist. In the other way, substance means "what a thing is," which is also called the nature of the thing. . . . Therefore it is said in the *Predicaments*, that second substances, which are genera and species, do not mean "this something," which is a subsisting substance, but they mean "what sort of a thing," that is, a nature in the genus of substance.

Thus, therefore, the Philosopher proved above, that "one" and "being" do not signify a substance which is this something, but we must seek for something which is one and being. In the same way, we seek something which is man or animal, like Socrates or Plato. Finally, he showed that these terms signify the natures of the things of which they are predicated, and not something else added like accidents. For in this, the common terms differ from accidents, though it is common to both common terms and accidents not to be this something, because common terms signify the very nature of supposits; but accidents do not, but rather they signify some added nature.

> Commentary on Aristotle's Metaphysics, Bk. X, lect. 3 (ed. Cathala, Nos. 1979–1980).

XII

Accidents in General;
Quantity and Quality

103. The nature of accidents

The investigation of predicamental accident is a further development of our study of predicamental being. To help us to locate this study properly we will summarily reconsider what we already know about accidents.

The thing-principle of (metaphysical) being designates the whole individual which possesses the act of existing. This thing-principle manifests itself as a substance inasmuch as an existent is a whole directly ordered to esse, is of a certain kind, can be subject to changes and modifications. Again, the thing-principle manifests itself as modified in various ways, some of which come and go, others of which are permanent; some of which pertain to the individual as such, others of which belong to the individual because of the kind of thing it is. These modifications are called "accidents." An accident, then, is that which is in another as in a real subject, *by which* that subject is (not simply, but) in a modified way; the proper character of accident is that of a real principle *by which* the thing-principle of finite being is constituted; this principle is really distinct from its coprinciple, substance.[1]

Secondly, accident is a direct principle of predicamental being. As we have seen briefly,[2] the analysis of predicamental being gives us the division into predicamental substance and predica-

[1] See above, secs. 39 and 40.
[2] See above, sec. 96.

mental accident. Predicamental substance is the absolutely considered nature according to which a real individual thing exists in
itself. Predicamental accident is a denomination predicable of
real individual existents because of the modifications which these
existents manifest to us. As a denomination, the predicamental
accident is taken *concretely;* for example, "white," "tall." The
concrete accidents implicitly include their subjects; for example,
"white" implicitly includes (some) subject. But by formal abstraction, we can consider the accident without its subject; for
example, "whiteness," "tallness." In this abstraction, we use a
manner of understanding and speaking about the abstracted accident *as if* it were a substance and a real thing (*per modum substantiae*).[3]

Hence, accidents can be thought about predicamentally and
spoken of in two ways. (1) Taken concretely, as direct predicates
(for example, "white"), all the accidents are predicated as forms
inhering in a subject. Taken in this way, they implicitly include
the subject. (2) Taken abstractly (for example, "whiteness"),
the accidents no longer include the subject. Because the concrete
accident explicitly includes the accident and implicitly includes
the substance, it is a compound (a *per accidens* unit)[4] that cannot be placed in any predicament. Only the abstract accident
can be placed in a predicament (for example, of quantity, of
quality). As abstract, the accidents are not predicated directly of
any subject but only indirectly (*in obliquo*). For example, we
predicate a concrete accident directly when we say, "John is
short"; but to predicate the abstract accident of John, we must
add a word which relates the accident to him, as, "John has short-
ness." But note that when we think of an abstract accident in
itself or use it as an indirect predicate, we deal with it as if it
were a substance or thing.

The predicamental accidents are understood as forms and dealt
with after the manner of substances. Consequently, we also refer
an essence and an act of existing to them, and we designate this
act of existing as an "accidental esse." As we saw above, being in
its first and proper sense is constituted by the two principles of

[3] On this point, see Selected Passages, No. 44.
[4] See above, sec. 89.

esse and essence, and the latter in turn is constituted by substance and accident. We also saw that predicamental being is analogously divided first into substance and accident and that these principles, in turn, are divided into substantial essence (essence in the strictest sense) and substantial esse, and accidental essence and accidental esse.[5]

Predicamental being is divided into substance and accident. Of these two principles, substance is being by itself, or by essence. Hence, when we are strictly speaking of predicamental substance as a principle of predicamental being, its substantial esse is our way of considering it as real. Thus, "man" is a predicamental substance; if we want to assert it as real, we say, for example, "Man is a substance or a nature." (This is per se predication.) Therefore, we can consider substantial essence and substantial esse as merely different considerations, for substance is predicamental being by itself.

But predicamental accident is not being by itself. By itself, or by its essence, the predicamental accident is abstract, and, as abstract, it cannot truly be signified to be—it is not true that "Whiteness is" all by itself. We can say, "Whiteness is," only inasmuch as it is related to, and dependent upon, substance; that is, it is true that "Whiteness is" only in the sense that "Some things are white by whiteness." Hence, predicamental accident *is said to be*, not simply but secondarily, in dependence upon substance. Of itself, it is not predicamental being, but it shares in the esse which is attributed to substance. From this point of view, accident is (predicamental) being analogously by the analogy of participation.[6] Therefore, it is also true that the accidental

[5] See the diagram above, sec. 96; see also, Selected Passages, No. 43.

[6] The analogy of participation in predicamental being is somewhat different from the analogy of participation in being in its proper sense. When we say, "God is being by essence, creature is being by participation," we mean that God's being and the creatures' being are really distinct. When we say, "Substance is predicamental being by essence, accident is predicamental being by participation," we do not attribute the same kind of distinct being to the accident as the substance has. Nevertheless, the *manner* of predication is the same.
Because many Thomists have not distinguished between being in its proper sense and predicamental being, they have said that substance and accident are analogous according to the analogy of proper proportionality (substance is to its esse as accident is to its own esse). It is true that there

esse is a completely different intelligibility from that of the
accidental essence. The essence of an accident is the particular
kind of modification it is;[7] its esse is an "inesse" or an inherence
in a subject.[8] Thus, when we want to give the formal definition
of a real accident, we begin by saying, "That which . . ." even
though in the real order an accident is not a being or even a thing.
Only the modified being properly exists, and the modification is
a principle *by which* something is in some way or other. Further,
the *is* which is attributed to the abstracted accident in its definition is not an existential act in the proper sense, for, if it were,
the abstract accident would be a being in the real order.[9] When
we understand an abstracted accident after the manner of a substance (for example, "whiteness"), and wish to signify that
accident as real, we *attribute* the act of existing to it. What does
this attribution rest on? It rests on the fact that for an accident to
be real in the way corresponding to its nature, it must be united to
an existing thing as act to the potency which is substance, and by
that union the accident "has" an act of existing, namely, the act
of existing of the being whose modification it is.

Because an accident does not have its own proper distinct act
of existing, it is not a being in the proper and first sense of that
word. St. Thomas sometimes says that an accident is not a being
but pertains to being (*magis entis quam ens*—it is rather *of* a
being than a being) and that it can be called "the being of a
being" (*ens entis*).

---

are several reasons for making this mistake. First, as we shall see, there is no
other way in which we can *signify* an accident as real except by attributing
to it an esse—we say, "It *is*"; but what is the meaning of "is" in this usage?
Secondly, there is a perfectly correct way in which we can speak of an
"accidental esse," as we shall also see; but the fact that we *consider* accidental
esse as other and distinct from substantial esse is not by itself a proof that
there are two varieties of existential act. Only a latent Platonism will attribute to the real order all the structures and distinctions found in the mind.

In the properly metaphysical way of understanding accident, the abstract
accident (for example, "whiteness") has no existential act at all; the concrete
accident (for example, "white") includes in its meaning the subject of
existential act and so "has" an existential act, not of itself but by reason of
the subject which is included.

[7] On the meaning of *essence* in accidents, see Selected Passages, No. 43.
[8] See also, Selected Passages, No. 45.
[9] Cf. Selected Passages, No. 42.

Note that accident is first of all an "addition" to substance in the order of essence. We can, as we have seen, talk of an "accidental esse" to indicate that a particular accident is modifying some thing which actually is. We can even say that the "accidental esse" adds to the substantial esse of a thing. To be learned is to have more being than to be without learning, though learning is "only" an accident. What we should understand by such expressions is not that another really distinct act of existing has been added to the act of existing of the substance but that the act of existing of the man (taken concretely in the real order) has now been extended, enlarged to be the act not only of the substance but also of the modification "learning." This is merely a particular application of the theorem, "Act and potency are proportioned to each other." If that-which-is (substance + accidents) is really more than it was before, then the act of existing is really more than it was, not in reference to itself but in reference to the increase of the potency whose act it is.

If we keep this in mind, we will not be tempted to think of accident and substance in terms of a pin and pincushion or of clothes and the man. An accident is really distinct from the substance, but it combines with the substance to form a composite subject (that-which-is) for the unique act of existing. Hence, an accidental modification of a being may be a profound modification of the very act of existing of that being (for example, moral goodness is "only" an accident).

As we shall see when we begin to consider the various accidents in particular, "accident" is an analogous term. The intelligibility (*ratio*)[10] of accident is that of a form, and even of a substantialized form. But this intelligibility "after the manner of a form" is not a mirror image of reality. The different accidents each realize this intelligibility differently. We shall see this more clearly as we go on, but it is necessary to be forewarned, lest a univocal notion of accident creep in.

104. Quantity and quality

To consider quantity in itself, what it is, what are its properties, and so on, belongs to the philosophy of nature. We are interested

---

[10] On the meaning of "intelligibility," see above, sec. 88.

in quantity only to the extent that it is a principle of being. By quantity we mean here "continuous quantity" or extension. There is another kind of quantity, namely, discrete quantity. (Discrete quantity is number, whose consideration belongs entirely to the philosophy of nature.) Continuous quantity or extension is defined as "that which has parts outside of parts" (this is a definition of the *abstract* accident, quantity).

The first question that arises is that of the distinction between matter and quantity. There seem to be no unequivocal instances of a change in quantity while the matter remains constant; hence we are not able to use the argument for a real distinction based on a real change. Moreover, matter does not exist without quantity, and quantity is not naturally found as an existing being without matter. It seems that the only way to approach this question on a philosophical basis is that of a deduction from the princples of act and potency. If we go back to the original evidence from which we found that there is a distinct substantial principle called primary matter, we recall that primary matter is the common, determinable element or principle in substantial change. It is, therefore, pure potency in the order of essence. Now, what is the nature of quantity? It is in potency to division, but of itself it is actually "spread out," such that in relation to place one part is here and another there. Therefore, quantity is an act. Hence it cannot be really identical with matter but must be really distinct from matter. On the other hand, by its nature as extension, it presupposes some substance, for the parts which are outside of other parts must be parts of something; they cannot *just* be parts (although they can be abstractly understood in that way). Therefore, quantity is an accident. Quantity is in a subject, or "inheres in" a subject, and can be correctly described as an intrinsic modification of a substance. Moreover, quantity is to be found in all the things of our experience, and all these things are material; hence quantity has an intimate connection with matter.

In relation to other accidents of material things, quantity is the basic accident. It is obvious that quantity is presupposed for the accidents of time and place, *situs* and *habitus*. It is also presupposed for qualities like color (which is a modification of a surface), figure, hardness, softness, and the like, and for the actions and passions of material things, as we can see from a rapid glance at some of them (for example, chemical activities).

The qualities of material things are generally considered to belong to four classes: shape and figure (which are "qualities of quantity"), power (and the lack of it), habit and disposition, and passions (that is, the affections of things which are changed, such as hot or cold, as well as such modifications which are similar to dispositions but are completely temporary, as blushing). These various accidents are similar in that they all designate some way in which a real thing is over and above its substantial determination. All of them presuppose a subject; that is, there must be something which is shaped, has power, has acquired a habit, and so forth. Any of them can be appropriately pointed out in answer to the question, "What sort of thing is it?" (hence the name quality, derived from the Latin interrogative pronoun or adjective *qualis* which means "what sort of?"). Thirdly, all of these various accidents are similar in that (*a*) they modify a substance absolutely or in itself, that is, not in relation to some other things, and (*b*) they can be directly conceptualized and defined. Hence, qualities are "formal accidents," that is, the analogy between form and matter on the one side and quality and substance on the other is very close from the point of view of the ways in which they are understood, and, as we have seen, the way in which these principles are understood is an essential characteristic or property of a predicament.

105. Digression: the substance-accident distinction and the theology of the Eucharist

A Catholic has a particular interest in this doctrine, because it is very closely related to the theology of the Eucharist. Revelation tells us that the apparent bread and wine of this sacrament are the Body and Blood of Christ. Theologians say that the accidents of what was the bread and wine exist, by the power of God, without inhering in their natural subjects.

It is of course important to remember that the distinction between substance and accident was first stated by Aristotle, obviously in entire ignorance of the revelation to come. So it is a purely philosophical doctrine. Secondly, it is important to see that the distinction of substance and accident does not "explain," or make the sacrament "easy" for God. This much is true: if we were to assert the identity of substance and accident, the revelation would be unintelligible.

106. Definitions

Accident is that by which a being exists in some modified way, that whose nature is to be in another, as in a subject.

Quantity is that by which a material substance has parts outside of parts.

Quality is the accident which modifies the manner of existing of a being.

107. Readings

James S. Albertson, S.J., "The *Esse* of Accidents According to St. Thomas," *The Modern Schoolman*, XXX (1953), 265–278; a textual study showing that accidents do not have a natural proper existential act really distinct from the existential act of the rest of the being.

St. Thomas Aquinas, *Summa Theologiae*, Pt. I, q. 3, art. 6 (substance and accident in creatures and in God), q. 54, art. 3 (the distinction between substance and accident even in angels), q. 77, art. 1 (including the arguments and their answers; the distinction between the substance of the soul and its accidents); Pt. III, q. 75, art. 5 (on the accidents of the Eucharist); Pt. I–II, q. 53, art. 2, ad 3 (the difference between the concrete and abstract accident); *Truth*, q. 3, art. 7, ad 2 (concrete and abstract accidents); *On the Power of God*, q. 7, art. 7, par. 1 (substance and accident as beings); *Commentary on the Metaphysics of Aristotle*, Bk. V, lessons 10, 15, 16, 17, Nos. 898–905, 977–1032, pp. 348–350, 374–389 (on the categories).

Clifford G. Kossel, S.J., "Principles of St. Thomas's Distinction Between the *Esse* and the *Ratio* of Relation," *The Modern Schoolman*, XXIV (1947), 93–99; this section is a very fine explanation of accident considered as a predicament.

SELECTED PASSAGES FROM ST. THOMAS AQUINAS

*42. Proper Being, Predicamental Being,
and Being Which Is Truth*

Is is said in three ways. The first way is that in which it signifies the truth of a proposition and is a copula; and in this sense . . .

"being" is an accidental predicate, and this "is" is not in the thing but in the mind which joins a predicate with its subject. . . . A second way is that in which we speak of the esse which pertains to the nature of the thing which is divided into the ten predicaments; and this esse is in the thing, and is the act of being resulting from the principles of the thing, as "lighting" is the act of "that which shines." Sometimes [in a third way] esse means essence, or that according to which a thing is.

> Commentary on the Third
> Book of the Sentences, dis.
> 6, q. 2, art. 2.

43. Essence with Respect to Substance and Accident

Simply and in the first sense, only substances are defined, and only substances have an essence. . . . But in a qualified sense, and secondarily, other things also can be defined. For substance, which absolutely has a quiddity, does not depend in its quiddity on another. But accident depends on a subject, although the subject is not of the essence of an accident, just as the creature depends on the creator, and yet the creator is not of the essence of the creature, so that it would be necessary to place an exterior essence in its definition. But accidents do not have esse except by this that they are in a subject, and thus their quiddity depends on a subject; and for this reason it is necessary that the subject be placed in the definition of the accident, sometimes indeed in the nominative, sometime in an oblique case.

The subject is used in the nominative case, when the accident is signified as an accident concretely with a subject, as when I say, "Snub is a concave nose." For then "nose" is placed in the definition of "snub" as if it were a genus, to indicate that the accidents do not have subsistence except from a subject. But when the accident is signified in the abstract, after the manner of a substance, then the subject is placed in the definition of the accident in an oblique case, like a difference, as it is said, "Snubness is the concavity of the nose."

> Commentary on Aristotle's
> Metaphysics, Bk. VII, lect.
> 4 (ed. Cathala, Nos. 1352–
> 1353).

44. Difference Between the Way of Knowing and the Way of Being

A great mistake is made about forms, for the reason that many judge about them as they judge about substances. This seems to happen because in the abstract forms are signified after the manner of substances, as whiteness, virtue and so forth. Hence, some, following the manner of speaking, judge about them as if they were substances.

On the Virtues in General,
art. 11.

45. Existential Act and Predicamental Being; the Relation of Substance and Accident to Existential Act

"Esse" taken in its second meaning is "the act of being inasmuch as it is a being," that is, by which something is denominated actually a being in the real order, and in this meaning, esse is attributed only to those things which are contained in the ten genera. Consequently, "being," which is denominated from this esse, is divided by the ten genera. But this esse is attributed to something in two ways. In one way, [it is attributed] as to something which properly and truly has esse, or is, and in this way it is attributed only to substance subsisting by itself. For this reason, that which truly is, is called substance in the first book of the *Physics*. But all those things which do not subsist by themselves, but are in another and with another, whether they are accidents or substantial forms or any parts whatsoever, do not have esse so that they themselves truly are, but esse is attributed to them. In the second way, [esse is attributed to something] as to that by which something is, as "whiteness" is said to be, not because it itself subsists in itself, but because by it something has "a being white."

Quodlibet IX, art. 3.

XIII

The Formalized Accidents

108. Relation

So far we have considered the predicaments of substance, quantity, and quality, which are similar in that they designate the subject in itself. The remaining predicaments, relation, action, passion, when, where, situs, and habitus, all refer to the subject but either directly or indirectly include a reference to something else. There predicaments will now be taken up in some detail.

The dictionary defines "relation" as the mode (or way) in which one or more things stand to another or others. In this definition, the word "things" is taken in a very wide sense to include not only real things, but anything conceived or understood after the manner of a thing. It can also be defined as the order or respect (as in the phrases, "in regard to," "in respect of") of one to another. In some cases, the whole reality of one thing is referred to another, such that the relation is really the same as that which is related. For example, the whole reality of potency lies in its order to act; so, too, matter is real inasmuch as it is the capacity of receiving form, essence is real inasmuch as it is wholly ordered to the act of existing, and so on. Such relations we call "transcendental relations"; we do not deal with them here, for they are only the things themselves which are related, and we have considered them as constitutive coprinciples of being.

The relations we are interested in now are those which are called "predicamental" relations. They are first of all accidents; that is to say, they do not constitute the reality of the thing related but are something other than the substance of the thing itself. For example, a "father" is not constituted a being by his relation to his child; a thing which is similar to another is not constituted a being by being similar, and so forth. The relations in these two examples are respectively "fatherhood" and "similarity."

In order that we can talk of a relation, there must be a subject (for example, the man who is the father), a term (the child), and the foundation, that by reason of which the subject is referred to the term (for example, in our case, the generation of the child by the father). If one of these three is missing, there is no relation (for example, between two things which are in no way comparable there is no relation because the foundation is missing, thus, "green," strictly speaking, is neither similar nor dissimilar to "cube root"—there is no foundation for a comparison).[1]

We can easily see that in some cases the subject, term, and foundation are each real. In such a case we speak of a *real* relation. In many cases, however, one of the three is not real but is supplied by an act of the mind; for example, we can speak of the "left" side of this paper, although the paper has no left side, and there is nothing in the paper which gives it the foundation for such a comparison to a man. In a man, we speak of a left side, for there is a foundation in the bodily structure between right and left. In other cases the term is not real; for example, when we say "Elmer is as moody as Hamlet" or "as simple as Li'l Abner." In such cases, we speak of a "relation of reason," and this kind of relation is a being of reason. (One of the relations of reason which we can easily overlook is the relation of identity; identity is a relation of reason because there is no term distinct from the subject).

Hence, relation is unique among the predicaments. For all the other predicaments have to be real, whereas relation can be real or not-real, and still be a predicament.[2]

Our particular problem then is: What is "relation" considered in itself? It is, of course, a predicate, and so something understood, an *intelligibility* (a *ratio*). But our question means more

---

[1] On the function of the foundation in relation, see Selected Passages, No. 47.

[2] On this point, see Selected Passages, No. 48.

than this; it means, Is a real relation as such and according to its mode of intelligibility to be found in the order of being? Why is this a problem? One easy way to see that this is a problem is to consider the fact that the relation of a particular subject can arise, change, and disappear without any efficient cause influencing that subject. For example, one white page of paper is *like* another, but if the other turns brown with age, the white page is *unlike* the brown one. The white page has changed from like to unlike without any cause influencing the white page. How can this be? Or again, there are thousands of eggs in existence, all of which are like each other. When a new egg is laid, all the other eggs are now similar to it. And how many relations of similarity does each egg have? It seems foolish to say that there are thousands of perfectly similar accidents in each egg, differing only in their term, and it is impossible to say that there is a general relation of similarity, because a general relation is abstract and cannot be found in the real order but only in a mind. These absurdities and impossibilities should be enough to show us that the question has been wrongly understood.

Let us go back briefly to accidents. The intelligibility, "accident," which is mentally understood after the manner of a form is variously and differently realized in existent material beings. In saying that accident is conceived after the manner of a form, we mean that it is thought of as a form or quasi form determining and modifying a substance, in a way somewhat like that in which substantial form determines and specifies matter. Since the intelligibilities which we thus conceive bear directly on real beings, they are first-intention intelligibles.[3] This does not mean, however, that there is always in the real order a form or quasi form. Both that which we understand and our manner of understanding of first-intention intelligibles must conform in some way to the real order; but this conformity is not mirror-like.

Let us recall a few examples. A quantified existent is quantified by a real intrinsic act, a quasi form, really distinct from the sub-

[3] Recall that first intentions are knowledges of that which we know directly, that is, of things or objects. Second intentions are knowledges about objects *as known* and are called "second" because they presuppose a previous act of knowledge to be known; cf. above, sec. 96, n. 7.

stance which it modifies and determines. We speak of such an act or determinant of a real concrete substance as an accidental form, and, in this instance, our manner of understanding is direct, for in the real order there is a determinant, a quasi form, modifying an existing substance and making it extended. So, too, qualities are understood as forms; we understand that in the red rose there is a form, which we abstractly call "redness," by which that rose is red. Thus, quantities and qualities, which are denominations understood after the manner of forms, are in the real order quasi forms or forms modifying a concrete substance.

Now let us take up the predicamental accident, relation. We will first examine that kind of relation which is based on quantity, since it can be analyzed very easily. Is there in a material existent a form or quasi form corresponding to the formal intelligibility, relation? It is true, that, like quantity and quality, relation is understood after the manner of a form. But what is there in the real order? For example, take these two lines:

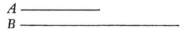

Obviously, we have here an instance of real relation, "longer than," and "shorter than." But are these formal principles inhering in the black ink, in the same way in which the blackness inheres in the ink? In the real order, there is line *A*, which is a collection of substances; for the purposes of understanding the situation, we will think of a being, which is one substance, one inch long, and symbolized for us by *A*. Similarly, *B* shall symbolize another substance which is a per se unit two inches long. *A* then is a substance, intrinsically modified by the quasi-form quantity, so as to be one inch long. *B* is a substance, intrinsically modified by another quantity, so as to be two inches long. Now it is the very nature of quantity that any one quantity *can* serve as the measure of every other quantity. This nature of quantity is *formalized* and actualized as soon as a mind apprehends these beings, quantified as they are, as respectively "shorter than" and "longer than."

This does not make these relations beings of reason. For what is understood is completely real. In the real order, there are (1) two subjects, one for each of the relations: (2) two terms, one for

each relation: (3) the foundation, which in itself is a real principle of the being and, at the same time, is such as to be "open"
to other realities of the same order.[4] The intellect recognizes
them for what they are and understands the subject by reason of
the foundation, as related to the term of the relation.

But the way in which these three principles of relations are
understood is unlike the way in which they are in the real order.
Relation is understood as a kind of form which is between two
beings, and joins or unites them like a bridge or a rope.[5] What is
there in the real order which corresponds to this intelligibility
conceived after the manner of a form? The answer is that there
is one real subject (a being) with a real foundation (quantified,
[acting, or being acted on]), and another real being. Corresponding to the conceived form there is a *situation* which includes
several beings. Yet in a real relation *what* is understood is truly
in the real order. In a relation of reason, on the other hand, the
mind precisely *contributes part* of what is understood; that is,
either the foundation or the term.[6]

In the relations based directly on quantity, and in those which
are based on quality through quantity, we have what may be
called a formal, static relation ("equal," "larger," "similar").
These relations are pure intelligibilities and do not imply any
kind of unification of subject and term in the real order.

There are other relations which are not so purely formal and
which imply some kind of union between subject and term. These
are the relations based on passion and action, and on tendency and
goal. For example, let us take the relation of "child." A child is
a human being who, being a substance (the subject), has been produced in its being by a parent (the term), so that at least for the
beginning of its existing it depends on another (the foundation).

[4] See Selected Passages, No. 47.
[5] Cf. Selected Passages, No. 49.
[6] It is traditional to speak of the "esse" and the "intelligibility" (*ratio*)
of a relation. Real relations and relations of reason have the same intelligibility (that is, they are understood as involving a subject, foundation, and
term). But only a real relation has "esse." This means, "Only of a real
relation is it true that there is in the real order a subject, a foundation,
and a term." (In the real order, relation is not a distinct form inhering in
some subject; as understood, it is a formalization; evidently, a formalization
cannot exercise an act of existing.)

To be produced by another is in some sense to be connected with another. Yet cause and effect are really distinct beings and do not by their very natures involve each other. An effect "includes" its cause, inasmuch as it is related to it; more precisely, inasmuch as it has received some influence from it. Yet it is a really distinct thing (according to its intrinsic principles of being). The child, considered in its intrinsic constituents, is a substance, with an act of existing proper to it and variously modified by its inherent perfections. But of this child it is also true that it is the child of these individual parents. When this situation is seen as a whole, immediately there is a relation. Again, the mind adds nothing to *what* is understood.

Let us take another example of the reception of some accidental perfection—let us say that the power of sight has been acted on by an external visible object. The subject is the person possessing the power; the term is the physical agent; the foundation is the reception of the influence from agent to patient. But note that a power is already ordered to the reception of such an influence prior to the action of the agent; in other words, passive powers are by their very nature oriented toward the corresponding agents. Consequently, there is a union—not substantial but accidental—through the tendencies of passive powers as well as through the reception of influences from agents.

The relation of a cause to its effect is not as simply handled as that of an effect to its cause. For, as we have already seen briefly and shall see more fully in the next section, the causality of the causes which we find in immediate experience is really distinct from them and flows from active (or operative) powers which, as accidents, are really distinct from the substance of the causes. Hence, in finite causes we can find the three elements of a relation as real and as really distinct from each other. For example, in the relation of "father," as we find it among men, there are (1) the man who is the subject of the relation; (2) his active powers and his activity by which the effect is produced; (3) the really distinct effect, the child. However, if in some being its powers and its activity are really identical with its act of existing, then we could not find the three really distinct elements which constitute a real relation. In God, the relation of

"Cause of the world" is a relation of reason, for we place distinctions in Him between the intelligibilities of power and activity although there are really no such distinctions. For the same reason, all relations of God to the world are relations of reason,[7] even though what we understand in them is true.

In the case of finite agents, relations based on causality are not merely formal, static ones. Like the passive powers, the active powers of created things are oriented to their objects. Moreover, active powers are tendencies, and so subject and term are united—again accidentally—through the tendencies of active powers toward their corresponding passive potencies. As we have seen before, act-potency correlations are based on the very nature of act and potency and, consequently, are not immediately and directly predicamental relations. For example, the tendency of any acid to react chemically with a suitable base is the very nature of the active power of that acid. So, tendency and orientation are not predicamental relations but are essential act-potency correlations. But that a particular acid reacts chemically with a particular base at some given time and place is the contingent and distinct actuality of action and passion.

Furthermore, action and passion may be transitory (for example, the generation of a living thing), but the relations based on them are permanent. How can this be? First of all, once it is true that A has caused B, it is always true, and so from the viewpoint of intelligibility the relation is permanent. But there is more to it than this. In all material things, the cause in acting loses something to its effect—not because it is a cause but because it is a material thing. For example, in local motion and in heating there is a loss of energy; in lighting, there is an emission of photons; in chemical activity there is a loss of energy (electromagnetism and gravity remain mysterious). In the generation of living things, there is a loss of some part of the material substance of the parent. Hence, a material thing is permanently different once it has caused an effect. And, for its part, an effect has its esse as received from its cause. This received esse remains permanently a received esse (and this is true of immaterial

---

[7] Except, of course, such relations as are involved in, or are a consequence of, the Incarnation.

effects, like a created angel, as well as of material ones). Hence, there is no question of relations based on passion or action ceasing merely because the actions or passions have ceased. Moreover, there are the basic, transcendental orders of active powers toward passive and of passive powers toward active ones, and these transcendental orders which are essential to the powers remain as a permanent ontological substrate for predicamental relations.

Thus, when we understand a complex situation by means of the intelligible form of relation, what we understand is truly in the real order: subject, term, and foundation. But the static relations based directly on quantity and those based on quality through quantity only assert these elements and do not imply any union of any kind between subject and term. However, the relations based on action and passion, although they also express in a unified way a complex situation of several beings, imply over and above that an accidental union of subject and term through goal orientation, tendency, and activity.

One of the important divisions of relations is that into mutual and nonmutual relations. By a mutual relation is meant one which is the same from both sides of that which is related; examples of such are similarity, equality, and the like. Nonmutual relations are those which are different on the two sides of the things related, for example, parent and child, larger and smaller, and that whole large group of relations which are real on one side and of reason on the other; for example, a table is at my right hand (real), but I am on the left of the table (of reason), or, I know this thing (real), but this thing is known by me (of reason).

There are various foundations of relation. We have already considered quantity and action and passion. Aristotle adds a third (*Metaphysics*, Bk. IV, 1020b30–31), that of being measured, as knowledge is measured by its object or a portrait is judged by its faithfulness to the person. There are, of course, related substances, for example, substances which differ specifically; and related qualities, for example, similar or different qualities. But substance and quality do not constitute independent foundations for relation, except through quantity or action and passion.[8]

---

[8] St. Thomas explains that substance and quality are absolute perfections; that is, they are the perfections of the subject itself. Substance and quality

109. Action and passion

Motion or change is in that which is moved or changed and is clearly the act (perfection) of that which undergoes change. Motion or change is already in itself an intelligibility; we understand the total process from initial stage to term (at least relatively in such instances as local motion), although what is actually real at any moment of time is not the total process but only one stage of it.

It is one and the same motion which is from the mover or agent. Therefore, when we compare or contrast action and passion, we are still referring to one and the same motion, not two. Exactly the same thing is referred to in the real order when I say "*A* moves *B*," and "*B* is moved by *A*," although in the first case action is predicated of *A*, and in the second passion is predicated of *B*. Hence, action and passion are identical in reality with the motion and with each other, but they are different intelligibilities: for to be the act or perfection of the changing in so far as that act is in the changing and to be the act of the changing in so far as the change is from the agent are different intelligibilities.[9]

Do not confuse this with situations which are expressed thus: "*A* moves *B*" and "*B* moves *A*," because here two actions are predicated of two different things. Likewise, "*B* is moved by *A*" and "*A* is moved by *B*"; here two (numerically) different passions are predicated of two numerically different things. These are not identical in reality with each other.

To have the situation of action and passion in the real order, only three "things" are required: an agent with an active power, a thing in which change takes place, and the change itself caused by the active power. Nothing else is necessary; in particular, there is no need for an acquisition or change in the agent.

Although motion or change is properly in the patient, we actu-

---

are related, either through quantity (so that we can speak of "one" or "many" qualities, the "intensity" of a quality, and so on), or through action and passion. See *In V Metaphys.*, lect. 17; *In I Sent.*, dis. 26, q. 2, art. 2, ad 4; *In III Sent.*, dis. 5, q. 1, art. 1, qa. 1. See also, Selected Passages, No. 46.

[9] Cf. Selected Passages, No. 50.

ally predicate the action of the *agent*. In doing this, we directly understand and name one thing—the agent—from another which is really distinct from it. We say, "An electric coil heats the water," though the heating is going on in the water, not in the coil. (Of course, there are other things going on: the electric current is heating the coil, and there is also some action of the water upon the coil. But we are abstracting from these other actions, and treating only the one action.) We understand the coil's influence upon the water in terms of something modifying the coil, and this modification itself we treat after the manner of a form. Hence, "action," strictly speaking, is a construct, and this kind of construct we call an *extrinsic denomination* (because the agent is named—*denominatur*—from the change it produces in the patient). Because action as a predicament is understood after the manner of a form, action is a univocal predicate.

"Passion" is predicated in a similar way, for "passion" is expressed in a predicate when we understand and name the patient from a change in it produced by the agent. For example, we say, "The house is being built by John." (Distinguish this predicate from the kind expressed in a sentence like "The house is being built"; in the latter sentence, not passion but motion or change is being predicated.) Hence, "passion," strictly also, is an extrinsic denomination (because the patient is partly named from a reference to the cause of the change). Because passion is understood after the manner of a form, it is a univocal predicate.

When we ask what is referred to in the real order, we designate the motion or change in the patient. But motion or change is a process-toward-the-act of being, and so is in the existential order; change is a way to come to be. Thus, change in itself, in the real order, is analogous. For example, one kind of change is alteration (change of quality), another is augmentation (increase in quantity), another is change of place, and so on. These various changes are different as changes, not by an external difference added to them.

Likewise, there is an act in the agent which grounds its reality as agent. This act in the agent is not its substantial form or its act of being or a quality but the act of an active power, which presupposes the act of existing. This act, concretely, is the "agent in act," or "the acting of the agent," and is itself not a univocal reality but an act which is analogous like the act of existing. "Acting" is known directly in a judgment, in a verb of acting (in a way similar to the act of existing), and we can have a concept of action, not directly by abstraction from the thing, for acting is by no means abstract; it is necessarily concrete and existential. We derive our concept of action by a "second-level" abstraction, from the judgmental knowledge previously expressed in a verb.

Note carefully that action and passion are correlated and that consequently they refer only to transient action. That is why we sometimes call transient action "predicamental action." Immanent action or operation strictly so-called is an act or perfection of the agent; it is not of itself a means to anything else or a way to come to be but an end. We see or understand, and so forth, and these operations are the perfections of the seer, the knower. Immanent action is like transient action only inasmuch as it is an analogous kind of "acting," the actuality of a power of immanent operation.

110. When, where, situs, and habitus

The predicament *where* states the relation of one material thing to others in regard to quantity. Note that *where* is not the same as space. Space is a pure abstraction, namely, three-dimensional extension abstracted from all accidental modifications, understood after the manner of a being in itself as a kind of container into which material things are placed. *Where*, on the contrary, is concrete. It designates a material thing (more accurately still, a quantified thing) in relation to other material things. But because *where* names one thing from other really distinct things, it is an extrinsic denomination. Recall that extrinsic denominations are not beings of reason; for *what* I name when I say "here," namely, this thing and other material things and the contact (direct or mediate) between them, are completely real. But the *way* in which they are understood, that is, like an inherent form, is a way of understanding.

When names the duration (the continued existence) of a thing in relation to the duration of some other thing or things. Strictly speaking, the duration measured by *when* is a perfectly continuous duration, capable of indefinitely repeated division. Hence, the duration which is the measure by which I name something to be *now* must be a continuous change, and that is why local motion serves as a convenient measure. Distinguish *when* from time. Time is a pure abstraction, namely, perfectly continuous and even successive duration (changing duration) as the measure ("number") of motion according to the sequence of priority and posteriority. *When*, however, is quite concrete; it names one real duration in relation to another.

Situs is a very complex predicament, adding to *where* the disposition or arrangement of different parts among themselves, for example, "head" or "foot" in an animal, "top" or "bottom" in a tree, and so forth. Note that the difference in the "different parts" is a difference of quality (figure and so on). Now, inasmuch as *situs* has this arrangement or structure or organization implied, to that extent it is an intrinsic perfection of the thing itself (some authors call this "internal situs," but more accurately it is a complex quality). But inasmuch as the proper notion of *situs* is a measure of the ordered parts in relation to place, it too, strictly speaking, is an extrinsic denomination.

Habitus, finally, designates place in relation to some human purpose, thus, clothed, shod, and so forth. Consequently, it is also an extrinsic denomination, naming one thing from its relation to another distinct thing.[10]

It will be noted that the predicaments which are extrinsic denominations cannot be applied to one individual in isolation. For example, if we supposed that only one material thing existed, it would have no predicamental relations, no predicamental actions or passions, would not be anywhere or at any time, would not have situs or habitus.

It is to be noted also that the last four predicaments (when, where, situs, and habitus) all depend on quantity in one way or another. Consequently, if there should be any nonquantified beings (spiritual beings), such beings will strictly speaking not be any *where;* nor will they exist during any portion of time; nor

[10] Cf. Selected Passages, No. 51.

will they have situs or habitus. Of course, we cannot imagine such beings to ourselves, and we have to understand them by analogy with the sensible things of our experience. Hence, we will apply these predicaments to them, but we should understand that this is done improperly.

111. Definitions

Relation is the way in which one "thing" stands to another or others. For the expression "stands to" we may substitute "is in a certain respect to," "is with regard to."

Transcendental relation is a principle of being whose whole reality lies in its orientation to another. (For example, matter whose whole reality lies in its orientation to form.)

Predicamental relation is the accident by which one thing (the subject) *is* contingently with respect to another (the term). (For example, fatherhood, similarity.)

Real relation is a relation in which the subject, foundation, and term are all three real. (For example, fatherhood is a real relation because the man who is the father, the person who is the child, and the act of generation are all three real; similarity is a real relation when the material quantified thing which is the subject exists, the term also really exists, and the foundation is a real modification of the subject.)

Relation of reason is a relation in which either the foundation or the term is produced by an act of the mind. (For example, the right side of a desk—the desk has two sides, the subject and the term, but no foundation in itself for having one side called "right." Or we may say that a certain person is "as inaccessible as Jupiter"—the person exists; no one can get to see him, but Jupiter is not a real being.)

Mutual relation is one of a set of relations which are such that the relation of subject to term is the same (specifically) as the converse relation. (For example, if A is similar to B, then B is similar to A; so, too, with equality.)

Nonmutual relation is one of a pair of relations which are not the same in each of the pair of terms involved. (For example, if A is larger than B, then B is smaller than A; if A is B's father, B

is *A*'s child; if I know a thing, the thing is known by me—and here the first is a real relation, the second a relation of reason.)

Action is the change (motion) of a patient as from an agent.

Passion is the change (motion) of a patient as received (from an agent) in a patient.

Extrinsic denomination is the understanding and naming of one thing from another thing really distinct from it.

When is the accident by which we name the duration of one thing from the continuous duration of another.

Where is the accident by which we name one thing from its contact with other material things distinct from it.

Situs is the accident by which we name the internal order of different parts of one thing in relation to where these parts are. (For example, top, bottom, middle.)

Habitus is the accident by which we name one thing as being in a certain situation in reference to a human purpose. (For example, clothed, shod.)

112. Proof

In our experience there are real things (subjects) which must be understood as related by reason of some intrinsic perfection in them.

But: when the intelligibility (*ratio*) of a relation expresses real and really distinct subjects, foundations, and terms, it possesses all the elements necessary for a real relation.

Therefore: there are real relations.

113. Readings

St. Thomas Aquinas, *On the Power of God*, q. 7, art. 9, ad 7 (distinction between the esse and the intelligibility of a relation), q. 7, art. 10, ad 8 (perfections which are not forms); *Summa Theologiae*, Pt. I, q. 13, art. 7; q. 28, art. 1 and ad 4 (meaning of real relation); q. 29, art. 4 (on relation, especially in God); q. 37, art. 2 (on denominations); q. 77, art. 6 (on accidents).

Clifford G. Kossel, S.J., "The *Esse* and *Ratio* of Relation," *The Modern Schoolman*, XXIV (1946), 19–24, 30–36, 96–107; "St. Thomas's Theory of the Causes of Relation," *The Modern Schoolman*, XXV (1948), 151–172.

SELECTED PASSAGES FROM ST. THOMAS AQUINAS

46. The Foundations of Relation

Since a real relation consists in a certain order of one thing to another, relations of this kind must be found in as many ways as it happens that one thing is ordered to another. But one thing is ordered to another, either according to its act of existence, inasmuch as the esse of one thing depends on another, and this is the third mode; or according to active and passive power, according as one thing receives something from another, or gives something to another, and this is the second way, or according as the quantity of one thing can be measured by that of another, and this is the first way.

But the quality of a thing, as such, regards only the subject in which it is. Hence, according to quality, one thing is not ordered to another, except in so far as quality has the nature of an active or passive power, inasmuch as it is the principle of action or passion; or because of quantity or something pertaining to quantity, as one thing is said to be whiter than another, or as something is said to be similar [to another], which has some one quality. But the other predicaments rather follow relation than cause relation. For "when" consists in some relation to time; "where," to place; "position," implies an order of parts; "habit" a relation of that which has to that which is had.

> *Commentary on Aristotle's*
> Metaphysics, Bk. V, lect. 17
> (ed. Cathala, Nos. 1004–
> 1005).

47. The Foundation and the Reality of Relation

Relation does not have an esse in the real order except from this that it has a foundation in the thing, and from this foundation it is found in a genus. Hence it is that the essential differences of relations are taken from the differences of other beings, as is clear from the Philosopher (*Metaphysics*, Bk. V), who says, that some relations are founded on quantity, and others on action, and so on. A further consequence is that the order of relations among themselves is according to the order of those things upon which they are founded. Therefore, as we find that in those things which are distinguished by their essences, that the principles of their substance distinguish them (namely, their matter and form), and other accidental things are signs which manifest this distinction, so is it also in those things that are distinguished by their relations, that the relations which are founded on the nature of the thing are distinguishing, and other relations are signs of distinction. But the relations which have a foundation in the nature of the thing are the relations of origin, for fatherhood is founded in the communication of nature.

Commentary on the First Book of the Sentences, dis. 26, q. 2, art. 2, ad 4.

48. *The Esse of Relation*

The intelligibility of a relation, like that of motion, depends on the end or term, but its esse depends on the subject.

Summa Theologiae, Pt. III, q. 2, art. 7, ad 2.

It is to be noted, that relation is said to be in another way than other beings. For in other beings, any thing is said to be in two ways: with regard to its esse, and with regard to the intelligibility of its quiddity, as wisdom according to its esse places something in its subject, and similarly according to its intelligibility places a nature in the genus of quality. But relation is something according to the esse which it has in its subject, but according to its intelligibility it is not a "something," but only a being referred to another. Consequently according to its intelligibility it does not place anything in its subject, and this is why Boethius says that relatives do not predicate anything of that of which they are said. Hence also it is that there is something related in which there is only a relation of reason, and there is not placed in it anything in the real order, as when the knowable is referred to knowledge. And this is true as well in the relations which are predicated of God as in those which are in creatures, but in different ways, for the relation which has an esse in creatures, has another esse than the esse of its subject, and so it is something other than its subject. But in God there is nothing which has an esse different from it; for the esse of wisdom in God is the divine esse itself and not something superadded, and similarly the esse of Fatherhood. Consequently relation, as far as its esse is concerned—and this is the only way in which it ought to posit anything—is the divine essence, but according to its intelligibility, by which it has the function of distinguishing one person from another, to express *something* does not belong to it, but rather [to express] "to something."

Commentary on the First Book of the Sentences, dis. 20, q. 1, art. 1.

49. *Is a Relation Related to Its Subject?*

. . . relations, by which a subject is referred to another, are not referred to the subject by another intermediate relation, nor to the opposite; for example, fatherhood is not referred to either the father or to the son by means of a relation; and if such relations are spoken of, they are relations of reason.

> *Commentary on Aristotle's*
> Metaphysics, Bk. V, lect.
> 20 (ed. Cathala, No. 1063).

50. Action and Passion

But if action and passion are the same in substance, it seems that they are not different predicaments. But it is to be noted that the predicaments are distinguished by the different ways of predicating. Hence, the same thing, according as it is predicated differently of different things, belongs to different predicaments. For place, inasmuch as it is predicated of the locating thing, belongs to the genus of quantity, but inasmuch as it is predicated denominatively of the thing located, constitutes the predicament "where." Similarly motion, according as it is predicated of the subject in which it is, constitutes the predicament of passion; but according as it is predicated of that from which it is, it constitutes the predicament of action.

> *Commentary on Aristotle's*
> Metaphysics, Bk. XI, lect.
> 9 (ed. Cathala, No. 2313).

51. Not All Denominations Arise from Forms

That from which something is denominated, need not always by its nature be a form. It is enough that it be signified after the manner of a form, grammatically speaking. For a man is denominated from action and from his clothes, and from other things like this and these really are not forms.

> *On the Power of God*, q. 7,
> art. 10, ad 8.

XIV

Correlations

114. Introductory note

A more accurate consideration of the nature of metaphysics can be made now that the basic fundamentals have been considered briefly. It is also now possible to draw together some elements which were first considered separately as they occurred, and this is especially true of the doctrine of analogy. Finally, more explicit comparisons can be made between metaphysics and other knowledges and between St. Thomas and some other philosophical positions.

This chapter is not intended to be taken in the ordinary class. As occasion offers, some references may be made to it; the better students can be directed to read parts of it and may even be inclined to read it on their own initiative. Because of this purpose, the treatment will be compressed and often schematic. It is by no means claimed to be exhaustive.

115. Ontological and constructural knowledge

We have briefly seen that knowledge can be divided and classified in many ways. We have seen that a knowledge is specified by its subject and, most accurately, by the formal intelligibility of that subject—what is known precisely in the way in which it becomes knowable to us. This formal intelligibility (*ratio formalis objecti*) is often called the formal object.

Many writers on philosophy apparently think that the formal object is something entirely on the *thing* known, as it exists in the real order. It is therefore necessary to state explicitly what

most Thomists (in fact, most philosophers) admit quite clearly
—in other contexts and connections. First of all, a sensible, material thing is not *actually* intelligible[1] either in what makes it to
be what-it-is or in what makes it to be simply, and therefore its
actual intelligibility must include the way in which it becomes
known to us. Secondly, immaterial, or spiritual, beings are indeed
actually intelligible to an intellect proportioned to them; they
are not directly intelligible to us but only by means of sensible
things in one way or another; therefore the intelligibility of
spiritual things for the human mind also includes the way in
which they become intelligible to it. That is why St. Thomas
speaks of the way of understanding (*modus et ratio cognoscendi*)
as well as of what is known in the thing.[2] Since the knowable as
such (*scibile in quantum scibile*) is what distinguishes and specifies a knowledge, we must take account both of what is known
and of our way of knowing it.

One aspect of the "way of knowing a thing" has become clear
only in recent centuries; it was not explicitly recognized even
by St. Thomas. Among Thomists, Jacques Maritain was the first
to make a detailed study of two different manners of knowing:
"intuitive"[3] (dianoetic) and "empiriological" (perinoetic).[4] We

---

[1] By the use of this phrase, "actually intelligible," implicit reference is
made, first, to the common Aristotelian teaching that an intellect which
knows by way of reception of an influence from material things cannot
know them directly precisely as material (cf. G. P. Klubertanz, *Philosophy
of Human Nature* [New York, Appleton-Century-Crofts, Inc., 1953], pp.
180–184); secondly, to the equally common teaching that the contingent
precisely as contingent is not the object of purely intellectual knowledge
(for the meaning of this teaching, see George P. Klubertanz, S.J., *The
Discursive Power* [St. Louis, The Modern Schoolman, 1952], pp. 192, 216–
219, 248–254, 284–286); for the need of finding some necessity in the scientific
consideration of contingent things and the way in which this is done, see
the article of Joseph Owens, C.Ss.R., "A Note on the Intelligibility of
Being," *Gregorianum*, Vol. XXXVI (1955), 169–193.

[2] For the *modus cognoscendi*—the way of understanding—note this list of
references given by Schütz, *Thomaslexikon: Summa Theologiae*, Pt. II-II, q.
48, art. 1; Pt. III, q. 9, art. 4, ad 1; *In Boethii de Trinitate*, lect. 2, q. 1,
art. 1, ad 3; q. 2, art. 1, ad 2, 3, 4; *In I Sent., prologue*, q. 1, art. 5, c. *In
Post. Analyt.*, lect. 1, princip., lect. 4, princip.; lect. 30, princip.; *Truth*,
q. 11, art. 1; *In II Metaphys.*, lect. 5, med.

[3] Particularly in his more recent writings, Jacques Maritain has been
using the term *intuition*. Inasmuch as this term is meant to indicate the
direct, nondiscursive character of the understanding, it translates *intellectus*

shall refer to the two kinds of knowing as "ontological" and "constructural."

An ontological knowledge is a knowledge that is directly and immediately of the thing known according to the latter's own proper reality. For example, we can immediately sense and understand[5] the shapes of objects that have definite outlines, and in those shapes can directly understand some simple, direct relationships—for example, seeing an extended thing like the page of a book, we can immediately understand that this is a four-sided shape, and that a part of such a surface is always and necessarily less than the whole. Again, other simple qualities can similarly be apprehended by us—colors, temperature relative to our body, resistance of bodies. Moreover, in the presence of a sensible ob-

---

or *intelligere*. But the implications and connotations of the term seem to be very unfortunate. What Maritain himself means by the term is not always clear. He speaks of an "intuition of being" which is had suddenly after long years of reflections; of an "intuition" of the existence of God. What is common to these two acts is their nondiscursive nature. It does not seem that either of them would have been called by St. Thomas an *intellectus*. For this reason, this book dissociates itself from the term "intuition" and uses instead terms like "insight," "*direct understanding*." What is meant by insight in this book has been explained several times; see also below, nn. 6 and 15.

[4] For this distinction, see Jacques Maritain, *Degrees of Knowledge*, trans. under the supervision of Gerald B. Phelan (New York, Scribner's, 1959), pp. 202–205; "On Human Knowledge," *Thought*, vol. XXIV (1949), 225–243; "Science, Philosophy, and Faith," in *Science, Philosophy and Religion* (New York, Conference on Science, Philosophy and Religion, 1941), vol. I, pp. 162–183. See also Louis de Raeymaeker, "The One Voice of Science and the Many Voices of Philosophy," *Philosophy Today*, vol. V (1961), 83–91; Jean Ladrière, "Freedom in Science," in *Truth and Freedom*, (Pittsburgh, Duquesne Univ. Press, 1954).

For more detailed expositions, see Alden L. Fisher, "The Contemporary Status of Scholastic Psychology," in *Proceedings of the American Catholic Philosophical Association*, vol. XXXI (1957), 144–156; John J. Fitzgerald, "The Contemporary Status of Natural Philosophy," *ibid.*, 132–144; and G. P. Klubertanz, S.J. "The Doctrine of St. Thomas and Modern Science," *Sapientia Aquinatis* (Rome, Catholic Book Agency, 1955), pp. 89–104.

[5] To *understand* does not mean "to name," or necessarily, "to define"; it certainly need not mean "to have a scientific knowledge of." In particular, if we see an object shaped like ⬤▬▬▭ , we can understand at once that it has such a shape, without being able to name or describe it, much less define it. This is by no means a mathematical, abstract knowledge; the experience is direct, immediate, and concrete.

ject, we immediately understand that it exists—at least under proper conditions of awareness.

Furthermore, ontological knowledge reaches to some minimal knowledge of natures: at least that this thing before me is a material thing, for example. To some extent, we have a direct ontological knowledge of what "man" is and of what "knowledge" is. Such direct knowledge is a knowledge of nature or essence, and it is very limited. We know the essence of man quite well; of living things generically; of most other things according to some remote genus (for example, as material substance). We also know that there are really distinct individuals and different kinds of things, whatever the differences between them may be.

Still further, we have an immediate knowledge of activity as a special kind of reality different from form, essence, and even the act of existing, although our first knowledge of these different kinds of reality will be very vague and inexpressible in words. Nevertheless, this knowledge is a direct knowledge of the thing known in its own terms. Together with this direct knowledge of activity we also have an immediate apprehension of change and causality[6] (again, at least in some instances); we experience some things causing other things, for example, ourselves causing something to happen.

So far, we have instanced kinds of ontological knowledge in the mode of immediate experience. We can also have ontological knowledge of some conclusions which are no longer immediate in the sense that their objects are not experienced in themselves. These conclusions can still be ontological in character, provided that all the terms entering into the reasoning process are directly

---

[6] This is not knowledge at the level of the philosophy of nature, or even, strictly speaking, of principles proper to that branch of philosophy. It is a direct and immediate knowledge presupposed for all philosophy.

One of the recent works which insists on the dependence of metaphysics upon the philosophy of nature, and proposes an organization of knowledge entirely different from the one proposed here, still admits that there is a prephilosophical knowledge of causality; see *Science in Synthesis*, by William H. Kane, O.P., Benedict M. Ashley, O.P., John D. Corcoran, O.P., and Raymond J. Nogar, O.P. (River Forest, Dominican College, 1952), pp. 197–198; Father Kane, the author of this section, does not believe that metaphysics can use this knowledge. The reason seems to be that this knowledge is prereflective. But why should metaphysics be the only scientific knowledge incapable of purifying an experience by direct reflection?

ontological, that the reasoning itself is direct (that is, is either direct deduction, direct induction, or a direct fact-proof [*demonstratio quia*]), and that the reasoning proceeds according to the directly ontological character of the terms involved.

Hence, the method of ontological knowledge is (*a*) intelligible induction and direct insight;[7] phenomenological description,[8] that is, direct, noninterpreted description; and (*b*) direct reasoning (as described above), that is, not hypothetico-deductive and not resting on extraneous elements.

Must there be *some* ontological knowledge? Yes, if there is to be *any* knowledge of reality at all. Otherwise, we would be in a complete subjectivism. This will become clearer if we take a look at constructural knowledge and see how it is developed.

Let us first look at pure constructural knowledge. Of course, there is no object of the human mind which is absolutely and entirely constructed by the mind without even any point of departure in experience. Mathematics offers the simplest and one of the best examples of a purely constructural knowledge. Given the barest starting point in experience—we are not concerned here with establishing the fact, much less with the way in which mathematics is originally connected with experience—the mathematician proceeds to construct mentally his figures, formulas, functions, and symbols. In constructing the objects of his knowledge, he knows them, or, conversely, he knows them by constructing them. These "mathematicals," as we may briefly call mathematical objects in general, do not exist; their being is a

[7] These terms, especially the latter, are used in many senses. For the precise way in which they are used here, see Klubertanz, *Philosophy of Human Nature*, pp. 385–401; Robert J. Henle, S.J., *Method in Metaphysics* (Milwaukee, Marquette University Press, 1951). Note that the term "insight" is sometimes used by experimental psychologists as equivalent to "interpretation"; interpretation, however, seems to be a clear case of constructural knowledge.

[8] See John Wild, *Return to Reason* (Chicago, Henry Regnery, 1953), pp. 35, 37–38, 48–49. Our acceptance of the term phenomenological does not imply that "phenomenology" as a distinct kind of philosophy is a part of Thomistic metaphysics, or even that it can be adapted or harmonized with it.
See also James Collins, "The Bond of Natural Being," *Review of Metaphysics*, vol. XV (1962), 552–556, 565–572; and John Wild, *The Challenge of Existentialism* (Bloomington, Ind., Indiana Univ. Press, 1955), 187–196.

being-known; they are beings of reason. When someone formally knows one of these "mathematicals," what he knows is precisely the mathematical and nothing else,[9] that is, the object constructed by him. The only laws that a mathematical is subject to are the laws of intelligibility: definability or constructability, consistency, and the like. So much for pure constructural knowledge; let us now consider the constructural knowledge of the real.

Constructural knowledge of the real has several characteristics. It is first of all—at the level of scientific knowledge which is our main concern here—selective ("abstractive"). The scientist concentrates on some particular and, therefore, selected evidence, and what is selected is univocal, "literal." This is a general requirement; it is strongly reinforced if instruments are used which by their nature allow only for certain types or kinds of activity to register. Therefore, constructural knowledge is of a whole according to some partial aspect; and, under this first consideration, the "constructurality" consists in this: that the partiality of evidence and reporting is understood and stated as if it were a total report.

Secondly, constructural knowledge of the real arises by *rational* induction.[10] We have already noted that ontological knowledge is severely limited in scope. In very many cases, we observe a fact, an event, and so forth, and all we understand is *that* this event occurs, once or several times; we see no connection that is directly intelligible. Hence, we are forced to a roundabout way of reasoning to come to anything like a general knowledge. We *argue* that we have hold of a necessity, on the ground of a relative consistency in an agent that is nonfree at least in this activity; we may also need statistics to achieve the generalization.

Thirdly, and most characteristically, constructural knowledge is indirect, that is, the knowledge of one thing in terms of another. This "other" is a construct or substitute-object. Now there are several types of constructs. An example of the first is in use when we understand the subatomic components of atoms in terms of

[9]Obviously we must distinguish mathematics as a science from such quite different operations as counting and measuring real things. This latter kind of knowledge is not constructural and seems to be prior, not posterior, to mathematics as a science.

[10] For a fuller explanation of the term *rational induction*, see Klubertanz, *Philosophy of Human Nature*, pp. 385–401.

"particles." Unless we had met a particle in direct experience, this word would be meaningless. Moreover, a subatomic particle is not a particle in the directly experienced sense of "particle." But the point is: if we conceive an atom as composed of particles, we can set up relationships between these particles that correspond with the selectively observed behavior of atoms. This kind of construction is construction in terms of a sensible model.

We can also make a construct in terms of nonsensible objects. Here, we begin with pure constructions, that is, with objects whose whole reality arises from their being built in such a way by the mind. Pure constructions are a special kind of knowledge all by themselves. But they can also be used instrumentally in the knowledge of the real, and when they are so employed a constructural knowledge of the real is obtained. Thus, mathematical physics is a constructural knowledge, in that it uses mathematical entities (as well as other types of construction) in the understanding of the real.

A third kind of construct is the operational definition. This is knowledge, not precisely *of* the thing but of what we must do to acquire "it" in the real order, whatever "it" may be. For example, "chlorine" is what you get at one of the poles in the electrolysis of salt water. This is a useful definition, and it has some connection with whatever "chlorine" is in itself, but the definition does not reveal that connection; such connection, if it is had, may be made by means of a model construction.

A fourth kind of construct consists in obtaining a surrogate of an essence or nature by the selection of what seems to be the most consistent of the various several attributes of a thing, which, at the same time, enables us to put some order into the rest of the attributes.

The third stage in construction—that of the four types of construction strictly so-called—is what is typically characteristic of constructural knowledge. It is by no means an arbitrary proceeding. At the very least, the construct must be verified—consequences deduced from the construct must be found to hold good in the real order. For example, the quantitative relations predicted by a mathematical formula in thermodynamics must be observed (verified) in the physical process. A closer type of relation is to be found in more physical theories which have some elements of description, or model, in them; here, the theory must not only provide good predictions but also must have some similarity with what is described, in so far as we know anything about it. For example, the atomic theory as a whole has many aspects which come closer to being descriptive than merely theoretical.[11]

116. Metaphysics, experience, and spontaneous knowledge

In the first chapter, we have seen that descriptively metaphysics is a kind of knowledge that differs from other kinds. The question readily arises: "What is the relation between metaphysics and these other kinds of knowledge?" Because there are various modes of knowledge and many distinct kinds of scientific knowledge, we must consider them one at a time in their relation to metaphysics. The relations in question are principally those of priority and dependence.

Does metaphysics depend on other knowledge? In other words, does metaphysics have any presuppositions? In one sense, metaphysics cannot have any presuppositions. It is a demonstrative knowledge of all being, and so no being is beyond its scope. Moreover, there cannot be any other knowledge which is strictly and formally presupposed by the very nature of metaphysics itself; Aristotle called it "first philosophy"; and we can say that whatever the scientific knowledge is which rests on no other knowledge, that is metaphysics.

In another sense, metaphysics cannot be the first knowledge. Aristotelian metaphysics—the first fully conscious attempt to build a metaphysics—was intended to be the last knowledge gained by a man. Formally, Aristotelian metaphysics rested on Aristotelian "physics." This historical fact has influenced other thinkers to say that metaphysics formally depends on other knowledge. Again, St. Thomas has explicitly said that metaphysics cannot be learned by a juvenile mind; a mature person is the only one who is capable of learning metaphysics. Usually some experience and at least a broad acquaintance with science are required

[11] In fact, the atomic theory even has some ontological elements within it; see George P. Klubertanz, S.J., "The Teaching of High School Chemistry," *Journal of Chemical Education*, XXXII (1955), 248–252.

before a student can successfully attack metaphysics. And, indeed, it would be totally impossible to begin the study of metaphysics without *any* preceding knowledge.[12]

The relation between metaphysics and spontaneous knowledge is further complicated by the fact that many statements (for example, that a real world exists, that there are real causes of sensible effects) seem to be found both in spontaneous knowledge and in metaphysics. And some knowledge of this kind necessarily exists in a person before he has had an opportunity to study metaphysics. What is the relation between the two knowledges? Or are they perhaps identical?

We can begin to solve this problem if we reflect on the kind of evidence that metaphysics rests on.[13] As we have seen, metaphysics

[12] The old adage says that whatever is in the intellect was *first* in sense— *prius in sensu*. Many Thomists (and others, too) seem to think that sensation and intellection are two distinct operations going on in us and somehow correlated; that sense precedes intellection in time; and that there is only a causal connection between the two operations. Introspection and analysis both show that as far back as a human being can recall, and clearly in adult life, human conscious activity is sensory-intellectual at once. There is no priority in time of sense over intellect to be discovered; only an analysis can discover the distinction between the two kinds of activity. Hence, to the objection, "Prior to metaphysics there is sense experience," the answer is, "Sense is indeed a *cause* of intellection, but sense experience is not an activity temporally prior to or descriptively distinct from intellection; perception is descriptively a single unified experience in which analysis discovers sensation and intellection."

Jacques Maritain, *Art and Scholasticism*, trans. F. J. Scanlon (New York, Scribner's, 1937), pp. 25–28, 161–173, speaks of "intellectualized sensation"; see also his *Creative Intuition* (New York, Pantheon, 1953), pp. 163–166.

On the dependence of metaphysics on other knowledge, see G. P. Klubertanz, S.J., "Metaphysics and Theistic Convictions," to be published in the *Proceedings of the Workshop on Teaching Thomism Today* (Washington, Catholic Univ. of America Press).

[13] For textual and historical studies on the nature of metaphysics as here expressed, see George P. Klubertanz, S.J., "The Teaching of Thomistic Metaphysics," *Gregorianum*, XXXV (1954), 3–17, 187–205, and "Being and God According to Contemporary Scholastics," *The Modern Schoolman*, XXXIII (1954), 1–16; Elizabeth G. Salmon, "What Is Being?" *Review of Metaphysics*, VII (1954), 613–631; Joseph Owens, C.Ss.R., "A Note on the Approach to Metaphysics," *The New Scholasticism*, XXVIII (1954), 454–476; Leonard J. Eslick, "What is the Starting Point of Metaphysics?" *The Modern Schoolman*, XXXIV (1957), 247–263; James Collins, "Toward a Philosophically Ordered Thomism," *New Scholasticism*, vol. XXXII (1958), 301–326; Robert J. Henle, S.J., "Metaphysics," in *Proceedings of the 1961 Workshop on Philosophy and the Integration of Contemporary Catholic*

rests on immediate or perceptual knowledge.[14] We find in immediate experience the presence of sensible being, and sensible being is the starting point of all metaphysical knowledge. Note that we do not derive this principle (namely, being) *from* experience; we find it in experience. We do not say, "We found being in our spontaneous knowledge, let us now analyze that knowledge." True, we did find (sensible) being in spontaneous knowledge; then it was accepted unreflectively and without any relation to anything else. When we begin metaphysics, we begin with a very careful description of sensible being. This preliminary description is carried on with a constant reflection on the evidence, looking at what we find and trying to understand and express it to ourselves bit by bit in harmony with what we find, no more and no less. This is a highly self-conscious process, quite different from the procedure of spontaneous knowledge. Secondly, the metaphysician studies sensible being from the point of view of being as being, and this formal consideration gives quite a special character to metaphysical knowledge. From this description, the metaphysician continues on to an analysis of the structure of that being (the constitutive principles of being), still in the light of that same formal intelligibility. The analysis of the structure of sensible being as being leads to the discovery of the existence of the cause of that being, that is, to the existence of God. The rest of metaphysics consists in pushing further the implications of these basic discoveries (the properties of being, the transcendentals; our predication of being, the categories, or predicaments; what is entailed by the nature of God as subsistent esse, the Divine attributes; and what can be elaborated concerning the relation of the

Education (Washington, Catholic Univ. of America Press, 1962); Joseph Owens, C.SS.R., *St. Thomas and the Future of Metaphysics* (Milwaukee, Marquette Univ. Press, 1957).

[14] By *perception* and *perceptual knowledge* we mean the total, unified activity whose object is an existing thing present to our senses and attended to by us; it is neither purely sensory nor purely intellectual. On the experience of sensible things as the starting point of philosophy, see Etienne Gilson, *The Christian Philosophy of St. Thomas Aquinas* (New York, Random House, 1956), p. 454, note 67; Jacques Maritain, *Degrees of Knowledge*, trans. Gerald B. Phelan (New York, Scribner's, 1959), p. 76; Robert G. Miller, C.S.B., "Realistic and Unrealistic Empiricisms," *The New Scholasticism*, vol. XXXV (1961), 311–337.

world to God, creation, providence, the co-operation of God with creatures, the Divine foreknowledge, and so on).

Spontaneous knowledge, for its part, consists partly of immediate experience, partly of some relatively simple, nontechnical conclusions derived from experience. Therefore spontaneous knowledge contains in some way the starting point of metaphysics. But only "in *some* way"—not as the metaphysician uses it. Spontaneous knowledge has no reflexly conscious point of view; it takes immediate experience as it finds it, obscure and confused. Secondly, spontaneous everyday knowledge reaches to some understanding of sensible being, to principles understood in a rough, or gross, unrefined sense. Among these principles we find the principle of epistemological realism (understood rather vaguely and generally), the principle of the plurality of distinct individuals in the world, the principle of the diversity of the kinds of being ("kinds" or "species" understood in a very vague way), the principle of change, of the diversity of the kinds of change, and of causality within change.[15] Thirdly, spontaneous knowledge includes some conclusions, such as the immortality of the soul and the existence of God (both of these understood not only vaguely but also through metaphor).[16] This part of spontaneous knowledge is both true and certain, although the certitude corresponds to the kind of knowledge we have and is only analogous to scientific certitude.

The relation of metaphysics to spontaneous knowledge therefore is somewhat complex. As far as the starting point of metaphysics is concerned, it is contained within spontaneous knowledge *materially* (it is not understood under the same intelligibility); it

[15] Cf. n. 5. The listing of principles here is not exhaustive. We should also include such items as the knowledge of obligation and of the difference between right and wrong, the notions of right and duty, of truth and falsity.

[16] In principle, there is no error in this kind of knowledge, for it rests on immediate evidence that is presented to the mind without the need of any investigation. It is not a careless or haphazard knowledge, even though it is not gained by a conscious methodology; for in this kind of knowledge overwhelming or massive evidence takes the place of methodological attention. Therefore, this knowledge is valid, that is, is true and certain; it needs no later justification or validation; consequently, also, philosophy need not begin with a universal doubt (and cannot so begin). But in fact spontaneous knowledge also includes much opinion, error, and sheer fantasy.

is not simply accepted *from* experience but is re-examined within experience with great care and in the light of being as being. As far as the principles are concerned, in the first place, the principles of metaphysics and of spontaneous knowledge are only *materially identical*. (Two propositions are materially identical when they have the same subjects and predicates—the same, that is, when they are considered apart from any added meaning they might have from their connection with a particular formal object of a habit, with particular principles, and with preceding reasoning on which they depend. St. Thomas calls a proposition isolated in this way a "position.") In the second place, metaphysics does not accept its principles uncritically *from* experience. There is, it is true, a special difficulty with metaphysical principles. The understanding of being which is expressed in the principles mentioned above is difficult to bring to awareness because of its great generality. They are implicit in *all* experience, it is true, but, because they pertain to all experience, attention cannot be focused on them by isolating them. Therefore the ordinary techniques of discovery are unavailing. These principles come to explicit awareness only by the sheer "massiveness" of their evidence, and this ordinarily takes quite a few years of experience and a sufficient maturity of the physical organism to permit some more than momentary reflection. Metaphysics thus presupposes a confused and general knowledge of its principles. But these principles are not blindly accepted by the metaphysician; the student of metaphysics carefully reexamines the derivation of these principles from sensible being directly in some experience of being, and in so doing brings to explicit knowledge their own intrinsic evidence (or "self-evidence"). This process we have called "intellective induction."[17] Thirdly, spontaneous knowledge includes some conclusions which are materially identical (as positions) with some conclusions of metaphysics, and chief among these is the existence of God. Again, metaphysics does not merely accept this conclusion. Neither does

[17] By an "intellective (intelligible) induction" we mean an intellectual understanding that is gained in experience by an insight, direct, nondiscursive understanding of a concrete, sensible instance present to us. See the references given in n. 7; see also Edmund H. Ziegelmeier, S.J., "The Discovery of First Principles According to Aristotle," *The Modern Schoolman*, XXII (1945), 132–138.

it reject or doubt it. But unless a person already has some knowledge of God in some way and firmly accepts His existence, it is ordinarily impossible to deal intelligently with the proof of His existence.[18] The human mind ordinarily cannot come to a knowledge of God in a single act—at least not to such a knowledge as would enable it seriously to inquire into the grounds of such knowledge or to investigate the Divine nature. Briefly, we can say that metaphysics neither accepts nor rejects the conclusions of everyday knowledge but critically examines the reasoning (which everyday knowledge did not do and could not have done) and very carefully determines the sense of the conclusion in the light of being as being.

117. Realism, doubt, and philosophical method

The order and interrelationship of the various kinds and levels of knowledge are of special importance in the problems and controversies that have centered on "realism." "Realism"—as far as metaphysics and theory of knowledge is concerned—means that position which holds that there is some being or reality which is independent of knowledge and can be known as independent.

Historically the problem was unintentionally raised by René Descartes, who intended something quite different, namely, to remove the causes of the disagreements among philosophers by eliminating errors and hasty judgments. He maintained that we ought to doubt everything except that which we can see to be true in a clear and distinct idea. From this starting point, he thought that we ought to doubt the existence of things "outside" of ourselves, and that we were sure only of our ideas and of ourselves as spiritual substances thinking these ideas. After several other philosophers criticized certitudes in the context of Descartes's principle and method, David Hume finally placed the problem in its sharpest and extreme form. He argued, first, that ideas are only faint copies of sense impressions (following John Locke) and, second, that sense impressions clearly and distinctly give us only themselves. In other words, what is certain is that experience

[18] That is why an atheist, a skeptic, or an emotionally disturbed person is not convinced by *any* proof of the existence of God. To doubt a proof because atheists reject it is to confuse rational necessity with subjective conviction. See also below, sec. 121.

of color, sound, and such qualities is going on; there is an instinctive impulse and habit to "believe" that these are the colors and sounds of things and that we are subjects who know them. For our purposes, we can consider Hume's position to contain, first, a statement of fact (ideas are only faint copies of sense impressions) and, second, a principle: knowledge cannot be knowledge of anything "outside" of itself—the so-called principle of immanence.

Most of modern philosophy must be understood in the context of Hume's position and analysis, though the influence of Descartes's original formulation is still present. One group has adopted Hume's position almost entirely, and this is the movement formerly called logical positivism and more recently linguistic analysis or, simply, analysis. One short-lived movement tried to counter Hume's conclusions; admitting that the Humean theory of ideas and impressions was right, its followers held that there was an additional power of knowledge, called "common sense," which directly gave us knowledge of the reality of a distinct world and of ourselves. Immanuel Kant mapped out a method which in some variant forms is followed today by many: first, he denied that ideas are only faint copies of impressions as Hume had alleged; secondly, granting the principle of immanence, he thought that we could escape from its limitations by a special procedure, the method of a priori deduction. Described briefly, and therefore only vaguely, the method is this: given an act of knowledge, we can assert not only that act of knowledge as an act, but also all the conditions without which that act would not be possible. The idealists of the nineteenth century followed Kant in distinguishing between sense and ideas, but gave up the hope of knowing a material world; rather they denied the independent existence of such a world, and tried to put an "ideal" or "spiritual" reality inside knowledge. Later, the principle of immanence was challenged by Franz Brentano and Edmund Husserl, among others. They insisted instead on another aspect of knowledge, that all knowledge is essentially and irreducibly "knowledge of . . ."; this aspect they called "intentionality." But what are we to say about the object that follows the preposition *of*? Many give it the reality of essence (what we have called earlier "real in the wide sense"). Intentionality is sometimes interpreted as a "creative activity," holding that the "object" *of* which there is knowledge becomes an "object" by being known.

This is a very general and schematic outline of modern positions on the so-called "problem of knowledge." In this context, anyone who holds that there are realities distinct from and independent of knowledge is called a "realist." What about Hume's problem (and back of it, Descartes's)? As for the alleged "factual" part of Hume's position, it is denied flatly that ideas and other intellectual knowledge are only faint copies of sense impressions. The principle of immanence is rejected as being itself merely asserted, contrary to the nature of knowledge as immediately given (hence, not self-evident, as Hume imagined, but constructed), and an instance of spatial thinking about a nonspatial relation—that of knower to thing known. Hume and Descartes both must be accused of limiting, without any reason, the scope of intellectual knowledge to the concept; if this limitation is unwarranted and false, their conclusions fall to the ground.

But realists differ considerably among themselves about the way in which we know that there are such distinct realities, what those realities are, and what we do philosophically about them. (1) As far as the method of knowledge is concerned, realism can be mediate (if it holds that the existence of realities distinct from knowledge must be proved) or immediate (if it holds that there is direct evidence of such realities). (2) If a realism holds that what is real and independent of human thought is primarily an essence, it should be called a realism of essence; otherwise, it is an existential realism. (3) If a realism holds that we know real existents in such a way that we can increase our knowledge of them by an examination of the things themselves, it is a scientific or objective realism; if it holds that, in spite of our having a direct knowledge that things independent of ourselves exist, we must proceed by way of an analysis of the a priori necessary conditions of such knowledge, it is epistemologically a realism, but metaphysically and methodologically an a priori deduction; if it holds that we know real things, but that philosophy consists only in an analysis of the knower, it is usually one of the forms of existentialism or subjectivity.

With regard to these three sets of "options," the position taken in this book is an immediate, existential realism, developed principally on the basis of objective experience. There will be no attempt here to prove or to justify these choices. For one thing, if the book does not justify itself on its own introductory level, nothing else will; on the reflective level, it would take another book—or several books—to do the job satisfactorily. But reasons can be indicated summarily. (1) A mediate realism is possible only if principles have an immediately evident objective reference; but it is much simpler to take the immediate evidence of the things themselves.[19] (2) Anything less than an existential realism is a second-best and fits less well with man as a body-soul composite.[20] (3) As for methods, the unique validity of the a priori deduction could be asserted only on the basis of the principle of immanence, as Kant in fact asserted it; if it is not a unique method, it could be either parallel, prior, or posterior to an objective analysis. As parallel or prior, it is open to the objection that it does uncover necessary conditions, but cannot distinguish between merely logical conditions (beings of reason) and principles within being. As posterior, it has a certain value in the second, self-reflective stage of scientific knowledge; and this, as we have previously indicated in dealing with the transcendental true, is precisely where it belongs. The subjective or existential analysis could be the unique method of metaphysics for a personalist or "Christian spiritualist" (one who believes that only spiritual beings exist, or at least that there is a knowledge of spiritual persons entirely independently of the knowledge of external sensible things), or for for one who thinks that mere things and persons cannot have anything in common. In any other case, it cannot be the unique method. It is to be praised for having re-emphasized the distinctive reality of the person against a defective metaphysics based on merely sensible being, but this means that it must be joined with an objective analysis to be metaphysically adequate itself. Finally, an objective metaphysics can be either experiential or based on

[19] Etienne Gilson, *Réalisme méthodique* (Paris, Téqui, 1935), and *Réalisme thomiste et critique de la connaissance* (Paris, Téqui, 1939); *Return to Reason*, ed. John Wild (Chicago, Regnery, 1953).

[20] Etienne Gilson, *Being and Some Philosophers*, 2d ed. (Toronto, Pontifical Institute of Medieval Studies, 1953).

the conclusions of another science; we have indicated in the preceding section why an experientially based metaphysics is preferable.[21]

118. Digression on "common sense"

Those who are familiar with other discussions of the problem raised in the preceding section will have noted the absence of the term "common sense." Sometimes, it is true, the term "common sense" means precisely what we have designated "spontaneous knowledge." In that case, the question, "What is the relation between metaphysics and common sense?" will already have been answered in our own terms of spontaneous knowledge. But this very special meaning of "common sense" has been avoided in this book for two reasons: one drawn from ordinary usage, the other from historical considerations. In our ordinary usage of the terms, *sense, good sense,* and *common sense,* we imply practical knowledge.[22] But metaphysics (and all philosophy except ethics) is not practical but theoretical, speculative, or pure knowledge. So, in answer to the question, "What is the relation between metaphysics and common sense?" we can say, "There is no direct relation." Common sense bases its practical judgments on experience and some simple inferences. Metaphysics is a speculative, scientific discipline concerned with the real as real. Indirectly, there is this relation: metaphysics is the elaborated, demonstrative knowledge of much of what is presupposed for common-sense judgments.

The historical meaning of *common sense* is complex. It received special prominence, as we have just seen, during the early stages of the controversies between realists and skeptics. The Scottish realists decided that we had a special faculty, distinct from reason, whose object was to know the reality of the sensible world and other basic truths. This solution was attractive in some ways; it would guarantee what, in fact, we all (somehow) know to be true; it was even tempting, because it would free us forever from

[21] See also below, sec. 120.
[22] According to *Webster's New International Dictionary*, 2d ed. (Boston, G. & C. Merriam, 1953), "common sense" has as its second meaning "Good, sound, ordinary sense; specif., good judgment or prudence in estimating or managing affairs, esp. . . . as not dependent on special or technical knowledge" ("3. Phil. *b.* The unreflective opinions of ordinary men").

the necessity of having to study and consider all other philosophies. Of course, in the sense of a distinct faculty, "common sense" could not be accepted by Thomists; so they identified "common sense" as "intellect working on obvious and necessary truths." But the historical specter of the Scottish realism followed the term about in spite of the attempted correction.

Moreover, the Thomists have compounded the problem of "common sense" on their own. Many of them were looking for a "starting point" for philosophy, and they wanted a ready-made one, a critically justified one, and one against which other philosophical positions could be compared and accepted or rejected as the case might be. The most widely accepted solution was that the human mind spontaneously and immediately knew three fundamental truths (the first principle—of contradiction; the first fact —"I exist"; the first condition—the ability of the mind to know truth).[23] On the face of it, the intent of these philosophers looks perfectly sound; its real value lies in this: that they correctly realized the need for some starting point. For, if a philosophy must begin by justifying its very existence, then it never begins; the demand for total self-justification of a philosophy as its first step toward being is the demand of a skeptic. Basing philosophy on "common sense" eliminates an infinite regress in the search for a foundation, but it brings about new problems. Some of the utterances of "infallible common sense" are uncouth, and some are obviously wrong, so philosophy shall have to choose among them. But on what basis? On the basis of common sense itself? Those who chose to take common sense as their starting point[24] had to answer the objection that they were dogmatic, likely to be fixed forever in error, at variance with the ancient tradition that philosophy is an *inquiry* into *every* object, not merely an inquiry about some objects. Moreover, science had made its progress precisely inasmuch as it got rid of common-sense notions,

[23] On this whole question of Thomistic epistemologies, see Georges van Riet, *L'Epistémologie thomiste* (Louvain, Institut Supérieure de Philosophie, 1946).

[24] For one of the few good treatments of "common sense," see Yves Simon, *Traité du libre arbitre* (Liège, Sciences et Lettres, 1951), pp. 59–69. Unfortunately, the wrong connotations and historical associations of "common sense" cannot be avoided even by one who treats the real problem intelligently and well.

and this was especially true of astronomy. Was philosophy to lose entirely its scientific character?

This approach did not please other Thomists.[25] They were struck with the obvious inability of common sense to make the critical judgments it was alleged to be making all the time. They saw that if common sense needs to be corrected, it cannot be the starting point and the criterion of truth. So they wanted to begin by *rejecting* common sense, as the only alternative to accepting it. But if one rejects common sense, one must find some area that is outside common sense, and only two such starting points seem to be available. One is the conclusions of science, and this starting point has always been, and is now, the starting point of positivists, and remains that. In a later section, we shall consider the relation between metaphysics and science which is abstract and constructural. So we need not delay long here to explain why science is not a starting point of metaphysics. The other starting point outside the area of common sense is the basic concept of metaphysics, the concept of being, of reality, of intelligibility, or whatever a particular kind of philosophy has taken as its basic concept. This starting point has always been that of rationalists and of idealists; it cannot be the starting point of realistic metaphysics; at best, such realism would have to be mediate, and at this late date it scarcely seems necessary to show that mediate realism cannot stand up. From this historical consideration the conclusion seems to emerge that both the acceptance and the rejection of common sense make a realistic metaphysics impossible. Hence, it seems much better to avoid the term entirely.

Closely related to the discussion of "common sense" is the attempt to clarify the starting point of philosophy in terms of "common experience."[26] The sciences, by way of contrast, are said to originate in "special experience." The choice of terms has unfortunate connotations. The use of "common and special" as

[25] On this point, see Louis-M. Régis, O.P., "La critique thomiste est-elle thomiste?" *Etudes et recherches, Philosophie II* (Ottawa, Collège Dominicain, 1938).
[26] This term was popularized by Mortimer J. Adler; see his *What Man Has Made of Man* (New York, Longmans, 1937), p. 139.

alternative designations seems to suggest that whereas science is based on methodological, careful, critical, highly accurate, and selective data, philosophy is based on opposite grounds, that is, on haphazard, careless, inaccurate, unrefined data. This is how the distinction has been understood by many, and so they have concluded that philosophy might perhaps have some value as a preliminary stage prior to science but that it should yield to the more careful results of the sciences. So the term "common experience" also seems misleading and inappropriate.

119. Metaphysics and humanistic knowledge (liberal education)

In examining, in the first chapter, human knowledge as it in fact presents itself, we discovered that it exists in three modes: that of spontaneous knowledge, that of humanistic knowledge, and that of scientific or demonstrative knowledge. We want here to consider the relation between the humanistic mode of knowledge and metaphysics; for this purpose we can briefly summarize the characteristics of humanistic knowledge. It is characterized by its effort toward the integration of knowledge through principles and through its appeal to the human being as a whole—as a sensory as well as a rational being, as a being with sensory emotions and rational tendencies as well as one with knowledge. As such, humanism is a distinct mode of human perfection, which cannot be omitted without harm to the development of the personality and cannot be substituted for or replaced by any other kind of perfection, without loss. Because it is a development of the total personality, humanism has an intrinsic value, and is by no means merely an instrument for other values. In fact, for many persons, humanistic perfection is terminal as far as the natural development and training is concerned.

In the liberal subjects, especially in literature and history, we find many things which are materially similar and sometimes even materially identical with the principles and conclusions of philosophy. For example, we might consider the humanistic presentation of the dignity of man; similarly, the drama of human freedom, the dilemma of choice, the difference between right and wrong are found in a marvelously rich fashion in the humanistic mode of knowledge.[27] Are these characteristic understandings different from philosophy? If we put the question concretely, we can see that they are. Can the understanding of man presented in *Macbeth* be successfully put into the scientific mode of philosophy or psychology? Can Newman's *The Second Spring* be adequately expressed in a graph, or the *Sonnets* of Elizabeth Browning be reduced to a series of experiments? Obviously they cannot; and, since this is so, the humanistic mode of knowledge must be admitted to be different from any scientific mode.

What is the relation of such humanistic understandings to the similar philosophical understandings? Both types of understandings rest immediately on experience and, therefore, not on each other. In this sense, the two are mutually independent. The principles of humanistic knowledge are essentially the same as the principles of spontaneous knowledge, but refined by some reflection and experience; they are concretely conceived and stated in a highly concrete and vivid way. In addition, where the principles as spontaneously conceived are vague or indistinct, in humanistic knowledge they are amplified and made definite through metaphor and imagery. What is more, in spontaneous knowledge the principles are present but scarcely function at all *as principles;* spontaneous knowledge remains fragmentary, disconnected. In humanism, the principles already present in spontaneous knowledge but unused are put to work to organize and unify. Inasmuch as humanistic knowledge is involved with what is concrete and sensory-imaginative, it will present through direct principles, metaphor, and imagery what philosophy considers on a purely cognitional-rational basis. But because humanistic knowledge is so highly concrete and so charged with emotion, it is incapable of complete clarification and of defending itself against certain kinds of attacks especially from technocrats, and error can easily be mixed in with its truth.[28] In this sense humanism needs meta-

[27] Much of both the Old and the New Testaments will be found to be in the humanistic mode. For example, consider the discourse of Jesus at the Last Supper as given to us in St. John's Gospel and see if this can be adequately expressed in technical, scientific terminology.

[28] Note that an understanding which is essentially metaphorical can *never* be used as a premise in a philosophical argument and cannot simply be *turned into* a philosophical statement.

physics, not precisely as a necessary intrinsic constituent but as an external norm possessed by at least some who also have the humanistic perfection.

On the other hand, though humanism is not by its nature a step on the way to metaphysics, a liberal education is in fact a good preparation for the study of philosophy.[29] For the personal experience of every man is very limited, and in many cases, if one could call only on that purely personal experience, it is doubtful if even a whole lifetime could provide him with all the experience necessary for an adequate understanding of philosophy. It is well known that in the absence of experience, a merely verbal and abstract presentation will never provide an insight into reality. But the humanistic presentation is far more than merely verbal and it is concrete; it can provide an imaginative reliving of another's experience, and this contribution is notably great with respect to the philosophy of human nature and to ethics. By providing such a great enlargement of experience,[30] a liberal education can make a successful study of philosophy possible much sooner than private experience could possibly do.

[29] For college students of philosophy, a good humanistic formation is an almost indispensable preparation.

Further developments of this notion of humanistic knowledge can be found in Robert J. Henle, S.J., "A Thomistic Explanation of the Relations Between Science and Philosophy: The Theoretical Presentation," *Bulletin of The Albertus Magnus Guild* (October, 1956); *ibid.*, "A Philosopher's Interpretation of Anthropology's Contribution to the Understanding of Man," *Anthropological Quarterly*, vol. XXXII (1959), 22–40; *ibid.*, "Science and the Humanities," *Thought*, vol. XXXV (1960), 513–536; see also, Victor Hamm, *Language, Truth and Poetry* (Milwaukee, Marquette Univ. Press, 1960), pp. 60–61.

However, it should not be thought that humanistic studies are to teach philosophy or to provide the proper materials for philosophical study. In the first place, such an interest would go far in destroying the real value of the humanities. In the second place, the method of discovering a philosophy by investigating the "Western tradition" or canvassing the "great books" is essentially fallacious as a philosophical procedure: (*a*) it confuses humanistic and philosophical modes of knowledge; (*b*) it supposes there is a "least common denominator"—the *"philosophia perennis"*—which can be discovered by a poll of philosophers. In the third place, this procedure would tend practically to ignore the philosophical significance of science.

[30] An enlargement which, incidentally, was scarcely known to St. Thomas himself.

120. Metaphysics and other scientific knowledges

There are many contemporary philosophers who are of the opinion that philosophy is built on the conclusions of some science or of all the sciences or on the specialized, *interpreted* evidence of the sciences. Still others think that metaphysics at least is built upon the conclusions of the philosophy of nature.

Can metaphysics be built on the conclusions of any or of all the sciences? All the sciences are abstract; and all modern sciences are at least partly constructural. Any knowledge built upon abstract and constructural conclusions must necessarily itself be abstract and constructural. But metaphysics is not an abstract science, as we have seen abundantly; and it is an ontological knowledge, a knowledge of the real as it is. Hence, it is simply impossible for metaphysics to be built upon the conclusions of any or all sciences. Furthermore, the specialized and *interpreted* evidence of the special sciences cannot serve to ground either philosophy in general or metaphysics in particular. True, the evidence metaphysics seeks can be found in almost any experience inasmuch as it is a direct experience. But, as scientists are becoming more fully aware, the scientific "fact" is not simply experienced; it is a theoretically *interpreted* statement of something experienced. But the theoretical interpretation of any science involves both abstraction and construction and, consequently, is thereby not suitable as a point of departure for philosophy. Thirdly, metaphysics cannot be built upon the conclusions of the philosophy of nature.[31] First of all, even the philosophy of nature is abstract. In particular, it presupposes without discussing the reality of its object.[32] It knows, accepts, but never mentions existence. The being which is the object of the philosophy of nature is predicamental being. For that reason, it can never serve to ground the study of the real as real, of that-which-*is*.[33] Secondly, the object

[31] Cf. Owens, "A Note on the Approach to Metaphysics," *The New Scholasticism*, XXVIII (1954), 454–476. See also "Metaphysics and Theistic Convictions," in *Proceedings of the 1962 Workshop on Teaching Thomism* (Washington, Catholic Univ. of America Press) which contains additional references.

[32] It is an axiom commonly admitted by all Aristotelians that "no science proves the existence of its object—except somehow, metaphysics."

[33] Cf. Owens, *loc. cit.*

of the philosophy of nature (as ordinarily understood) is intrinsically connected with change;[34] metaphysics at its crowning point reaches a being which is immune from change, and so its knowledge cannot successfully be based on the philosophy of nature.

Moreover, it is unnecessary to look for a foundation for metaphysics in any of the specialized sciences. Why seek such a foundation? Most of those who do so, give as a reason that they must keep metaphysics in touch with reality, as if the only alternative were to begin with sheer unattached ideas of nothing in particular. But, in fact, metaphysics is grounded in the immediate experience of sensible being; it is based directly on reality. It already has a better foundation of its very nature than could be given it by any abstract science.

Quite a contrary point of view is taken by those who assert that all the special sciences are based on metaphysics. On the ground that metaphysics alone can formally treat of the most universal principles of knowledge, they maintain that all the sciences which use those principles are thereby based on metaphysics. This, however, is an overstatement. It is true that only metaphysics can discuss certain universal principles correctly. But that does not make the other sciences formally depend on metaphysics. Any particular science starts with a certain number of assumptions, and, as far as the internal necessities of that science are concerned, these assumptions can remain unproved assumptions. As long as a thinker works within that particular science, he need never go back beyond those assumptions. True enough, if the thinker wants to find the foundation of his science outside that science and continues his search far enough, he will ultimately come to metaphysics. But this search is precisely no longer within his science.[35]

[34] "Nature" according to the Aristotelians is "the first principle of motion and rest"; therefore, it is material, changeable, and composite.

[35] This is not meant to deny that there is an order among scientific knowledges. There is such an order, or "hierarchy"; but this order is not such that we can deduce one science from another, substitute one for another, or tell from one science what another must say in detail. On the other hand, the more universal and abstract knowledges are prior to the lesser in logical sequence; sometimes the logically posterior sciences borrow principles from the prior in the form of axioms or postulates (assumptions); prior sciences can resolve conflicts among posterior ones.

We have thus seen that there is no direct dependence of metaphysics upon any other scientific knowledge.[36] Is there any dependence at all? Can metaphysics be helped by other organized knowledges? To some extent, yes. Mainly, it is a matter of avoiding error. Avicenna in the ninth century tried to prove that there could be only ten intelligences because he thought that there were in fact only nine spheres. When astronomy showed that the spheres did not exist, later philosophers were no longer tempted to prove how many intelligences there are. Similarly, the problem of the *primum mobile* simply vanished. The positive help given by science to philosophy is almost nonexistent for metaphysics, but it is somewhat more important for ethics, and even more for the philosophy of nature.

Thomists may be surprised that there is no use of the doctrine of the "three degrees of abstraction" in dividing the sciences and that there are even derogatory comments about the doctrine in the footnotes in various places. The doctrine is this: there are three kinds of objects, (1) those which exist and are known in matter and motion; (2) those which exist in matter but are known in abstraction from matter; (3) those which exist separately from matter and are known in abstraction from matter. The first degree abstracts from individual matter, but includes common sensible matter; the second degree abstracts from sensible matter but includes "intelligible matter" (which is the same as "qualityless material substance" or "extension conceived of as a subsistent form"); the third degree abstracts from all matter. Thomists use this doctrine to classify the sciences: dealing with the first degree there are all the natural sciences including the philosophy of nature and of man as sensible; with the second degree, all the branches of mathematics; with the third, metaphysics (including natural theology) and our knowledge of intellect, will, and the spiritual soul.

The doctrine is a systematization by the Commentators on St. Thomas of St. Thomas's systematization of Aristotle's criticism of

[36] In the philosophy of nature, we investigate the nature of knowledge, and this investigation is of great help to metaphysics when the latter studies the nature of God.

In "Metaphysics and Theistic Convictions," *loc. cit.*, additional arguments are given, as well as a number of references.

Platonic separationism. According to Aristotle's account, Plato held that sensible things were in matter and to that extent unreal; the real beings were not in matter: souls (whose status is somewhat uncertain), mathematicals, and the ideas. Aristotle attacked this scheme of reality by arguing that one had to distinguish between the status of these items in knowledge, where they were separated, and in reality or being, where some of them were separated from matter and others were in matter.

The arrangement is a very confusing one because it works at the same time from two bases of division. It is not a division of reality simply, because the mathematicals are not a distinct group in reality. Nor is it strictly a division of knowledge, except reductively and partly by way of a division of the subject matters of knowledge. Materiality does indeed have something to do with intelligibility, but indirectly only. Nor is the polemical value of the arrangement very great, since it is doubtful whether any contemporary philosophers are holding for separated, subsistent ideas.

121. Metaphysics and the faith

Does revelation need metaphysics? Does the act of faith in a revelation need metaphysics? Absolutely speaking, no. Revelation can be accepted and understood on the basis of spontaneous knowledge alone. The truths necessary for faith, such as the existence of God, can be known with certitude by spontaneous knowledge, as we have seen. A Faith can be held and carried out in practice, even to a very high degree of perfection, without any philosophy (or theology)[37] whatsoever. There may be accidental and extrinsic reasons why some individual may need to learn metaphysics in order to save his soul, just as there may be a reason why some one needs to learn biology or astronomy. But such necessities are entirely extrinsic to the nature of revelation and of faith.

Does a Christian culture need metaphysics? Historically speaking, it would seem necessary that such a culture (*not* any given individual, as was just said) somewhere actively possess a metaphysics. In general, it seems to be a characteristic of the human

[37] Unless the term *theology* is used in a purely etymological sense to mean "any kind of knowledge about God."

mind to want to push into every possible area that can be known. If some major area of knowledge is left without its proper corresponding scientific knowledge, some other kind of knowledge will tend to take it over, with unfortunate consequences. This necessity is not because of the faith but because of the natural tendencies of the human mind. Similarly, if a culture fails to meet one of its problems because of some defect, that culture will suffer the consequences. If a Christian culture lacks medical knowledge, it may be destroyed by a plague and, ordinarily, will not be saved by a miracle. So, too, if a Christian culture lacks metaphysics, it may be upset by some problem of order—frequently an intellectual one—and, ordinarily, this consequence will not be prevented by a miracle.

Does theology need metaphysics? Here a distinction must be made. If we reserve the term *theology* for some kind of organized knowledge, theology will be seen to be of two kinds: positive or humanistic theology and scientific theology. Humanistic theology of itself does not need metaphysics, although there may be indirect necessities because of the culture or because humanism in general needs metaphysics as an external help, as we saw above. Scientific theology is the scientific (demonstrative) understanding of a revelation, and such an understanding becomes scientific through the application of rational, scientific understandings and methods[38] to revealed truth. Hence, scientific theology strictly needs metaphysics for its very existence as scientific knowledge.[39]

[38] Naturally acquired knowledge seems to enter into theology in several different ways. (1) Some knowledge is preliminary or preparatory: archeology, linguistics, knowledge of the pertinent languages, and so forth. (2) Other knowledge supplies factual premises for arguments; for example, biology may tell us that a certain material substance is a deadly poison, so the theologian concludes that to administer such a substance is murder. (3) Some knowledge enters into theology as materially constitutive; thus, philosophy enters in as determinable to the goal of the theologian and supplies him with both organizational principles and means of at least a partial understanding.

[39] It is a pedagogical question whether metaphysics should be learned first, and then the theology, or whether the entire understanding of reality could be taught together as "Christian Wisdom." The latter way seems more ideally perfect; the former is practically advantageous both in regard to the time needed and in view of the fact that students have to be prepared to live in an unbelieving world and so must be able to answer objections with naturally valid answers and to give natural arguments. Each

On the other hand, does metaphysics need the faith? If we are speaking of the rational necessities of an organized knowledge, no. Metaphysics is a natural knowledge; it is constituted by principles discovered in experience and is elaborated by natural reasoning. Historically speaking, metaphysics has been helped considerably by the faith, and it can be seriously contended that Thomistic metaphysics would not have taken the form it did without the faith. Nevertheless, Thomistic metaphysics remains a rational discipline, subject to strictly rational laws and necessities.

Finally, does the thinker who wishes to penetrate deeply and truly into the nature of being need the faith? Here the answer is almost an unqualified yes. Certainly it seems impossible for a young person to make much out of metaphysics unless he has a rather firm grounding in the Christian tradition and firmly believes in the existence of a distinct, personal God. Absolutely speaking, it might be possible for a virtuous and religious person, who does not accept the Judaeo-Christian revelation through no fault of his own, to come to something like a Thomistic metaphysics after years of experience and reflection. But such a limiting case serves, it seems, only to bring out the fact that metaphysics as a discipline is not based on the faith. Basically, the reason why the thinker who understands Thomistic metaphysics and, much more, the thinker who brings about advances in metaphysics ordinarily must also be a Christian is the unity of personality. One cannot at the same time deliberately attend to the conclusion that God exists and rationally will to reject Him.

122. Thomism and other philosophies

We have already indicated in various sections of this book— and presumably the fact is sufficiently well known—that there are many philosophies, which approach reality in quite different ways and, at certain points, differ irreconcilably. This is the so-called "problem of diversity." What can briefly be said about it?

One approach to philosophy is to choose a reasonably good

---

method also has its disadvantages: the total approach is easily turned into a nominalistic process where the "philosophy" appears at best as mere opinion and often as mere words; in taking metaphysics (and philosophy, generally) first, there is some danger of rationalism. For more detailed analysis and references, see "Metaphysics and Theistic Convictions," *loc. cit.*

guide, on the basis of authority and tradition, and begin the study of philosophy. As we get into a philosophy, we will find our guide offering evidence for what he says, and we have the right and the duty to consider (*a*) whether there actually is such evidence; (*b*) whether significant contrary evidence has been sufficiently considered; (*c*) whether the evidence really supports the conclusion, leads to such an insight, and so on. If it does, we can accept it unconditionally. If we cannot precisely conclude that these three conditions are fulfilled but also cannot see that they are not fulfilled, it is prudent to accept the doctrine conditionally, that is, until we see that it is otherwise. Once we have worked through a relatively complete philosophy, we can go ahead to a deeper study which will also put us into contact with other philosophies. This further study is almost entirely a matter of acquainting ourselves with the history of philosophy in a very thorough fashion—not merely by way of memorizing dates and doctrines but with a solid grasp of the problems, methods, and presuppositions each philosopher has. On this basis we will be able to make a final decision about the philosophy we hold. This is a difficult program, and it is ordinarily possible only for those who intend to specialize in philosophy. Those who cannot complete such a program will find no adequate *philosophical* solution to their problem.[40]

Another approach to the problem of diversity of philosophies is through the history of philosophy. One could begin with the earliest recorded philosophies and follow the history of philosophy to the present day and, on the basis of what he finds, make up his mind. This is a relatively impractical way to go about solving the problem; it would entail a lifetime of study before one knew where he stood in metaphysics.

[40] There are perfectly *reasonable* nonphilosophical grounds for solving the problem. For a Christian, there are relatively few difficulties in solving the problem on the basis of the harmony between his faith and the philosophy he accepts. For a Catholic, there remains only the problem of choosing between the various "Scholastic" philosophies. In principle, this problem is solved *philosophically* just like the more general problem of diversity. If he cannot solve his problem philosophically himself, it should be pointed out that he is really concerned only with philosophical *positions*, and the positions are sufficiently common that the problem is not of major importance for him.

A popular contemporary approach is to take and accept the diversity of philosophical positions in connection with each philosophical problem. This way of solving or rather *meeting* the problem of diversity is indeed often used, but it is not very philosophical. For a philosophical position cannot be philosophically understood apart from the evidence, the principles, and the reasoning leading to it. Yet the system of seeing what all the important philosophers have to say on each point, as that system is ordinarily carried out, is merely a recounting of the positions, with a lot of rhetoric thrown in favor of the one the teacher happens to be (surreptitiously) advocating. The result of such an eclecticism is not philosophical thinking at all; it might perhaps lead to what Plato would call "right opinion," and again it might not.

123. The constructural knowledge of being

Can there be a constructural philosophy? There have been such philosophies; there still are. By a constructural philosophy we mean one whose basic principles and concepts are constructural, although in most cases they also contain some ontological knowledge (which may result in an internal tension in the philosophy itself). To take a simple case, we need but consider the "being" of Parmenides. This immobile, simple, all-inclusive form is not a reality; to some extent it does help us to understand reality indirectly. But since being as being is directly (ontologically) intelligible to some extent, a constructural philosophy is unnecessary and to some extent useless. On the other hand, an ontological knowledge of reality can be helped out at certain points by constructs. To give an instance outside of metaphysics: we can understand certain things better when we deal with habit-groups in terms of matter and form, although the term "matter" is not used in its proper sense. In metaphysics itself, we deal with pure intelligibilities; this is especially true in the case of the predicaments. For example, *relation* as a form is a construct; in the real order there is no *form* of relation, as we have seen. But we can understand relational reality by means of such a mentally constructed form. The use of such constructs does not make the whole knowledge constructural, since the basic knowledge in metaphysics is ontological. We can therefore legitimately speak of "primary constructs" (when they are the basic concepts of a science) and "secondary constructs" (when the constructs appear in auxiliary positions).

In passing, we have referred to "second-level abstractions." Ordinarily, when we speak of abstraction, we indicate a direct but incomplete way of understanding a thing. For example, when we understand Peter as a "man," our concept *man* is abstract, inasmuch as it does not explicitly include Peter's individuality. However, we can also abstract the intelligible form of "man" itself. Here, we indicate a partial way of understanding what we had previously understood. This is an abstraction performed, not with regard to a thing, but with regard to what we know about a thing. Such an abstraction we have called a "second-level abstraction." For example, we abstract from Peter's individuality to get the concept "man"; we abstract from the general subject included in "man" to get the concept "humanity." This kind of abstraction is in quite common use, and usually people are not confused by abstract terms of this kind. Sometimes, however, they are; the "state," for example, is a second-level abstraction that sometimes is mistaken for a reality as such. We have seen other instances of misunderstanding with regard to the predicaments, especially that of relation.

Another type of second-level abstraction that we have already referred to is the "concept of existence as a form." We know that the act of existing, although it is the basic and primary act, is definitely *not* a form. We can help ourselves to understand esse better by an analogy with form. But when we go further and think that esse is a form, then we have developed a full-blown construct. It is true that we can do certain things with the "form of existence"; for example, we can say that properly real things have the form of existence, whereas mental fictions do not possess such a form. Provided we know what we are doing, such a proceeding would not be harmful, although it might be somewhat useless. But if we think that this is indeed what esse really is, then we are making use of a primary construct and will most likely soon be in difficulties.

Similarly, in the course of our study of being, we have referred to various *concepts* of being. These concepts, inasmuch as they were supposed to be the primary and basic understanding of that-which-is, played the role of *primary* constructs. The philosophies based on them are therefore constructural, and in considering them, we have rejected them as inadequate.

But is there room at all for any constructural knowledge of being in an experientally based metaphysics? Let us recall what we saw earlier in considering being as a transcendental. We saw there that there are several conceptions of being: the primitive conception of being which is prephilosophical; the essential conception of being as whatever is real in the wide sense ("being" as the object of the intellect); the metaphysical conception of being. As far as this third conception is concerned, we saw that when an analogon is named without explicitly designating its analogates, then it is understood as the conception of the prior analogate (prior, that is, with regard to our knowledge). On this score, "being," named without any further qualification, is "a subsistent sensible substance having an act of existing." Not included in this "being in common" except by relation are non-sensible substances, the accidents, and God as transcendent cause. In a direct conception we cannot achieve any greater unity.

Is it possible in any other way to have *one* conception of being which would be compatible with the direct conceptions of being? We can do this, not by any further reflection on the things themselves, but by a reflection on our knowledge of being. In every case, including the beings that are not in being as a direct transcendental, we know each and every being as "something which is." In spite of the fact that this knowledge is different, the pattern in which it is expressed is the same, so that we can finally make this statement about our knowledge of the being of metaphysics: "Whenever we understand something which is real as real, we understand it as something-which-is."

We can now, by a second-level abstraction, express this statement in a concept which is a definition: being is that which is understood as something-which-is. Because this definition expresses what we do when we understand a being, it can also be called a "law" or a "rule."[41] Because it is a second-level abstraction, the "rule of conception of being" is a construct, not a direct knowledge of any real thing. Because it is not a primary but a derived concept and by no means is it the basic concept or judgment on which metaphysics is built, it is a secondary construct. As it stands, this "concept of being as a rule of understanding" is absolutely universal and can be used, if we wish, as a point of reference to give an external unification to our manifold direct knowledge of being.

Moreover, this constructural concept of being has some direct use as a predicate. It may be extremely significant to say, in some contexts, that "X is a being." For example, there are some who hold that the First Principle of reality, though eminently real in some sense, is nonbeing (Plotinus, Erigena). To say, in the context of an analysis or criticism of such a position, "God is a being," means "God can be truly understood by us as something which is." In some other contexts, to say, "This is a being" is equivalent to saying, "This is a fact" or "This is not a fiction."

124. The analogy of *analogy*

The Thomistic tradition concerning the nature, divisions, and kinds of analogy has not been followed in this book, both because our study of reality has revealed different types of analogy, and because a careful study of the sources has shown that the tradition has been schematized and oversimplified.[42]

Analogy, in general, is unity-in-multiplicity; it is not an unqualified unity either in being or in knowledge. Moreover, analogy is not an absolute quality or attribute of being in abstraction from knowledge. Consequently, analogy is not a relation which pertains to the order of the concept, but one which pertains to

[41] This may sound Kantian to some, but there is a difference. The Kantian "rules" (categories) are constitutive of objects as they appear and so are primary constructs; the "rule of the conception of being" is derived from objects ontologically constituted by internal principles and already known directly as beings in the first sense of that term; hence, it is a secondary construct.

For further considerations of the idea of being, see Stanislas Breton, *Approches phénoménologiques de l'idée de l'être* (Paris, Vitte, 1959).

[42] This conclusion is textually established in my *St. Thomas Aquinas on Analogy* (Chicago, Loyola Univ. Press, 1960).

the order of the judgment. We can then say that analogy is judgmental knowledge which is partly the same, partly different (and therefore we must suppose that we are talking about at least two analogates). What distinguishes the analogous judgment is that it is proportional predication: the meaning of the "predicate" is proportioned to the different subjects of which it is predicated.

Analogy can be divided in three different ways. (1) The perfection, or analogon, can be either intrinsic to all the analogates or extrinsic to all except one; (2) it can be in them according to some relational structure; (3) it can be qualitatively described in general ways. According to the first basis of division, we find extrinsic and intrinsic analogies. An extrinsic analogy is a pure multiplicity in itself, which is *considered* by the mind in some unified way. An intrinsic analogy is one which is inherent in the very things themselves that are known. An extrinsic analogy is *made* by the mind; an intrinsic analogy is to some extent found in the things in the real order.

Secondly, analogy can be divided according to its form, that is, according to the kind or type of relation in the various analogates. The "many" which are analogously one can be directly related to each other, the "one-to-one" structure; they can be related to a third which is somehow different from them, the "many-to-one" structure; they can be without a direct relationship as such, but there can be internal relationships in them which are related, the "many-to-many" structure. (Some "many-to-one" structures can be reduced to a group of "one-to-one" analogies, if the "one" of the "many-to-one" is itself the primary analogate of an analogy of the same order; otherwise they constitute a distinct type of relationship.)

Thirdly, analogies can be divided according to general qualitative differences. Thus, "one-to-one" analogies fall into three different groups: (1) the relation of the one analogate to the other is fixed and finite—the analogy of proportion, strictly so called; (2) the analogon is indefinitely greater, more perfect in the prior analogate, but is deficiently, less perfectly, in the posterior analogate—the analogy of eminence; (3) the analogon is identical with one analogate, so that that analogate is the analogon by essence, whereas it is possessed in a limited way by the posterior analogate(s)—the analogy of participation. "Many-to-one" analogies are of two kinds: the "one" can either be simply outside the order of the analogates (the analogy of individual communication) or it can be the whole composed of the analogates (the analogy of composition). "Many-to-many" analogies do not admit of any further division.

These analogies are applied to concrete groups of analogates; some of them can be used of analoga other than being. The analogy of proportion is found in all act-potency relationships: substance and accident, matter and form, the power-act-object series—for example, the conception "understanding" used of the power of the intellect, the habit of first principles, and the act of simple intellection, or "sight" used of the power, the act, and the object. Similar to this analogy, and based on it, is the analogy according to which a possible can be said to be: for a possible can be said to be inasmuch as there is an essence capable of receiving an act of existing and an actually existing cause to produce it. Another kind of proportion is that between finite non-univocal causes and their effects. This proportion can be extrinsic if the cause is strictly equivocal; it is intrinsic if the cause is strictly analogous.[43] Thus, in the case of health, the food is an equivocal cause of animal health; it does not possess as an inherent perfection the special disposition which it helps to bring about. Yet an equivocal cause is truly a cause; it possesses some perfection which unhealthy food does not possess, and it is because of this perfection also that it is denominated healthy. Note that in this second case, the meaning of "proportion" is slightly different from that of the first type (potency-act proportion); here, it means "apt to produce, yet not the same and not less." A third kind of proportion is that whereby a product of the mind is

---

[43] The meaning of the pair of terms, "extrinsic" and "intrinsic," is somewhat different in the cases of the different kinds of proportion. Thus, in the proportion of act and potency (for example, *sight* as an act and as a power), the analogy is an intrinsic analogy, in the sense that the potency is by its own intrinsic nature a potency to this specific kind of act and no other. In causal analogy, an intrinsically analogous cause possesses in itself a higher perfection which is similar to the perfection of the effect; an extrinsically analogous, or equivocal, cause contains an equivalent but not a similar perfection.

made similar to something real. Thus, a "being of reason" is made by the mind, and it is conceived after the manner of real being, although it is not such. Similarly, "predicamental being" is considered by the mind after the manner of real being, although what is known in this way is only a principle of being. These proportions are clearly extrinsic, and the relation between the two analogates is that the prior one is the model.

The analogy of eminence is a distinct kind of analogy, as long as the "excess" of the prior analogate over the posterior is indefinite. It seems, however, that the indefiniteness is due to the imperfection of our knowledge, and that when we find out more about the two analogates, the relation will turn out to be either definite (and so the analogy will become an analogy of proportion), or properly infinite (and then it will be an analogy of participation).

The third kind of two-term analogy is the analogy of participation. In this analogy, one analogate is by essence (or nature) what the other is by participation. In other words, one analogate is by identity what the other analogate has. The most fundamental instance of the analogy of participation is the analogy of being between God and creature, which, as we have seen, is not the first analogy we discover between the two analogates but can be known only when God is known to be a subsistent act of existing. In the analogy between God and creature, the analogate which is by essence what the other is by participation is also the total efficient cause of the other. The analogy obtains with regard to being, goodness, truth, beauty, life, intelligence, and the like. Another kind of analogy of participation can be found where one analogate is by its essence what another is by participation, without any causal relation between the two. For example, angels are intellectual by nature, men, by participation. Here, the analogy is real and intrinsic, but it is known in a very indirect way. An extrinsic analogy of participation[44] is that whereby the predicamen-

---

[44] An analogy of participation is intrinsic when the participant possesses the participated act as its own (as a creature really possesses its own act of existing). An analogy of participation is extrinsic when the participant does not possess the participated act as its own but refers to the act of that which is by essence—for example, "predicamental accident" extrinsically participates the being of "predicamental substance" (which is predica-

tal accident shares in the being of predicamental substance.

The second type of analogy is the three-term analogy. The analogy of individual communication is that found between the various individual beings as beings, inasmuch as they individually and uniquely communicate in the conception of being in common. This analogy is a distinctive kind of analogy principally on account of the condition of our knowledge. As we learned later on, individual beings are so many distinct participants in the subsistent being of God, Who is being by essence. But because we do not directly grasp God in His own being, the conception of being in common does not disappear, even after we learn that God is Being by essence. The analogy of composition is that of the intrinsic components of a whole, where the whole is the "one" to which the "many" are related. This we find between being and the principles of being, substance and the principles of substance. Thus, the whole concrete individual is that-which-is; its components, substance and accident, unequally share in the nature of that which they compose, yet they can properly be called beings by reason of their role as components. (Notice here that in consequence of these unequal roles, substance and accident also stand in the analogy of proportion.)

The third basic type of analogy is the four-term analogy, the analogy of proportionality. It is the analogy we find, first, between persons as beings and things as beings. It supposes an independent knowledge of each of the analogates between which no intrinsic order is discoverable precisely as analogates. We can extend this analogy to the so-called grades of being: merely inanimate things, plants, animals, men. The three degrees of life, vegetative, sensitive, rational, are also analogous with the analogy of proportionality. Another very important instance of proportionality is the series of pairs of intrinsic constituents of finite being, considered as act and potency, which we have called "the act-potency correlation." Finally, the analogy of the proper good is a proportionality, which is important not only for metaphysics but also for ethics. (The traditional instance of proper propor-

mental being by essence), in the sense that accident includes substance in its definition (for example, "color" is the quality of a material thing; "shape" is a quality of the surface of a material thing; and so on).

tionality between substance and accident is an extrinsic one, made by the mind and not found in reality; as we noted above, this analogy arises from an extrinsic analogy of participation.)

Schematically, we may consider the picture of analogy thus:

form	relation to reality	quality	application
two-term "one-to-one"	intrinsic	*definite:* proportion	substance and accident / act and potency / actual and possible / analogous cause and effect / matter and form (in substance)
		indefinite: eminence	nonunivocal (de facto analogous) cause / God and creature
		"infinite" participation	God and creature / (human vs. angelic intelligence) / (reason and "reasoned" appetition)
	extrinsic	*definite:* proportion	equivocal cause and effect / being of reason and real being
		indefinite: eminence	nonunivocal (de facto equivocal) cause
		"infinite" participation	predicamental accident in predicamental substance
three-term "many-to-one"	intrinsic	individual communication	many individual beings as beings
		composition	substance and accident to entire being / matter and form to entire substance
four-term "many-to-many"	intrinsic	proportionality	persons and things as beings / grades of being (etc.) in general / act-potency correlation
	extrinsic	proportionality	predicamental substance to predicamental accident

125. Thomism and the Thomists

Repeatedly in the footnotes and in the course of this chapter, reference has been made to interpretations of St. Thomas which differ from the one presented here. The appeal has been primarily to experiential evidence; an introductory book is no place to conduct an historical and textual argument. It is to be hoped that the studies cited in this last chapter will supply to some extent this part of the total demonstration.[45]

To anyone who already has some knowledge of Thomism before he reads this book, the position will appear as more or less of a departure from what he has learned. "More or less"—for in fact there are many Thomisms. Some hold that there is a quidditative concept of being, a concept of the act of existing itself, that judgment is a composition of two concepts, that we have a conceptual knowledge of what God is, that the proper point of departure is the concept of being itself. Others, Thomists too, deny all this. On another point, that of analogy, there are also several positions: that there is only one type of analogy; that there are several types all combined at once in the analogy of being; that there are several irreducible types of analogy, even of the analogy of being. There are differences in the interpretation of the categories and of their relation to real being. There are some Thomists who admit constructural knowledge; others who do not. There are all sorts of positions on the relation of metaphysics to experience, to other parts of philosophy, to other disciplines.

In recent years, differences of starting-point and method have been stressed more than before. Most of the earlier Thomists, and traditional Thomists today, base their metaphysics on the results of the philosophy of nature. Some have tried to base it on a system of concepts. Some—not only recent ones—have based it on the direct experience of being. Still others base it on the experience of personality and freedom. The differences of

[45] In addition to the studies cited above, in footnotes 4, 7, 8, 12, 13, 14, 19, 23, 25, 30, 42, reference should be made to the still valuable work of André Marc, S.J., "L'Idée de l'être chez S. Thomas et dans la Scolastique Posterieure," *Archives de Philosophie*, vol. X, cahier 1 (1933), and to the unpublished dissertation of Edmund W. Morton, S.J., "The Doctrine of Ens Commune in St. Thomas," (University of Toronto, 1954).

method are as great and perhaps even more noticeable. Traditional Thomism and those who start with a concept of being usually make use of a standard Aristotelian kind of deduction. Those who begin with an experience of being can use mainly an objective, analytic reduction to principles of being, or a phenomenological analysis, or a transcendental reduction to the a priori conditions of the knowledge of being. Those who start with the experience of personality and freedom have used an objective, analytical reduction or what is called an existential analysis.

In the presence of this historical situation, it seems legitimate to ask that this book not be judged on the basis of its agreement or disagreement with any commentator on St. Thomas, no matter how exalted the historical position of that commentator and no matter what his merits be in theology or history or in other branches of philosophy. Does the evidence appealed to square with experience? Is the understanding of that experience, and the conclusions drawn from it, in harmony with the actual philosophical understanding of St. Thomas *himself* as he has chosen to express it in the solution of the problems as they came to him in the context of his own time?

The concern for the authentic understanding of St. Thomas has been called by some an authoritarian one, by others a dogmatic and intolerant one. Two remarks can be made. The first is in the nature of a retort: Often enough those who object to the authority of St. Thomas themselves make use of authorities, only lesser ones—their teachers, the author of a striking book, and so forth. Sometimes, they laud originality, as if a philosophy were a good philosophy to the degree that it is different—a strange criterion indeed. As for dogmatism: tolerance and charity are exercised toward *persons;* in the order of ideas one looks for truth, adequacy, depth; though it is fashionable to believe that any kind of rational conviction must be fanatical, it takes both courage and humility to say, "This is what I think is right, and here are my reasons."

The second answer is, of course, the important one. St. Thomas's thought has a directness and a four-square fit with experiential evidence, a profundity, and an all-encompassing power that seem to be unique among philosophers, Christian as well as non-Christian. For many reasons his writings are not readily intelligible to the modern student, so that the mediating role of a textbook is a practical necessity. If this book can bring forth in the student the ability and the desire to read St. Thomas for himself, it will have fulfilled its immediate aim: to enable the American college student in the 1960's to win for himself the fundamental insights of St. Thomas. Then St. Thomas will be the guide that will lead the student to a philosophical understanding of being and, in that, to a knowledge and love of God.

Index of Passages
From St. Thomas Aquinas

Index

Boldface numbers indicate definitions; italicized numbers, footnotes

relation, 68, 218-219, **281**
  as intelligibility, 270-271
  causal, 274-275
  esse and intelligibility of, *273*
  esse of, 284
  foundation of, 283
  intelligibility of, 284
  mutual and non-mutual, 276, **281**
  of action and passion, 273-274
  of quantity, 272
  predicamental, 269-270, **281**
  real and of reason, 272-273, **281**, 283
  transcendental, 72, 269, **281**
religion and philosophy, 15-17; *see also* faith and reason

Russell, *160*
Salmon, 57, *294*
sameness, 80
Sartre, *66*
Schmitz, 57, 76
Schrödinger, 57
science, 3, **21**, 33
  and philosophy, 308-309
Scotism, 36
sense and intellect, *294*
self-evidence, *154*
semantics, general, 32
sensible, 49, 287
sensible thing, **22**
sentimentalism, 187
separation, *8*, *45*, 50-51, **55**, 56, 59-60
series, infinite, 194-195
  of causes, 192-193
  ordered, 193, 266
Sertillanges, 140, 182, 208
Sheldon, 57
Simon, *303*
simple, **236**
sin, 229-230
singularity, 36, *108*
situs, 280, **282**
Smith, 57
something, *44*, 216, **236**
soul, separated, *108*
subjectivity, 39, 72, *223*

subject matter, *see* matter of knowledge
subsistent, 252
substance, 95, 96, 101, **114**, 115, 118-119, 122, 126, 201, 238, 243, 246, **253**, 256, 258, 276
  angelic, *250*
  as being, 130
  Divine, 211
  first, 250-251, **254**, 258
  predicamental, 249-251, **253**, 260
  primitive meaning of, 250
  second, 246, 251, **254**, 258
succession, 83
supposit, 251-252, **254**
syllogism, 191

teleology, 114, 170, **182**
  of nature, 205
  principle of, *177*, **182**
tendency, 139, 145, 147, 174, 175, 177, 228, 231, 275, 276; *see also* appetite, purpose
term, 7, 62-63
  common, 76
  see also univocal, equivocal, analogous
that-which-is, **115**, 116
theism, 186
theology, 26, 311-312
thing, **22**, 73, 216, **236**
Thomas Aquinas, St., 17, 20, 23, 45, 56, 76, *100*, 116, *127*, *137*, 139, *146*, *151*, 165, 182, *188*, *194*, *198*, 201, 207, *214*, *226*, 237, 254, 266, 276, 282, 287, 294, *307*, 310, 325-326
Thomism, 19-20, 40-42, *66*, *71*, *111*, *261*, 287, *294*, 303, 310-311, 313-315, 324-326
Tournier, 57, 76
transcendental, 200, **236**
transient activity, *see* action, transient
truth, 59, 223-226
  logical and transcendental, **236**

understanding, way of, 287

unity, 68, 92, 220-222
  kinds of, 221
  per accidens, 96
  see also one
universal, 9, 63, 102, *103*, 220
  existence of, 64
univocal, 6, 7, 9, **22**, 63, 68, 71, **74,**
  118, 166, 291; *see also* knowledge, universal

Van Riet, *303*
Van Roo, 117, 140, 254
verb, *44*
virtual, *46*, 135

Vogel, 166

Walton, 117
Ward, 182
way of understanding, *see* understanding
Weltanschauung, 19
when, 279, 280, **282**
where, 279, **282**
whole, **236**
Wild, 24, 58, 89, 140, 166, *290*, *301*
wisdom, 25
world, 42-43

Ziegelmeier, *297*

Made in the USA
Middletown, DE
20 August 2018